Organizing
European
Space

Organizing
European
Space

Christer Jönsson, Sven Tägil and Gunnar Törnqvist

SAGE Publications
London • Thousand Oaks • New Delhi

SAGE Publications Ltd
6 Bonhill Street
London EC2A 4PU

SAGE Publications Inc.
2455 Teller Road
Thousand Oaks, California 91320

SAGE Publications India Pvt Ltd
32, M-Block Market
Greater Kailash – I
New Delhi 110 048

British Library Cataloguing in Publication Data
A catalogue record for this book is available from the British Library

ISBN 0 7619 6672 2
ISBN 0 7619 6673 0 (pbk)

Library of Congress catalog card number 131516

Typeset by Keystroke, Jacaranda Lodge, Wolverhampton.
Printed in Great Britain by The Cromwell Press Ltd, Trowbridge, Wiltshire

Contents

Acknowledgements

This book represents a truly collective effort. It has grown out of seminars and a series of meetings over a number of years among the three co-authors around the theme of the future European political and economic order. Originally the focus was on a 'Europe of regions', but gradually the scope widened. At the same time, the original format of seminars with colleagues and graduate students eventually gave way to a 'trialogue' between the co-authors, where we compared and critiqued the perspectives of our respective disciplines on the territorial state and its alternatives. Out of this process of mutual teaching and learning, the idea of a multidisciplinary book on 'organizing European space' emerged. As we began drafting chapters, a new series of meetings was devoted to scrutinizing and rewriting drafts. Thus, even if the original drafting of individual chapters has been distributed among the co-authors (and the insightful reader may guess who drafted which chapters), we stand collectively behind the final product.

The whole process was triggered by a generous grant from the Erik Philip-Sörensen Foundation at Lund University. Without it, we would never have had the opportunity to take time away from our busy schedules and commitments within and outside our respective departments. We are therefore extremely grateful to the Foundation and to Erik Philip-Sörensen himself, who has taken a personal interest in our project.

A number of other individuals have been helpful in bringing our project to fruition. Jasmine Aimaq has translated parts of the manuscript; Tomas Tägil has designed the historical maps; Jonas Johansson has assisted in preparing the references and index; and Lucy Robinson has been an encouraging and supportive editor. In addition, seminars and discussions with our colleagues and PhD students have generated valuable ideas and insights for this book. Rather than producing a long list of names, we express our sincere thanks to all those who have contributed in different ways to our joint undertaking. Whatever the weaknesses of our final product, they would have been far greater without your help.

Christer Jönsson • Sven Tägil • Gunnar Törnqvist

Lund, Sweden

Introduction

'How many states are there in Europe today?' An academic colleague of ours likes to pose this question in his lectures. It invariably triggers a certain amount of confusion and prompts diverse answers. It has proved to be quite a pedagogical question, insofar as it spurs a discussion of what we mean by 'state' and by 'Europe'. Should the answer be restricted to those entities that have been recognized as states by all other European states, or include entities that have proclaimed statehood and have been recognized by some – and, if so, how many? – other states? And should we count the trans-Caucasian republics of the former Soviet Union among the European states? What about Turkey? Where, in short, does Europe begin and end? Moreover, are states really the most important organizational actors in contemporary Europe?

A deceptively simple question thus opens up some fundamental problems concerning European space and identity. In this book, we will carry the question one step further by not restricting it to one organizational entity, the state. Instead, we are concerned with the various ways in which European space has been organized in the past and present as well as possible future developments. Our overarching question thus concerns the different bases for organizing Europe politically and economically throughout the ages and into the new millennium.

The cartographer's dilemma

Three simultaneous and intertwined processes – which we usually try to capture with the labels 'globalization', 'European integration' and 'the end of the Cold War' – have transformed the European political landscape in the past decade and have added dynamism and uncertainty to the previously stable political map. The collapse of the Soviet empire resulted in a substantial number of new states, the destabilization of the Balkans and the dissolution of established alliance patterns. Intensified integration efforts in Western Europe have engendered supranational authorities as well as greater regional autonomy. At the same time, the continued deepening and widening of European integration, represented by the European Monetary Union (EMU) and the impending eastern enlargement of the European Union, raise a number of questions about the future map of Europe. Finally, the effect of globalization, however understood, is a matter of intense dispute. At issue is the significance and future role of the state, the very foundation of the kind of political map we have become accustomed to.

These and other discontinuities and uncertainties create problems for the modern cartographer of Europe. Gone are the days when cartographers did not have to worry about changing state boundaries, and when representing the members of NATO and the Warsaw Pact in different colours captured the essential political configuration of the continent. Not only must the present-day cartographer adapt to constant change, but he/she also needs to address a host of intricate questions. How do you depict the dynamics of the European Union? Which regions qualify to be mapped? More fundamentally, how informative is a map based on state boundaries, and how can you delineate the significant flows across state boundaries?

Some historians would argue that a comparison of maps of Europe just before and just after the First World War might yield important insights into present political configurations and tensions. Others prefer to go back even further in history and draw parallels between developments today and the Middle Ages. They highlight the geopolitical uncertainties, the contradictory impulses of centralization and decentralization, competing organizational forms after the end of the Cold War, as well as the long-term tendency towards overlapping loyalties and identifications among contemporary Europeans. Others still speak of an emerging 'Europe of regions'. They allude primarily to the encouragement of regional cooperation by the European Union, but also point to the fact that Europe was a continent of cities and regions long before the borders of the present states were fixed. We shall return to these simplified characterizations in the following chapters. Let it only be said at this juncture that the coexistence of divergent images points to the complexity and diversity of the current European map, and that our treatment will emphasize the diversity, variability and contingency of the organization of European space through the centuries.

Transdisciplinary trialogue

This book is a collaborative effort between a historian, an economic geographer and a political scientist. While we bring to the joint venture the preconceptions of our respective disciplines, our trialogue provides an opportunity to question and reconsider ingrained knowledge structures. To our mind, this is what *transdisciplinary* research – that much used and abused catchword – is all about. In today's highly specialized and information-rich academic world, it is impossible for any individual researcher to be transdisciplinary in more than a superficial sense. Yet it is often in the border area between disciplines that new knowledge is to be found. The obvious answer to this dilemma lies in collaboration between scholars who are firmly grounded in their respective disciplines while having open minds to criticism and new ideas from other fields.

The preparation of this book has taken the form of a continuous seminar, where each of the authors has prepared first drafts of chapters that have been subjected to the critical scrutiny and piercing questions of the others. Successive revisions have taken into account the input by the co-authors, which means that we are collectively responsible for the final manuscript. Our transdisciplinary trialogue over the past few years, which has involved mutual teaching and learning, has revealed somewhat different, but complementary, emphases within our respective disciplines. For geographers, *territory* is a key concept in addressing the problem of the modern state and its alternatives (how can territory be divided, shared or transcended?); political scientists tend to highlight *organization* (which ways of organizing space for political purposes are feasible?); and historians put emphasis on *identity* (through which historical processes are collective identities formed?). This triad – territory, organization, identity – constitutes our conceptual compass, as we embark on our common intellectual journey.

Organization, Europe, space

The three words in the title of the book, which reflect its triadic disciplinary foundation, warrant a few words of explanation. Space is a generic geographical concept which subsumes territory, a politically laden term. Similarly, organization is a general phenomenon, whereas the state is a specific and prominent form of political organization. The term 'Europe' suggests geographical boundaries and the limitations of our empirical scope, but refers to identity and cultural heritage as well. As will be amplified below, space, identity and organization are interrelated concepts.

Space

Maps, key instruments in geographic research, are expressions of the importance of distance, direction and spatial relations to understanding situations, possibilities and limits. However, there are various restrictions and possibilities that no ordinary map can accurately capture, such as those related directly to the individual and the manner in which he/she organizes his/her work and social life.

The concept of *space* is in reality a three-dimensional phenomenon, but within geography and related disciplines is generally perceived as a two-dimensional surface. The concept itself implies nothing about size. In principle, space is continuous and has no external boundaries. Operationally, it may be either large or small. In these respects, *area* may be considered synonymous with space.

The concept of *territory* is central in this book. A territory is defined as a cohesive section of the earth's surface that is distinguished from its surroundings by a boundary. The term territory is generally used to emphasize the question of 'political space', or a 'power sphere', an area under the control of a given ruler. The *territorial state* and the *region* are examples that will figure prominently in our discussion.

Human behaviour and social relationships have, throughout history, been linked to territory – to the local environment, a region or a state that forms the basis for a common identity and source of livelihood. Territoriality is probably inherent in human perception. Perhaps the manner in which human beings think and operate requires the existence of boundaries. The aim of this book is to investigate whether the boundaries we have become accustomed to, and conventional territorial concepts, are as self-evident as is often assumed. To understand the ubiquitous processes of drawing boundaries and organizing space, three concepts may be helpful: proximity, likeness and linkage.

PROXIMITY Physical proximity has always been a key principle behind decisions as to where to draw boundaries. We usually think of space as spreading from a centre, in the same way that individuals are prisoners of egocentric perceptions. 'I' – and by extension 'we' – constitute the centre interacting with my/our environment. For example, the Chinese used to call their land the 'Middle Kingdom'. When France was divided into *départements* after the Revolution of 1789, the new boundaries were based on how far a horseman could ride in the course of one day, a round trip either to or from a centre. Contemporary divisions into counties are founded on observations regarding commuting, purchasing habits and telecommunications patterns.

LIKENESS All social interaction includes a conception of boundaries that is founded on likeness. Self-images tend to be based on a sense of belonging to a certain group. Our identity rests on our ability to single out 'us' in relation to 'them'. Common interests, kinship, racial affiliation and religious and political convictions foster a powerful sense of community among individuals, yet at the same time may trigger bitter hostilities. The sense of belonging, exclusion and collective identity does not require that the individuals reside in physical proximity to each other.

This applies to intellectual boundaries as well. For instance, the Swedish botanist Carl von Linné was a master of drawing boundaries, but his division of the plant kingdom was based not on physical proximity, but on likeness and kinship between individuals in a population. This form of classification permeates today's education system, our research and, most likely, our way of thinking. Commonality within the more than 500 contemporary academic disciplines, for example, has little to do with territorial proximity. Yet when the boundaries of a discipline are overstepped, it often becomes clear that also in the wide world of scholarship there exist perceptions of a 'Middle Kingdom'.

LINKAGE The difference between likeness and linkage is that linkage has to do with geography. In this book we will discuss linkage chiefly with reference to the *network* concept, which depicts the geographic space as discrete points (nodes) bound together by lines (links). The network discriminates between nodes that are connected to it and those that are not. The implications and significance of this difference will be expanded on later. As will also be elaborated subsequently, the network concept can be used to portray non-territorial ways of organizing space in the scientific and economic as well as the political sphere.

Organization

Organizing refers to the way roles, procedures, culture and space are structured within a collective. It involves distributing preferences and resources among different actors (individuals or groups within the collective). As a consequence, the collective acquires certain priorities and capabilities.[1] A division of labour (roles), methods of coordination, decision-making and conflict resolution (procedures), common values and beliefs (culture) and a delimitation of geographical scope (space) thus characterize organizations. For instance, when we speak of the modern European state as a territorial organization, we highlight space as the defining variable. When we distinguish between parliamentarian and presidential states, we focus on roles, or the division of labour between sub-units. Alternatively, organizations – including states – may be labelled democratic or authoritarian with respect to procedures, and homogeneous or heterogeneous with respect to culture. It is precisely these underlying foundations of established organizations and organizing attempts in Europe that are the focus of our attention in this endeavour.

The word 'organization' derives etymologically from *organum* in Medieval Latin which, in turn, is related to *organon* in Ancient Greek. These words have the double meaning of 'instrument' or 'tool', on the one hand, and 'organ' or 'organism', on the other. This hereditary duality is reflected in our way of thinking and speaking of organizations. On the one hand, organizations are often seen as machines, featuring standardized operation and clockwork precision. It may be argued that 'the mechanistic mode of thought has shaped our most basic conception of what organization is all about'.[2] On the other hand, it is commonplace to use organisms as metaphors for organizations. We speak of different species of organizations, of organizations adapting to their environment, of organizational needs, health and life cycles, etc. The personification tendency is especially evident in the common way of speaking of organizations as if they were information-processing and learning individuals.

The obvious lesson from this preliminary effort at specifying the meaning of organization is that we are dealing with a multifaceted phenomenon. The process of organizing involves several variables – we have identified roles, procedures, culture and space – and the structures we label organizations have features that are imperfectly captured by machine and organism metaphors. Therefore: 'If one truly wishes to understand an organization it is much wiser to start from the premise that organizations are complex, ambiguous, and paradoxical'.[3]

Another caveat concerns the common tendency to equate organization with *formal* organization. But there is an *informal* side to organizations as well, which is not caught by the constitutions and organizational charts of formal organizations. In fact, the argument has been made that most organizational charts of boxes and arrows are not very informative and often misleading. Behind the facade of formal organizations informal structurations of roles, procedures, culture and space tend to emerge. Moreover, informal organizations may exist not only in the shadow of formal ones but also as autonomous alternatives to formal organization. As we shall see, some of the organizational challengers of territorial states today have this informal nature.

The words 'organization' and 'institution' are frequently used interchangeably. Yet a distinction can and should be made. Institutions can be understood as 'social practices consisting of easily recognized roles coupled with clusters of rules or conventions governing relations among the occupants of these roles'. Organizations, by contrast, are 'material entities possessing physical locations (or seats), offices, personnel, equipment, and budgets'. Organizations generally possess a legal personality, which means that they are authorized to enter into contracts, own property, and so on.[4] According to this distinction, the market is an institution, while the firm is an organization. Marriage is an institution, the family its organizational manifestation. By the same token, sovereignty is an institution and the state an organization, as will be elaborated in coming chapters.

Institutions persist over time. Strong institutions tend to be taken for granted and do not require continually mobilized support to sustain them. They confer identity to individuals and tend to colour their perceptions and thinking. Thus, institutions lend order and predictability to human affairs. The process of *institutionalization*, whereby short-term social practices jell into long-term institutions, is therefore of special interest. How did sovereignty practices become institutionalized in consolidating the state? To what extent are the social practices of the European Union institutionalized? These kinds of questions will be addressed in our enquiry into the organization of European space.

Europe

The concept of Europe has different implications depending on context and the observer's perspective. The simplest definition is the physical geographer's description of Europe as a continent, configured as a peninsula delimited by oceans to the north, west and south, and a more diffuse eastern boundary to Asia.[5] In early Antiquity, the boundary to Asia was drawn at the river Don (Tanais),[6] but more recently the Urals have been construed as the dividing line between Europe and Asia. Today, the symbolic border runs even east of the Urals, which never in history have proved to be an obstacle to the flow of ideas and human contacts.

Other portions of Europe's eastern boundary have also lacked real significance: the Ural River, the Caspian Sea, the Black Sea and its outflow into the Mediterranean. The Caucasus mountain range[7] has for centuries been considered part of Europe. Indeed, several of the post-Soviet trans-Caucasian republics today insist that the boundary between Asia and Europe lies further east, and that they are thus potential members of the European Union.

Nor do the Straits of Bosporus constitute a self-evident boundary between the European and the Asian part of Turkey. The Aegean islands, which today belong to Greece, are considered part of Europe, as is Crete, while Cyprus is generally counted as part of Asia. The southeastern boundary also reflects an early Greek perception of Europe as the Greek territories that lay west of the Aegean and were separate from the ancient Greek core areas in Asia Minor.[8]

The Mediterranean, Europe's boundary to Africa, in cultural terms has been quite the opposite of a barrier. Phoenicians, Greeks, Romans and many other peoples of Antiquity used the Mediterranean as a route for commerce and cultural exchange. During the Roman Empire, the Mediterranean was essentially a Roman inland sea, while northern Europe lay entirely outside the scope of the then-civilized world. When, in the centuries after the death of Mohammed, Islam began its expansion along the southern Mediterranean coast, the Mediterranean ceased to function as a link.[9] Today, the boundary between Africa and Europe is strictly upheld, not least to prevent mass immigration of impoverished North Africans to the wealthier European countries.

Nor is Europe's western border, the Atlantic, an impenetrable natural barrier. The Vikings were able to sail long distances over the open seas. In the early sixteenth century, naval powers of Europe conducted voyages of discovery and began to build a worldwide colonial system with Europe at its centre.[10] Although these empires were dissolved during the latter half of the twentieth century, substantial ties remain between the former colonial powers and their erstwhile overseas possessions. Only the northern border of Europe has functioned as a natural boundary historically, although this has not prevented boundary disputes between the coastal states, for instance, in the Barents region.[11]

Europe as a geographic concept can thus be reasonably delimited and defined. It is far more problematic to determine the scope and range of a 'European' culture. The idea of Europe as a cultural community is a relatively recent construction, although its roots can be traced back to Antiquity. Herodotus in the fifth and Hippocrates in the fourth century BC distinguished 'Europe' and 'Europeans' as separate categories in relation to the Greek world, which thus was not considered part of Europe. Yet the concept of Europe was not particularly significant in this era.[12]

It was only in the Carolingian period (c. 800) that the concept of Europe came into more frequent use, to describe not the continent as a whole, but the West Christian realm of Charlemagne, his *Imperium Christianum*. East Rome, Byzantium, which emerged in connection with the division of the empire in the late fourth century, lay outside the West Christian, 'European' sphere,[13] as did Scandinavia and the Muslim-dominated Iberian peninsula.

The perception of Europe as a political entity based on a Christian community survived the Carolingian era. The medieval German emperors and the Catholic Church continued to define Europe in this manner. In later centuries, European unity has remained a goal for both visionary thinkers and politicians, and numerous proposals and plans to unite the continent have been launched and rejected, and in some cases tested, albeit so far without lasting success. The history of Europe until now has been characterized by a perpetual tension between efforts at integration, on the one hand, and diversity and fragmentation, on the other. Both tendencies will be analysed and discussed in the following chapters, which will highlight the role of individuals as well as territory and forms of organization.

To disentangle the substance and scope of a 'European culture' would be a formidable task. For our purposes, it is sufficient to point to a few premises, basic to our understanding of Europe: first, Europe is relatively well defined geographically; second, Europe exists as a political entity, although its demarcation to the east and in relation to Asia continues to be rather diffuse; third, political organization on the continent must be understood in a cultural context of a multitude of nations, states and organizations interacting within this European space, facing a perennial choice between variegation/fragmentation and integration.

Structure of the book

To repeat, our focus is on change and variability rather than permanence, and we apply a long historical perspective in studying the organization of European space. Proceeding from the recognition that human perception is selective and theory-driven, Chapter 1 points to the privileged position of the sovereign state in contemporary historical research and social science theories as well as in the layman's understanding of international relations. Chapter 2 develops an analytical framework for the book – a 'territorial field of tension' – based on the contradictory processes of integration and fragmentation or, taking the state as the point of departure, between globalization and regionalization. Chapter 3 traces the origin of the concept of Europe and ana-lyses the different ways of organizing European space from the Roman Empire to medieval feudalism in terms of integration and fragmentation.

The sovereign state is the focus of the two next chapters. Chapter 4 traces the origin of the modern state. What were the alternatives to territorial states? And why did sovereign states, rather than any of the alternatives, become the predominant mode of organization? After addressing these questions, we discuss the fundamental concept of sovereignty. In Chapter 5 we ask why the state has persisted through more than three centuries, and identify contemporary challenges to the sovereign state as well as state responses to these challenges.

Chapter 6 discusses networks as alternatives to territorial organization. Networks constitute an organizational form that is radically different from states, insofar as they are understood as nodes and links rather than cohesive territory. European unification as an alternative to sovereign states is considered in Chapter 7. By relating the European integration process after the Second World War to earlier attempts at uniting Europe, the chapter aims at an understanding of the organizational nature of the present European Union. We conclude that the dynamics of the EU are more in accordance with the network logic than with the territorial logic.

In Chapter 8 the focus is on regions, understood as meso-level organizations between the national and the local. Various forms of regionalization are discussed, and the popular notion of a 'Europe of Regions' is scrutinized critically. Amplifying the relationship between regions and networks, Chapter 9 suggests the metaphor 'archipelago' to catch the tendency in today's Europe to link up dynamic regions in transnational networks. In Chapter 10, finally, we attempt to summarize, and extrapolate into the future, the tendencies described in the preceding chapters. Unlike the others, the concluding chapter is organized along disciplinary lines. What kind of conclusions does this joint enquiry suggest to a historian, a political scientist and a geographer?

NOTES

1 Lennart Lundquist, *Förvaltning, stat och samhälle* (Lund: Studentlitteratur, 1992), 104.

2 Gareth Morgan, *Images of Organization* (Beverly Hills, CA / London: Sage, 1986), 22.

3 Ibid., 322.

4 The definitions are taken from Oran R. Young, *International Cooperation: Building Regimes for Natural Resources and the Environment* (Ithaca, NY: Cornell University Press, 1989), 32.

5 In modern geographical research, classifications of Europe as a subcontinent or western appendix of Asia can be found. See Norman Davies, *Europe: A History* (Oxford: Oxford University Press, 1996).

6 Jacques Jouanne, 'L'image de l'Europe chez Hérodote et Hippocrate: essai de comparison', in *L'Idée de l'Europe au fil de deux Millénaires*, ed. Michel Perrin (Paris: Beauchesne, 1994), 22–38.

7 For the eastern boundary of the Roman Empire, see C.R. Whittaker, *Roman Empire: A Social and Economic Study* (Baltimore, MD / London: Johns Hopkins University Press, 1994), 49–59.

8 Davies, *Europe*, xv–xvii.

9 Fernand Braudel, *The Mediterranean and the Mediterranean World in the Age of Philip II* (Berkeley / Los Angeles, CA: University of California Press, 1995).

10 See, for example, John Horace Parry, *The Age of Reconnaissance* (London: Weidenfeld & Nicolson, 1963).

11 John M. Kvistad, *The Barents Spirit: A Bridge-building Project in the Wake of the Cold War* (Oslo: Institutt for forsvarsstudier, 1995).

12 See Jouanne, 'L'image de l'Europe'.

13 Rune Johansson, 'Idéer om Europa – Europa som idé', in *Europa – Historiens återkomst*, 3rd edn, ed. Sven Tägil (Hedemora: Gidlunds, 1998), 50ff.

1

State of Mind

All human perception is selective. We all process information through pre-existing 'knowledge structures' – systems of schematized and abstracted knowledge which scientists tend to label 'belief systems' or 'schemata' when referring to people they study, 'theories' when referring to their own scientific activity and 'prejudices' when referring to their rivals and enemies. Without these knowledge structures, 'life would be a buzzing confusion'; at the same time, 'a price is paid for this mental economy' – knowledge structures 'are not infallible guides to the nature of physical or social reality'.[1] Our preconceptions help us structure, but may also distort, what we see, understand and remember.

To a great extent, we are prisoners of our own preconceptions. Cognitive scientists have shown that knowledge structures are resistant to change. Rather than abandoning cherished theories, beliefs or prejudices, we tend to reinterpret contradictory information to fit pre-existing knowledge structures. This is no less true of social science theorists than of 'the man in the street'. The main difference between scientific and intuitive theories is that the former are formalized and available for public scrutiny, whereas the latter are implicit and lie below the level of awareness.

Human perception, in short, is theory-driven, whether or not the 'theories' are conscious and formalized. 'There is nothing as practical as a good theory' is an often-used quote, attributed to the German psychologist Kurt Lewin. Theories represent good cognitive economy, insofar as they allow us to sort out what to pay attention to in the overwhelming flow of stimuli and data. Theories are like floodlights that illuminate one part of the stage but, by the same token, leave other parts in the shade or in the dark. They sensitize us to certain aspects of a phenomenon or problem while desensitizing us to others. To use another metaphor, 'conceptual models not only fix the mesh of the nets that the analyst drags through the material in order to explain a particular action, they also direct him to cast his nets in selected ponds, at certain depths, in order to catch the fish he is after'.[2]

The state in focus

It is this dark side of theories that is our principal concern. Have our floodlights illuminated the wrong part of the stage, and/or have we cast our nets in the wrong ponds? The state has long had a privileged position in historical research and social science theories. The division of the world into sovereign states with mutually exclusive territories is a fundamental premise of social, economic and political life. In our understanding of the current world, 'states have become (second) nature, and come to seem inevitable'.[3] Most disciplines have upheld a clear distinction between what goes on inside the state, on the one hand, and activities that cross state boundaries and are referred to as international relations, on the other.

The predominance of the state in social science thinking is, for example, reflected in the German (and Scandinavian) labels for political science (*Staatswissenschaft*) and economics (*Nationalökonomie*). Similarly, state boundaries are prevalent in the maps of geographers, and a majority of historians write national histories. Moreover, the statistics that social scientists use are normally collected on a national basis. In fact, the etymology of the word 'statistics' reveals its close relation to 'state'. The state, in short, has become the ordering principle of several disciplines, all of which take the state for granted. State boundaries have come to represent intellectual boundaries as well.

It should be noted that the words 'state' and 'nation' are often used interchangeably in contemporary political and analytical language – in fact, you need go no further than to the previous paragraph to find an example. For instance, we speak of international relations when referring to interstate phenomena; the United Nations is a misnomer for an association of states; and we often allude to states acting 'in the national interest'. We shall return to the subject of nationalism and nation-states in Chapter 5. At this point, suffice it to say that the tendency to confound state and nation is another sign of the expansive nature of the state concept.

The prominence of the state constitutes the obvious common denominator of the disciplinary knowledge structures of the three co-authors, and the idea of this book has grown out of a shared conviction that this theoretical foundation needs to be reconsidered and that past, present and future efforts at organizing European space provide a fertile ground for such reconceptualizations. We are drawing on the growing realization within our respective disciplines that the structural basis of territorial states is, if not disappearing, then at least changing in character. In this sense, present-day scholars may find themselves in a situation similar to that of

> the late medieval political theorists who thought the choice was between the papacy and the empire as the primary unit of political organization. The best of these theorists realized that something new was emerging – the modern state; but they lacked the categories for understanding the new reality. We now are in a similar position.[4]

At the same time, we are sceptical of the tendency to overemphasize the newness of recent developments in Europe. We don't subscribe to proclamations of 'the end of history'[5] and 'the end of geography'[6] – or, for that matter, 'the end of the nation-state'[7] and 'the end of sovereignty'.[8] If anything, the end of the Cold War (here it is more legitimate to speak of an 'end', although there are sceptics on that score as well) taught us the dangers of theorizing on the basis of a narrow time frame. Theorists of international relations who used the Cold War as a yardstick of normality now face what Susan Strange has labelled 'Pinocchio's problem'. The strings that were attached to Pinocchio made him a puppet of forces he could neither control nor influence. His problem at the end of the story, when he was magically transformed into a real boy, was that he had no strings to guide him. Similarly, students of international relations in the post-Cold War era have been shorn of the intellectual strings that tied them to existing power structures, and are groping for orientation in the new world.[9]

The obvious lesson is that a longer historical perspective is warranted, if we want to avoid that our knowledge structures make us prisoners of the unique features of present realities. Thus, when we explore alternative ways of organizing European space, we rely to a great extent on historical experiences and structures. To be sure, history does not repeat itself, but we pay a heavy price if we ignore its lessons. And recent developments in Europe have involved the return, not the end, of history.[10]

More than half a century ago, E.H. Carr concluded: 'Few things are permanent in history; and it would be rash to assume that the territorial unit of power is one of them'.[11] Similarly, our enquiry proceeds from the assumption that the system of territorial states, which was formed in Europe with the Peace of Westphalia of 1648 and which eventually spread to cover the entire globe, is contingent. The state does not represent the only way of organizing European space, nor is it the inevitable conclusion of an evolutionary process. By problematizing the state and putting it into historical context rather than taking it for granted, we aim to remove the blindfolds that state-centric theories have furnished to our respective disciplines.

A constructivist approach

Our focus on perceptions and theories puts us in the 'constructivist' camp. We adhere to the view that what we refer to as political, social, economic and historical 'realities' are to a significant extent socially constructed by cognitive structures that give meaning to the material world. However, we do not subscribe to the extreme relativism of 'postmodernism' which holds that material reality cannot be known outside human language; thus, everything is reduced to 'discourses' or 'texts', and science is but one among these discourses with no privileged position. Rather, we agree with the emerging view of constructivism as occupying the 'middle ground' between rationalist, positivist approaches and interpretive, postmodern approaches.[12] On the one hand, constructivists, like positivists, believe in the existence of a material world which is independent of our accounts and which provides opportunities for, and puts restraints on, human action. On the other hand, constructivists, like postmodernists, hold that the material reality does not fully determine human action and thought and that social reality emerges from the attachment of meaning to physical objects. International relations, to constructivists, are based primarily on social facts, which are facts only by agreement. A metaphor may help to illustrate the constructivist position:

> Suppose you toss a rock into the air. It can make only a simple response to the external physical forces that act on it. But if you throw a bird into the air, it may fly off into a tree. Even though the same physical forces act on the bird as on the rock, a massive amount of internal information processing takes place inside the bird and affects its behavior. Finally, take a group of people, a nation or various nations and metaphorically toss them in the air. Where they go, how, when and why, is not entirely determined by physical forces and constraints; but neither does it depend solely on individual preferences and rational choices. It is also a matter of their shared knowledge, the collective meaning they attach to their situation, their authority and legitimacy, the rules, institutions and material resources they use to find their way, and their practices, or even, sometimes their joint creativity.[13]

Our enquiry into the organization of European space will focus on what Emanuel Adler calls 'cognitive evolution', the adoption by policy-makers – and scholars – of new interpretations of reality. This means trying to understand 'how institutional facts become *taken for granted*', how 'as certain ideas or practices become reified, competing ideas and practices are delegitimized'.[14]

Symbols and metaphors of statehood

The use of symbols and metaphors is central to processes of cognitive evolution in international relations. The term 'metaphor' comes from the Greek verb *metapherein*, 'to carry from one place to another', to transfer. 'The essence of metaphor is understanding and experiencing one kind of thing in terms of another'.[15] Metaphors are not merely figures of speech or ornaments; they are 'pervasive in everyday life, not just in language but in thought and action'.[16] We typically conceptualize the unfamiliar in terms of the familiar, the non-physical in terms of the physical, the less clearly delineated in terms of the more clearly delineated. We tend to structure the less concrete and inherently vaguer concepts (like those for mental processes) in terms of more concrete concepts (like those for physical processes) with a clearer experiential basis. For instance, many of the terms used to characterize intellectual activity are based on the metaphor of seeing with the eye – 'observe', 'see', 'view', 'point of view', 'outlook', 'focus', 'perspective', etc.[17]

By the same token, abstract political phenomena are strikingly often treated in metaphorical terms by practitioners and theoreticians alike. 'Since metaphor is transference of meaning from the familiar to the unfamiliar, the pervasiveness of metaphor in political speech is a sign that political things are somehow less familiar or accessible than the things from which political metaphors are taken'.[18] We have already pointed to the prevalence of mechanical and organic metaphors in descriptions of organizations. Other examples include the frequent use of spatial metaphors in political language. Ordering political parties and groupings along a left–right axis is a metaphor that dates back to the seating of the various fractions in the French National Assembly at the time of the French Revolution. Another equally common – but less conscious – spatial metaphor concerns our use of 'up' to denote power and high status and 'down' to denote powerlessness and low status (we speak of leaders being at the *height* of their power, of *high* command and of *climbing* the social ladder; conversely, you *fall* from power, and are at the *bottom* of the social hierarchy).[19] The 'up–down' imagery seems to be universal, transcending time and space, as indicated by the systematic use of it in the Amarna letters, the cuneiform tablets containing correspondence of the Egyptian court with neighbouring rulers in the mid-fourteenth century BC.[20]

The reliance on metaphors applies, *a fortiori*, to states and their relations. It is hard to imagine a vocabulary of international relations free from metaphors, analogies and symbols. Personification of the state – as of any organization, as pointed out in the Introduction – is a basic metaphor, which guides our thinking about international relations. As noted by one prominent scholar,

> if state behavior is to be intelligible and to any degree predictable, states must be assumed to possess psychological traits of the kind known to the observer through introspection and through acquaintance with other human beings. States must be thought capable, for example, of desires and preferences, of satisfaction and dissatisfaction, of the choice of goals and means.[21]

States/persons are members of a society; they maintain relations with each other; they may be friends, enemies, neighbours, allies, protectors, clients and so on. States behave, they express their interests, they perceive each other's actions, they interpret world events. We ascribe different personalities to states – they may be reliable or unreliable, aggressive or peaceful, strong or weak, decisive or wavering, stable or paranoid, cooperative or recalcitrant, and so forth. This kind of linguistic usage is sometimes defended as shorthand for persons acting in the name of the state, but the root metaphor – the state is a person – nevertheless tends to colour our thinking about international relations.

The state as a home is another common and powerful metaphor. The state's territory is a home, which needs to be protected from intruders. This spatial metaphor conjures up a limited, enclosed space with a clear-cut border between inside and outside. Within the home there is community and solidarity from which outsiders are excluded. Phenomena that do not tally with the home metaphor are perceived as unnatural. Homeless nations, such as the Jewish nation in the past and the Kurdish nation today, are anomalies, which, like homeless people, evoke mixed feelings of compassion and threat.

The two metaphors of states as persons and homes seem to be derived from a common preconceptual 'container' schema, deeply embedded in everyday language. It has three elements: interior, boundary surface and exterior. 'This schema is the basis of our understanding of "inside" and "outside", of human bodies themselves and of nation states'.[22] Moreover, 'the state is a person' and 'the state is a home' belong to the category of metaphors which are systematic, and which form 'coherent systems of metaphorical concepts and corresponding coherent systems of expressions for those concepts'.[23] They have a series of metaphorical entailments and a spillover of analogous connotations. In fact, it is difficult to talk and think of international relations without using these metaphors. By the same token, they limit our vision.

> The very systematicity that allows us to comprehend one aspect of a concept in terms of another . . . will necessarily hide other aspects of the concepts. In allowing us to focus on one aspect of a concept . . . , a metaphorical concept can keep us from focusing on other aspects of the concept that are inconsistent with that metaphor.[24]

While systematic, metaphors are often unconscious. With frequent usage, expressions will no longer be conceived of as metaphorical but as natural. Therefore they can be seen as necessary and inevitable, which of course they are not. There are always alternative metaphors, but new approaches to familiar phenomena may require 'frame restructuring', that is, relying on a different 'generative metaphor' which directs attention to new features and relations of the phenomena.[25] The metaphorical expressions we use when talking and thinking about states and relations between states tend to be both systematic and unconscious. Thus, personification renders it natural to see states as calculating actors and the home metaphor makes us take for granted exclusive territoriality.

In this book, we will question these ingrained metaphors and make some initial efforts at frame restructuring. In our discussion of alternative ways of organizing European space, the concepts of region, union and network loom large. The metaphorical nature of 'region' and 'union' are not immediately obvious. 'Union' stems from *unus*, the Latin word for 'one' and signifies anything that is constituted as one by the combination of elements previously separate. The word 'region' derives from a Latin verb, *rego*, which means 'to steer'. The original meaning of *regio* was thus 'direction', and only in a figurative sense did it come to denote border and a delimited space or district. Network is a more recent and increasingly popular metaphor in science as well as everyday language. As a metaphor of human organization, 'network' transcends territoriality; it substitutes horizontal, decentralized organization for vertical, hierarchical organization; it associates to complex, open-ended systems rather than to simple, closed systems; and it focuses on the interplay between technology and human beings. In these senses it challenges the very aspects of states that we have come to take for granted. In fact, it challenges the 'container' schema, which forms the basis of our metaphorical understanding of states.

In international relations, individual acts and events often assume a metaphorical or symbolic character. The fall of the Berlin Wall in 1989 and subsequent developments, which contributed to the end of the Cold War, have become powerful symbols. These events are seen as turning points, heralding a new era. There has been an avalanche of books speculating about the nature of post-Cold War international relations. Insofar as the events of 1989–90 spurred our joint rethinking of the organization of European space, we are no different from most of our colleagues. However, we diverge from many of them by applying a much longer historical perspective. In a way, it is a question of 'punctuation': in the same way as punctuation marks indicate beginnings and endings and give structure to otherwise fluid processes, social scientists and historians tend to single out which events in a sequence are stimuli or causes and which are responses or effects. While no doubt profound and significant, the events of 1989–90 should not blind us to other processes of change with different time horizons. Thus, in our 'punctuation', the Treaty of Westphalia of 1648 – another event of great symbolic and metaphorical significance – plays a more prominent role than the demolition of the Berlin Wall. Westphalia created the modern state. While the end of the Cold War did not eradicate or invalidate the state, it provided the impetus to start thinking more profoundly about its nature and its future.

NOTES

1 Richard Nisbett and Lee Ross, *Human Inference: Strategies and Shortcomings of Social Judgment* (Englewood Cliffs, NJ: Prentice Hall, 1980), 7.

2 Graham T. Allison, *Essence of Decision: Explaining the Cuban Missile Crisis* (Boston, MA: Little, Brown, 1971), 4.

3 R.B.J. Walker, *Inside/Outside: International Relations as Political Theory* (Cambridge: Cambridge University Press, 1993), 179.

4 W. Magnusson and R.B.J. Walker, as quoted in Thom Kuehls, *Beyond Sovereign Territory* (Minneapolis, MN: University of Minnesota Press, 1996), 37.

5 Francis Fukuyama, *The End of History and the Last Man* (New York: The Free Press, 1992).

6 Richard O'Brien, *Global Financial Integration: The End of Geography* (London: Pinter, 1992).

7 Jean-Marie Guéhenno, *The End of the Nation-State* (Minneapolis, MN: University of Minnesota Press, 1995).

8 Joseph A. Camilleri and Jim Falk, *The End of Sovereignty? The Politics of a Shrinking and Fragmenting World* (Aldershot: Edward Elgar, 1992).

9 Susan Strange, *The Retreat of the State: The Diffusion of Power in the World Economy* (Cambridge: Cambridge University Press, 1996), 198–9.

10 The 'return of history' idea is elaborated and applied to Europe in *Europa – Historiens återkomst*, 3rd edn, ed. Sven Tägil (Hedemora: Gidlunds, 1998).

11 E.H. Carr, *The Twenty Years' Crisis 1919–1939: An Introduction to the Study of International Relations* (London: Macmillan, 1939; reprinted 1984), 229.

12 Cf. Emanuel Adler, 'Seizing the Middle Ground: Constructivism in World Politics', *European Journal of International Relations* 3 (1997), 319–63; Jeffrey T. Chekel, 'The Constructivist Turn in International Relations Theory', *World Politics*, 50 (1998), 327.

13 Adler, 'Seizing the Middle Ground', 320–1.

14 Ibid., 340.

15 George Lakoff and Mark Johnson, *Metaphors We Live By* (Chicago: University of Chicago Press, 1980), 5.

16 Ibid., 3.

17 Ibid., 48; Eugene F. Miller, 'Metaphor and Political Knowledge', *American Political Science Review*, 73 (1979), 166.

18 Miller, 'Metaphor and Political Knowledge', 163.

19 Cf. Lakoff and Johnson, *Metaphors We Live By*, 14–16.

20 Kevin Avruch, 'Reciprocity, Equality, and Status-Anxiety in the Amarna Letters', in *The Beginnings of International Relations: Amarna Diplomacy*, ed. Raymond Cohen and Raymond Westbrook (Baltimore, MD: Johns Hopkins University Press, 1999).

21 Arnold Wolfers, *Discord and Collaboration: Essays in International Politics* (Baltimore, MD: Johns Hopkins University Press, 1962; reprinted 1988), 10.

22 Paul A. Chilton, *Security Metaphors: Cold War Discourse from Containment to Common House* (New York: Peter Lang, 1996), 50.

23 Lakoff and Johnson, *Metaphors We Live By*, 9.

24 Ibid., 10.

25 Donald A. Schön, 'Generative Metaphor: A Perspective on Problem-Solving in Social Policy', in *Metaphor and Thought*, ed. Andrew Ortony (Cambridge: Cambridge University Press, 1979).

2

Mapping Space

Physical foundations

Europe is a small continent in terms of physical area. On a world map or a globe, Europe appears as a western protuberance of Asia. It is difficult, if not impossible, to discern any natural boundary between the large eastern part of Eurasia and its small western portion. Europe meets the oceans with deep bays and prominent tongues of land. Large inner seas – the Mediterranean in the south and the Baltic in the north – cut deep into the continent. The coastline of Europe is extensive. There are no deserts, few impenetrable forests, marshes or mountain ranges, and thus scarcely any concrete obstacles to human advances. The land is essentially level, and interrupted in parts by navigable rivers. The climate varies depending on season, latitude and distance from the sea. Much of Europe is highly favourable to human settlement and livelihood.

The waterways were long the most convenient and comfortable form of transportation for both people and goods. They also provided the foundations of Europe's economic and cultural development. Foreign trade was conducted mainly from areas along the Mediterranean, the Black Sea, the Baltic, the North Sea and the Atlantic coast. Several of the continent's most important cities emerged along rivers with intersecting land trade routes.

During the thirteenth and fourteenth centuries, cities sprang up around Europe at an unparalleled rate. Several hundred cities in central Europe obtained political and economic privileges. Cities also became larger as a result of improved means of transportation. The cities, some with roots dating back to well before the Middle Ages, demarcated the strategic positions of Europe, defined by watercourses and topography. The Romans had laid the foundations in many instances. Along the Danube and the Rhine, forts were built and military camps were equipped. The *limes* marked the boundary between the barbaric peoples of north and east, and the civilized populations of south and west. Emanating from a gilded post on the Forum Romanum in Rome, roads branched out toward these forts. There were at least 4,800 km of paved roads in the Roman Empire, and still longer stretches of good-quality roads without permanent surfaces. These roads represented the best communications on land until the nineteenth century. That Napoleon could not travel faster than Julius Caesar was not only a figure of speech, but a reality.[1]

Over time, many of Europe's most important cities – Bucharest, Belgrade, Budapest, Vienna, Basle, Zurich, Frankfurt, Strasbourg, Mainz, Bonn, Cologne, Paris and London – emerged in connection with this 'physical infrastructure'. The Romans were in Maastricht already by 100 BC. They called the city *Trajectum ad Mosam*, the place where one can cross the Maas. Similarly, and mainly in connection with the waterways, cities later evolved in the Germanic and Slavic parts of Europe.

Generation upon generation invested in, and anchored themselves into, these patterns. When railroads, highways and telephone networks were built much later, the basic pattern had already been established. No wars, revolutions, plagues, economic crises or border regulations have essentially altered the picture. The functions of cities and the speed of transportation, however, have changed radically. In the most densely populated parts of Europe with ancient urban cultures, the cities function as mirrors of society. New features from every era in the area's history are reflected in the life of the city and leave their mark on remaining physical structures and architectures.

In earlier times, the *marketplace* was the core of the city. During Antiquity, the *agora* in Athens, and later the *forum* in Rome, served as political, commercial and religious centres. The medieval, and to a still greater degree, the Renaissance cities functioned as marketplaces, meeting points and scenes of action. They were the core of the far-flung, yet narrow stream of goods, information and people. Venice, Florence, Genoa, Antwerp, Bruges, Amsterdam, Lyons and some seventy Hanseatic cities in northern Europe are well-known examples.

The *factories* typified the cities of the new industrial world. In conjunction with natural resources and access to energy, industrial workers were recruited to large plants. Great developments in transport paved the way for uncontrolled urban growth. In England and Scotland around 1800, there were four cities with more than 50,000 inhabitants; a single generation later, the number had grown tenfold. Fordistic methods of production soon came to dominate the areas that stretched from the English Midlands, across northern France, southern Belgium, the Ruhr district and northwestern Italy. Smaller industrial districts emerged in different places. The process culminated around 1960.

After a period of decline and decay in several traditional industrial centres, European cities in recent times have experienced a sort of renaissance. The cities that are generally considered successful are distinguished by the fact that they serve as meeting places, liaison centres and arenas more than others. The function once filled by the marketplace has been moved indoors, and the media are key instruments for the city's contacts with the rest of the world. The advantages of the city have to do with the fact that it offers *proximity* in terms of density and sociality, but also in terms of the ease with which other cities can be reached through the wires and lines that facilitate communication and transport. The city is not only a place where goods and services are exchanged, and where people meet and collaborate. It is also the birthplace of new ideas, lifestyles, fashions and technologies. Cities, in short, are the ganglions of the European nervous system.

Against the background of great geopolitical changes in Europe, the settlement pattern emerges as the most stable spatial organization over time. It is to this pattern that the population, production and all forms of transportation are connected. From a wider perspective, the cities are thus at the heart of much of the geographic continuity of Europe.

Power over territory

The actions and social relations of human beings have always been tied to a territory, be it a local environment, a region or a state. The territory provides the basis for their common identity and the source of their livelihood. Territoriality may be inherent in human perception, and the instinctual need to protect one's preserves seems primordial. In agricultural society, owning a plot of land was essential to survival and reproduction. Physical distances long hindered the movement of people and goods. Information could only be exchanged between people within sight and earshot. In modern times, technological advances have entailed dramatic increases in informational range and geographic mobility.

In modern societies there is a tension between global and local forces. Two apparently incompatible trends point in different directions (see Figure 2.1). *Globalization* points to increased dependence on the outside world. Global networks, extended spheres of interest and increased mobility presage a society of flows on a global scale. *Regionalization* points in another direction. It implies that human beings and activities are, and will remain, tightly bound to a local and regional environment. These ties are considered fundamental

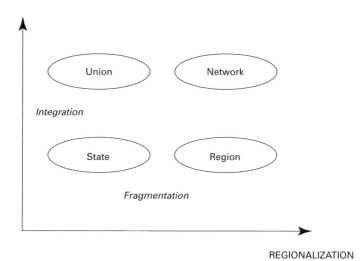

FIGURE 2.1 *The territorial field of tension*

and stand out in striking contrast to a world characterized by widened horizons and increasing mobility. History is full of examples of cultural, economic and political forces that have moved in different directions. As a result of the rapid changes that have occurred in Europe since 1989, these tensions have now become acute and are the subject of a lively debate and an extensive literature. As we have discussed in Chapter 1, the state is at the centre of this debate. The state is also the benchmark in the territorial field of tension depicted in Figure 2.1.

The sovereign state

The territorial state is the framework within which most political activity has been organized. The contemporary way of looking at the world assumes that states cover the surface of the earth and significant parts of adjacent waters. Legally defined borders distinguish the territories from one another, and within these boundaries the state exercises uniform and unbroken sovereignty over every square foot. This may be the reality today, but things were not always so.

In earlier epochs, there existed no uniform, comprehensive division of the geographic space. Today's territorial states were born in a world of geopolitical disarray void of any well-defined territorial order. Political, economic, religious and cultural areas overlapped with one another in a remarkably irregular pattern. For most people, the immediate environment constituted the framework for consciousness and the domain of experiences on which their identity rested. The states that did exist were vague constructions with nebulous boundaries. They were defined by a centre whose authority decreased with physical distance. The territorial spheres of power frequently changed in both substance and scope, and were combined into constantly shifting constellations.

The first territorial states in Europe emerged in the late Middle Ages, and the last important ones – Italy and Germany – in the latter half of the nineteenth century. The Hundred Years War between England and France (1337–1453), the Peace of Westphalia (1648), the French Revolution (1789) and the Napoleonic Wars (1800–1815) are generally seen as key moments in the history of the territorial state. The industrial revolution, general education, mass armies, national romanticism and universal suffrage – major phenomena of the nineteenth and early twentieth centuries – also figure in the picture. The emergence and evolution of the sovereign state, as well as the relationship between state and nation and between state and territory, are discussed in greater detail in Chapters 4 and 5.

An important factor contributing to the massive breakthrough of ideological nationalism in the past two centuries was that the movement stipulated objectives that coincided with strong economic interests. More important, however, was a series of parallel events that, from the dawn of the nineteenth to the middle of the twentieth century, engendered new preconditions for larger territorial spheres of organization. The new markets and modes of production of the industrial revolution constituted one such prerequisite. Explosive growth in technology was another. In addition, politics and the exercise of power increasingly came to be tied to geographically demarcated territories. The scope and application of rules and laws were now fenced in by physical boundaries. Within this framework, the state established a monopoly on the legitimate use of force and on the collection of taxes. Barriers to trade and customs controls were erected along the external parameters of the state. National banks were created to regulate interest rates and the national currency. Uniform school systems and career paths in the public sector evolved within the state's borders. Universal suffrage was granted to the citizens of the state, who in turn became obliged to defend the motherland. Collective welfare and social security were linked to the territory. A form of welfare nationalism emerged. A growing portion of democratic power and public decision-making authority has, during the twentieth century, been tied to the national level. In most of Europe, states are today the prevalent forums for decision-making.

The view that economics are a national matter evolved under mercantilism. Among the classicists and neo-classicists of economic theory, the nation (read: the territorial state) was not only a political and military unity, but also an economic 'being' that created the welfare of its citizens. Welfare was created and lost through the economic competition between large territories. Gross national product, national balance of trade, national growth, national welfare and national savings are still considered concrete and meaningful economic measures.

The territorial state today appears to be a firmly grounded construction. Consecutive generations have founded and strengthened the set of rules on which it rests. The industrial revolution and technological advances laid the material foundations for the centralization of power and state sovereignty. Education and propaganda, professional activity and career paths have given rise to 'imagined communities' shared by many.[2] The question to be pursued in this book is whether other spheres in Figure 2.1 contain forces that might eventually challenge this powerful construct.

The European Union

The dream of a united Europe is not new. Over several centuries, different empires brought under their supremacy significant parts of the continent for longer or shorter periods, and at times also areas on the other side of the oceans. Yet not all efforts to integrate Europe have taken place under the mantle of imperialism. Sources suggest that hundreds of plans for the peaceful unification of Europe have been presented throughout history.[3] In the sixteenth century, humanists of various nationalities demanded that the European rulers unite, primarily as a response to the then imminent Turkish threat. In the late seventeenth century, an outline was drawn for a European league of nations. Some hundred years later, the German philosopher Immanuel Kant argued that a lasting peace in Europe required a federation of states based on the principle of international law. In the revolutionary year 1848, the idea of a united Europe gained a broader following. French writer Victor Hugo advocated for the creation of a United States of Europe based on political democracy and respect for the rights of man. The outbreak of a world war in 1914 shattered any such hopes, however. Between the First and the Second World Wars, new plans were drafted for integrating Europe.

The European Coal and Steel Community (1951), the Rome Treaty (1957) and the Maastricht Treaty (1991) all indicated that Europe was on its way to a functioning union, corresponding to the upper left-hand sphere in Figure 2.1. Maastricht signalled a new phase in the quest for 'an ever closer union between the peoples of Europe'. Some states prefer the word *federation* to union, however. If all the provisions stipulated in Maastricht are implemented, then member states will relinquish a significant part of their traditional sovereignty. Maastricht calls for not only a closer economic and monetary union, but also a common regional policy, police cooperation, coordinated border controls, and common foreign and security policies. The path toward a European union indicates that different issues have been prioritized at different times. At first, peace dominated most discussions. Then, the rise of the global economy and international competition came to predominate. Today, unemployment and environmental problems are receiving most attention. Another major question is the European Union's boundary to the surrounding world, and its potential expansion eastward.

The European Union is supported by several of the same elements that were critical during the construction of sovereign states. Among factors that are lacking, however, are far-reaching social communication and identity at the supranational level. Is it reasonable to assume that an overarching European identity can be forged? Is it possible, or indeed desirable, to construct an imagined community within such a large area, with a multitude of deeply rooted ethnic and cultural particularities?

Autonomous networks

Whereas a territory is a continuous part of the earth's surface, a network depicts the geographic space as discrete points (nodes) bound together by lines (links). A network discriminates between nodes that are hooked up to the net and those that are not. As will be discussed further in Chapters 6 and 7, the tension between the two concepts becomes manifest when networks that are important to our welfare become autonomous in relation to the individual territories to which democratic control is confined.[4]

There are different types of networks. One may distinguish between physical, institutional and socio-cultural networks, to mention three pertinent dimensions. *Physical networks* are composed of constructions, lines and channels for the transportation of goods, people and information. Networks of highways, railroads, waterways, airways as well as electric grids and telecommunications constitute examples. These are physically tangible, and 'ground' all flows and contacts in the terrain. Since the end of the hunter–gatherer society and the creation of fixed settlements, these networks have come to constitute our principal geographic space. In the physical networks, the nodes are stations, the only places in which access to the network is granted. The network properties are particularly apparent when the nodes are comparatively distant from one another, such as in airline and maritime networks, and less apparent when they are closer, as in road networks and telecommunications systems. Physical networks are intimately related to wider patterns of settlement. Cities and places can at an aggregated level be viewed as nodes where channels of transportation and communications come together.

Institutional networks, or, as they are sometimes called, *organizational* networks, bind together the different sites and entities of economic and political life – those that produce goods, those that administer and those that offer services. Such networks can be internal, that is, links exist within an organization, be it a firm, a political party, or some other form of economic or political unit or collectivity. *External* or *interorganizational* networks tie together places of work that belong to different organizations. To apply the concept of network in this context, there must exist enduring interdependence between the participant entities. The relationship may be based on agreements and contracts between, for instance, providers and clients in a comprehensive system of production, or on established trust between different organizations.

Social and cultural networks unite individuals, and therefore also fields of knowledge and social environments. They convey ideas and impulses. Kinship or some other form of social relationship may serve as the tie that binds. So can various communities of interest, shared knowledge and mutual understanding. Social and cultural networks involve complex structures that together forge a virtually impenetrable network morphology. Because people can change roles and positions, these networks are in principle flexible. In practice, however, they reveal remarkably tenacious patterns, as will be discussed later. The concept of 'social web' or 'fabric' will be used as a synonym for network, to indicate that a network structure is quite dense.[5]

Many of the most important societal functions are today organized in networks. Within the world economy, modern industrial production and successful research, network structures are so prominent that one may speak of an emerging *network society*.[6]

Regions

With economic globalization, the outline of a boundless global society of flows can be discerned. In this new world, the traditional territorial state tends to lose some of the importance it has enjoyed in the past centuries. Another, more limited geographic entity is surfacing as a key actor – the region. Today, regions are considered the emblems of what is unique to Europe: its diversity and variation. As will be discussed further in Chapter 8, regions tend to be strengthened, as territorial states become weaker. Globalization is accompanied by regionalization, and the two trends reinforce one another.

In this context, the concept of region designates an area that is smaller than the typical territorial state, but larger than a municipality. In other words, the region is an entity smaller than the national context but larger than the local one, and may also be called a province or a district. With this definition, we are choosing not to use region to describe large territorial units, so-called macro-regions, such as 'the Mediterranean region', 'the Pacific region', 'the Baltic region' or 'the Barents region'.[7]

As will be elaborated in Chapter 8, regions appear in various guises and shapes. There are also different forms of regionalization, ranging from the decentralization of political and economic power to separatist tendencies threatening the disintegration of states. Political scientists, economists, geographers, historians and ethnologists have all begun to pay greater attention to the regional level.

The territorial field of tension

When the Berlin Wall crumbled in the autumn of 1989, a period of great change set in. So dramatic was the upheaval that many drew comparisons to the aftermath of the French Revolution in 1789. Eastern Europe began a massive transformation. The Soviet Union disintegrated. Former people's democracies in the Soviet sphere of influence regained their sovereignty and could once again go their own ways. Three states – the Soviet Union, Yugoslavia and Czechoslovakia – became twenty-two. With the exception of Romania and Yugoslavia, the changes proceeded peacefully.

In the heart of Europe, Germany was reunified. The European Community began to expand from its western core. The Maastricht Treaty of 1991 signalled an important step in creating a supranational European Union. Following referendums in their countries, Austria, Finland and Sweden joined the integration process. The Norwegians opted to remain outside the European Union. Meanwhile, regional identities and separatist movements gained momentum in various corners of Europe.

Amid the confusing dynamics of integration and fragmentation, questions regarding territories and their boundaries have come to the fore. The up-heavals of 1989 changed not only the map of Europe. The former political and economic parameters were altered, as were the premises for governance and planning. Theories and knowledge structures have yet to adapt to the new circumstances.

The assumption guiding our enquiry is that there is a tension between the globalizing and regionalizing trends that stimulates pressure for change and transformation. In the context of this tension, the three territorial entities discussed earlier are particularly important. Sovereign states remain the most important territorial units today. In much of the world, most political life is organized within state parameters. States provide the frame of reference for economics, social life and thinking. They are the foundations of the individual's identity. The European Union, as mentioned, stands out as a contemporary and readily accessible example of supranational integration. Self-confident regions are physically demarcated entities smaller than most states, and are roughly equal to districts or provinces. Alongside these formations, there exist autonomous networks that in various ways transcend the traditional territorial, political, economic and social frameworks. The corporate and organizational world as well as science, culture and social relations display transnational networks.

The ovals in Figure 2.1 can also be seen as four organizational spheres that compete with one another: sovereign states caught between supranational integration, autonomous networks and self-aware regions. The tension among them becomes apparent in contemporary discussions about the foundations of political power, democracy and legitimate normative systems. It influences the scope of national economies. And it becomes manifest in debates on the environment, management of resources, welfare and employment.

There is yet another thought behind the positioning of the four spheres. Against the background of the sovereign state, supranational integration is assumed to point unambiguously to the widening of the territorial sphere, if not to a global, then at least to a European level. Similarly, the rise in regional self-confidence is considered to lead unequivocally to the strengthening of the regional level. Words like 'Eurocracy' and 'regionalism' are used to capture each of the two trends. In reality, the two trends interact and reinforce each other. There is indeed a rise of the regional in close step with the rise of the global. As will be elaborated in Chapter 6, the development of autonomous networks is not as readily reduced to a single, obvious direction. Numerous studies indicate that the transnational networks that have developed within the corporate and political world, higher education, research and cultural life at the same time are dependent on regional and local support. 'Local embeddedness of transnational networks' is an expression used to describe the situation.

While the challenges that Europe has been faced with in recent years will be a focus of our enquiry, it should be recalled that the tensions depicted in Figure 2.1 are not new. Rather, these tensions have created more or less constant stimuli for change in our history. What is new is that the tensions have changed direction. From the Middle Ages to today, the emerging states challenged the older regions and networks and prevented far-reaching integration or fragmentation. Today, it is the state that is under fire.

Like regions and cities, networks of different types have long histories. Long before Christ, the Phoenicians, for instance, developed a network of trade routes that tied together commercial stations, and, over time, important commercial cities. The basis of this network was a narrow coastal sliver between Lebanon and the sea, while the nodes of the network lay scattered around the beaches of the Mediterranean and, most likely, also along the western coasts of Africa and Europe. The Greeks later constructed a similar realm of networks, as did the residents of Venice in the early Middle Ages. In northern Europe, some seventy cities forged a commercial league during the thirteenth, fourteenth and fifteenth centuries. This Hanseatic League functioned as a northern European great power without actually controlling a compact territory.

Concerning the influence of Venice during the fourteenth and fifteenth centuries, the French historian Fernand Braudel writes that the Venice-centred world economy, which was the source of its power, is not easy to demarcate on the map of Europe. The central zone in the city's power sphere consisted of an 'archipelago of cities', in the south demarcated by a line between Florence and Ancona, and in the north by the Alps. But these areas marked by fixed stars had in the north, on the other side of the Alps, an extension through a sort of milky way of commercial cities – Augsburg, Vienna, Nuremberg, Regensburg, Ulm, Basle, Strasbourg, Cologne, Hamburg and even Lübeck – and ended with the still powerful Dutch cities (where Bruges still shone brightest) and the English ports of London and Southampton.[8]

There were also cultural and social ties that wove together different parts of Europe. The Roman Catholic Church created a highly influential network of order routes and information channels with thousands of churches and monasteries as nodes of support. Universities were founded in close connection to many of these as local units, linked to a 'republic of the learned' by various contacts and a common language. Ruling dynasties and aristocratic families reinforced their exclusive ties to each other through strategic marriages, the use of languages their subjects could not understand, and fine manners. Journeymen, master-builders, artists, musicians and students imparted their competencies during their travels.

With the benefit of hindsight, it is clear that geopolitical developments at the dawn of the modern period, c. 1500, were at a turning point, an intersection with several paths from which to choose. One path would have allowed the continuation of far-reaching local and regional independence, closed feudal entities and scattered, free cities interconnected by trade routes. Another road might have led to the creation of some overarching European community. The Catholic Church and the Holy Roman Empire preferred this path. Both the local and the universal paths were trod; but it was another route, a middle course, that became most important over time. Around cultural, economic and political core areas in different parts of Europe, medium-sized territories emerged. One after the other, the regions and networks of the Middle Ages were engulfed by the territorial claims of the growing central powers.

The challenges illustrated in Figure 2.1 imply that we are today moving toward geopolitical patterns that existed before the dawn of the large territorial state. Indeed, some observers speak of 'a new Middle Ages'. The analogy has been made, by, for instance, the French journalist Alain Minc in his book *Le Nouveau Moyen Age*.[9] He argues that present-day developments exhibit characteristics of medieval Europe. The new Middle Ages, he claims, is a world order that is coming together in the aftermath of the collapse of communism. The upheaval did not affect only Eastern Europe. Western Europe also was confronted with new realities upon the dissolution of the Soviet Union. The threat from the Eastern bloc colossus once forced solidarity of Western states, which has not yet been replaced by a new form of cohesiveness.

According to Minc, Europe has not experienced anything similar since the fall of the Roman Empire. The consequences of the fall of communism and the destruction of the Berlin Wall surpass those that followed the decline of the Ottoman and the Habsburg empires. In the new order uncertainty reigns, and Europe is once again characterized by geopolitical complexity which at worst might degenerate into chaos. Nebulousness, incertitude, the absence of a centre and the lack of common purpose mark the world that is rising from the ashes of fifty years of superpower conflict. It will become increasingly difficult for economics, politics and military strategy to live in territorial harmony with each other. While the parallels with the Middle Ages should not be exaggerated, Minc and other 'neomedievalists' have alerted us to the fact that recent developments in Europe have paved the way for a new game between the territorial entities of different sizes depicted in Figure 2.1.

NOTES

1 Norbert Ohler, *Reisen im Mittelalter* (Frankfurt am Main: Artemis Verlag, 1986); in English translation *The Medieval Traveller* (Woodbridge: Boydell Press, 1989).

2 The term 'imagined communities' was coined by Benedict Anderson in his book *Imagined Communities: Reflections on the Origin and Spread of Nationalism*, revised edn (London/ New York: Verso, 1991).

3 Denis de Rougemont, *Vingt-huit siècles d'Europe: La conscience européenne à travers les textes* (Paris: Gallimard, 1961).

4 Our understanding of networks draws on the discussion in Gunnar Törnquist, *Sverige i nätverkens Europa* (Malmoe: Liber-Hermods, 1996).

5 See Torsten Hägerstrand, 'Resandet och den sociala väven', in *Färdande och resande* (Stockholm: KBF, 1995).

6 Cf. Manuel Castells, *The Rise of the Network Society* (Oxford: Blackwell, 1996).

7 Among students of international political economy, for example, the terms 'region' and 'regionalization' usually refer to the emergence of three major trade blocs or macro-regions (the Western Hemisphere, Europe and Southeast Asia). See, for example, Robert Z. Lawrence, 'Emerging Regional Arrangements: Building Blocks or Stumbling Blocks?', in *International Political Economy: Perspectives on Global Power and Wealth*, 3rd edn, ed. Jeffrey A. Frieden and David Lake (London/New York: Routledge, 1995).

8 Fernand Braudel, *Civilization and Capitalism*, 3 vols (London: Collins, 1981–1984).

9 Alain Minc, *Le Nouveau Moyen Age* (Paris: Gallimard, 1993).

3

Historical Space

People and territory

When Europe emerged into history a few thousand years ago, it was the Phoenicians on the eastern coast of the Mediterranean who coined the term 'Europe'. According to one popular theory, the term contains the Semitic word *ereb*, which means 'sunset', or 'darkness', and Europe was thus the land of the sunset, which is similar to later distinctions between the Orient and the Occident.[1]

The ancient Greeks, the first to really use the term 'Europe', were also unclear on the geographic demarcation of the area. The one thing they were sure of was that they were not part of Europe. Europe was the land of the barbaric peoples of the north and northwest, distinct from the Greek core-area in Asia Minor and from the culture and civilization of the Mediterranean world.[2] The perception of Europe as a continent, separate from Asia and Africa, is of later origin (cf. Figure 3.1).

Europe's first site of higher culture was the southern parts of the continent. During the Roman Empire the Mediterranean functioned as a Roman inland sea. North of ancient Rome lay a belt of Celtic peoples and cultures, which we know relatively little about but which none the less are often considered the first Europeans. The Celts initially separated the Germanic groups from the more developed southern parts of Europe. The Celts subsequently found themselves sandwiched between the Germanic tribes from the north and the Roman legions from the south. Today, the vestiges of what was once a dominant European people can be found only in the coastal extremities of the Atlantic – in Brittany, Wales, Ireland and Scotland.[3]

Northern Europe was remote from ancient Rome in several respects. In Rome, people told wildly exaggerated tales about the peoples to the north. Later, during the Great Migrations, the Romans became somewhat more knowledgeable about their neighbours. Germanic peoples, such as the Visigoths, the Ostrogoths, the Lombards and the Vandals, contributed to the dissolution of the Roman Empire. New cultures emerged in the border-areas, such as France, where elements of different cultures were fused over time. It was also here that the first post-Roman project for a united Europe was launched, under Charlemagne, King of the Franks. On Christmas Day 800 AD,

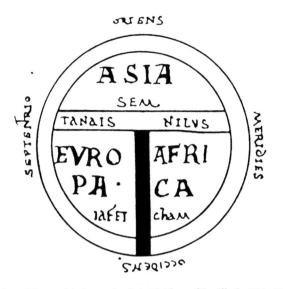

FIGURE 3.1 *Map of the world, drawn by Saint Isidore of Seville (c. 560–636): copy from the eleventh century (from J.B.F. Kormos, 'The Geographic Notion of Europe over the Centuries', in* Europe. Dream – Adventure – Reality *(New York, Greenwood Press, 1987)*

Charlemagne was crowned emperor, and obtained control over an area that he called Europe and that comprised the entire West Christian world.

Already in Roman times, there was remarkable ethnic diversification in Europe. The Germanic tribes in the north, the Celts in the middle and the Romans and Greeks in the south spoke languages that had evolved from an ancient Indo-European tongue spoken some 4,000 years earlier by nomadic peoples north of the Black Sea. It remains unclear how this language spread to Europe. Scholars debate whether a single people successively conquered Europe and exterminated all native populations, or whether a cultural expansion accounted for the eventual domination of Indo-European over other, earlier languages.[4]

Language is not necessarily equal to ethnicity. But the linguistic map of Europe clearly suggests that the different societies were not isolated, but were in contact with one another. The Great Migrations involved a long series of different groups including Germans, Celts and Slavs.[5] One group that appears quite late in the history of Europe was the Hungarians, who reached their present-day homeland in the early tenth century. The Hungarians wedged themselves into the Slavic world and formed a barrier between the Roman Catholic and the Greek Orthodox missions, with cultural consequences that are tangible still today.[6]

Naturally, the ethnic and linguistic diversity of Europe has been an important factor in all attempts to unite the continent. Religious developments also influenced such efforts. Christianity has occupied a central position in the

European culture-area, providing a shared foundation that strongly influenced value systems and ethics.[7] Religion has also played a disintegrative role, however. Early on a rift appeared between Rome and Byzantium, between Catholicism and Orthodoxy, which was to become a crucial event in the history of Europe. The division deepened over time, and finally left Europe divided into two separate Christian camps.[8]

There have been numerous attempts to bridge the gap between Western and Eastern Christendom. The crusades during the Middle Ages were in the beginning driven by the desire to unify Christianity. The different Christian groups needed a common enemy, and could unite against an Islamic expansion that from the seventh century brought under Muslim control the entire Orient, North Africa and later also penetrated southwestern Europe. The Islamic conquests in the west were conducted by the Arabs and Berbers, while the Turks completed the pincer movement against Europe by subduing Constantinople and the Balkans.[9]

For centuries, Islam constituted the principal threat that could be exploited in Christian propaganda. The Muslims were portrayed as a deadly menace to European culture. Yet in reality, Islamic culture could easily measure itself with Europe, since Muslim groups, especially the Moors in Spain, had preserved much of the culture of antiquity.[10]

Another dividing line, this one within the West Christian world, emerged in the sixteenth century when Luther and other reformists rebelled against the Catholic Church. The Reformation fractured western Europe into a Protestant north and a Catholic south, creating a schism that continues to play a role in discussions on present-day European integration.

Both the ethnic and the religious differences in Europe influenced the political structure and organization of this part of the world. A perpetual theme in the history of Europe is the contrast between the ideas of uniting and integrating Europe, on the one hand, and actual fragmentation and divisions on the other. Both tendencies have been apparent throughout recorded history, with varying significance and impact.

The Roman Empire

In early history, the economic, political and cultural centres of Europe were in the south, in an empire founded by the Romans, an impressive creation in terms of social organization and state formation. From a modest beginning in the city of Rome and the province of Latium, the Romans successively expanded through territorial conquests, military superiority and diplomatic skills. The enlargement of the empire was long directed toward the Mediterranean, where the Romans initially established junction points for trade, and then asserted their control over surrounding areas. The creation of this Mediterranean empire was in principle completed during the late Republic (133–31 BC), but reached new heights during the reigns of Augustus and Trajanus. The Roman Empire reached its geographic peak in the second century (see Figure 3.2), when the boundaries to the barbaric north were fixed and various buffer zones were established in the east as protection against the rampages of bordering nomadic peoples.[11]

Scholars have been engaged in extensive debates as to the determinants of the expansion of the empire. All disagreements notwithstanding, most agree that economic factors played an important role. The government of the provinces, which was in the hands of elites and kin-group confederations in Rome, produced a surplus that the central authorities welcomed. In principle, the Roman system of domination can be described as imperialistic.

The forms and structures of government of the empire varied both over time and from area to area. Only native Romans had initially the right to full citizenship, while the remaining residents of the empire had varying positions. In some cases, friendship treaties were signed with local rulers who were formally permitted to retain their power. In other instances, conquered territories were treated as Roman provinces and placed under direct rule.[12]

The administration of the provinces was crystallized already during the late Republic, when the system of Roman governors was established. These positions were filled only by high-ranking Roman officials, who served first as consuls and praetors in Rome and then were dispatched to the provinces as governors with extensive authority. Under Augustus, provinces that were directly subordinated to the emperor were distinguished from provinces administered by the Senate.[13]

One of the emperor's principal responsibilities was to defend the territory against outside enemies in the east, which lacked natural borders, and, more importantly, in the north, where Germanic and other barbaric groups constituted a significant pressure against the empire's boundary. A substantial part of the Roman army was committed to safeguarding the border areas, while few troops were needed for maintaining order within the central parts of the empire.[14]

For a long time, the northern boundary of the Roman Empire ran alongside the Rhine and the Danube and along a line between these rivers, where garrisons were stationed permanently. The boundary was successively fortified with ramparts, walls and other defences, originally of wood, then of stone. These so-called *limes* were complemented by strategic roads designed to rapidly transport Roman military units to vulnerable areas (see Figure 3.3).[15]

The Roman border defences required significant resources, both human and material. The Roman legionaries soon proved insufficient for the mounting demand. As a result, troops to defend the boundaries were enlisted from the border areas themselves. These soldiers settled with their families south of the *limes*, often while cultivating the land. Several of these military installations thus became permanent settlements, and formed the bases of later urban developments with lingering effect to present times.[16]

During the late Roman era, the border defences began to erode and the *limes* lost their stable structure. Over time, it proved impossible to repel the repeated

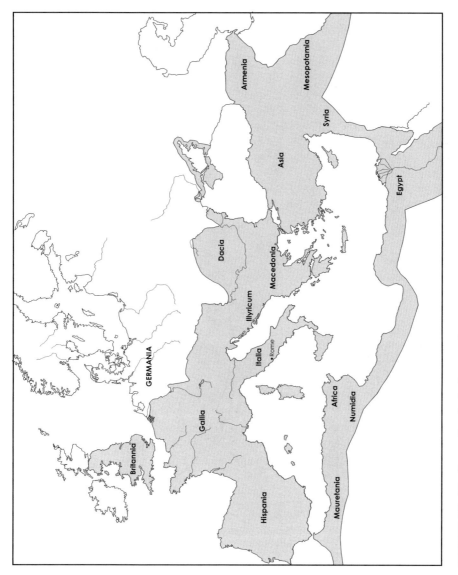

FIGURE 3.2 *The Roman Empire in the second century*

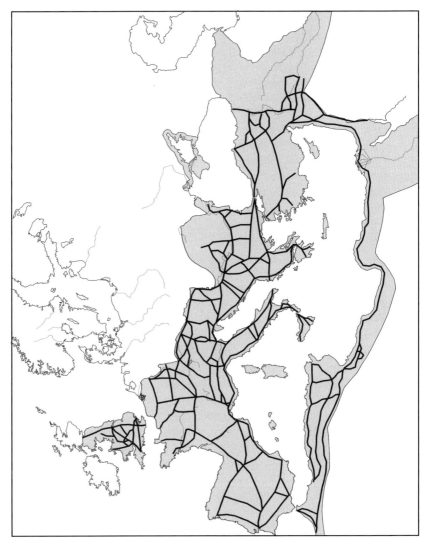

FIGURE 3.3 *The roads of the Roman Empire*

attacks of bellicose neighbours, who were drawn to the sophisticated culture and higher standard of living of the Roman Empire. The failure to defend the boundaries provides only part of the explanation for the decline of the Roman Empire, which was triggered mainly by internal factors.[17] At the risk of oversimplification, one could argue that the economic resources of Rome did not suffice to keep together the empire, in any case not in western Europe. Already in the fourth century, the empire was divided into a western and an eastern half. The West Roman part existed officially until 476, while Eastern Rome survived for almost another millennium.

The Roman Empire was in many ways a unique construction in the history of Europe. The Roman state was administered with a high degree of sophistication, and its methods of organizing and managing society became a model for later states. The empire took long to build; yet it also took long to dismantle. Wars, both expansionist and defensive, were a major feature of the Roman Empire, but for much of its population, especially in the central areas, the empire brought enduring peace; for them, *Pax Romana* was not a mere catchword.

Since the history of the Roman Empire is both long and complex, it is difficult to identify the distinguishing features of the Roman manner of organizing territory. One consistent trait seems to have been the establishment of a solid structure ensuring central control over the peripheries, without exaggerated attention to bureaucratic detail. Political power rested on the principle of citizenship, which was expanded from originally including only the upper strata in Rome, to comprising other key groups in the provinces. Citizenship was thereby effectively dissociated from ethnic criteria. While the Romans never deliberately conducted assimilation policies, Roman culture and the Latin language were so prevalent that many peripheral cultures in the multi-ethnic empire inevitably became part of a Romanizing process. This was true also of the tribes that in the latter stages of the empire were permitted to settle along the boundaries as allies and defence forces.

The Great-Migration states

Since the dawn of history the world north and east of the Roman Empire was characterized by remarkable demographic mobility.[18] Even those tribes that were not nomadic tended to leave their original communities, to migrate, and eventually settle in new environments.[19] The Roman border defences were for a long time an almost impenetrable barrier, even if occasional forays into Roman territory could not be prevented.

In the fifth century, the imbalance increased dramatically. From Asia, peoples such as Alans and Huns rode into Europe and through their ravaging raids set in motion a demographic chain reaction.[20] During the Great Migrations (*Völkerwanderungen* in German), the Germanic invasions altered the social realities of the West Roman Empire, not by threatening to eradicate the Roman institutions, but by adapting them to Germanic patterns.

Roman culture was thus 'barbarized', although the blame cannot be assigned exclusively to the Germanic peoples.[21]

The situation stabilized in the early sixth century. The most important change was that what remained of Roman unity was definitively dissolved, and that the empire was superseded by a number of loosely organized states, where ethnic factors played a greater role than before. In the Roman successor states, citizenship and territorial affiliation were no longer key. Instead, the state was defined by the relationship between the leaders and the people of the ethnic group or tribal confederation. Even after territorial possession became comparatively stable, the kings in the Great-Migration states sought legitimacy in the personal relationship between ruler and people. This was reflected, for instance, in their choice of titles, which referred directly to ethnic groups rather than to territory: *Rex Vandalorum, Rex Visigothorum*, etc. The Merovingian kings never labelled themselves king of France, but king of the Franks.[22]

The Great-Migration states differed from each other in various respects, however, and it is therefore difficult to draw any general conclusions. Research has nevertheless tended to distinguish between two main types: those besieged by military forces, and those conquered by peoples. In states besieged by military forces, Germanic peoples (tribes and tribal confederations) settled far from their earlier homes. These groups were not particularly large, and at first remained aloof from the surrounding majority population. Their power was based on military capacity, which did not prevent cooperation with the educated Roman upper class of landowners and administrators that resided in the areas. Examples of this type of Great-Migration state include the kingdom of the Ostrogoths in Italy,[23] the Visigoths in Spain[24] and the Vandals in North Africa.[25]

In central Europe, the Great Migration had quite different results. Here, entire populations had moved to new areas but often had maintained contact with their kindred tribes in the Germanic world. The newly arrived populations blended with the groups already residing in the area. This was especially apparent in the kingdom founded by the Germanic Franks in Gaul, originally a Celtic area but strongly influenced by Roman culture and administration.[26] Further east, the Slavs were progressing toward the Elbe and the Danube.[27]

While the immediate consequences of the Great Migrations varied in different parts of the former Roman Empire, the long-term outcome was uniform. The Germanic elites became merged in the landowning and official classes. Christianity, while no longer an entirely homogeneous faith, nevertheless provided a common religion. Ethnic differences were neutralized in the process. In southern Europe, the Great-Migration states became parentheses and the Germanic peoples left little in the way of a cultural legacy. Social changes in central and southern Europe were also quite similar. A system of large landowners and subordinated peasants emerged in most areas, in part as the result of growing legal insecurity. The peasants were made to pay for their protection by the landowners, through work and submission.

Despite the many differences in the widespread Roman Empire, between centre and periphery and between the many peripheries, there had been unifying forces. The administrative system, the Latin language and Roman culture all helped consolidate the empire. An effective infrastructure had been created, including a network of roads, whose outlines remain today, and a system of Roman colonization centres in the provinces.

Much of this system crumbled during the Great Migrations. The roads were left to decay and many of the emerging cities, such as those along the Danube and in former Gaul, were left desolate. Foreign trade either was reduced dramatically or ceased entirely. However, the turmoil did not signal a complete break from the past. The Mediterranean world remained a specific culture area bound together by common interests after the fall of Rome, and Byzantium continued to play an important role in this framework. This was especially true in the Great-Migration states in southern Europe, but also in the Germanic world of central Europe.[28]

From the perspective of integration/fragmentation, developments in late Antiquity exhibit a marked pattern: the Roman integration project, in many respects successful, was followed by a fragmented system with several parallel state-formations. Of these, only the Frankish Empire was robust enough to survive. Under the Merovingians, the territory was extended south in the sixth century. The Frankish Empire brought together elements of Germanic, Celtic and Roman culture, engendering a new culture that served as a basis for an ethnic identity that could be tied to a specific territory.[29] This takes us to the medieval world, characterized by new principles for organizing society and structuring territory.

Medieval feudal society

Just as it is impossible to draw clear boundaries between ancient Rome and the Great-Migration societies, it is difficult to specify when feudalism, the political and economic system that prevailed in much of Europe during the Middle Ages, emerged. Once it was fully developed, feudalism was the overarching system within which all territorial organization, control and administration was determined.[30]

Feudalism rested on possession and usage of land in a predominantly agrarian society. A system of landowners and subordinated peasants had been evolving since Antiquity. Agriculture was the principal livelihood and produced small but significant surpluses that could be exploited by a small elite of warriors and landowners. After the Great Migrations, the cultivated lands of central Europe were probably smaller in terms of area than during the Roman era. Reclamations and new agricultural technology gradually altered the picture, however. The feudal manor was typically not a cohesive area where farming was effectively organized for large-scale production, but a complex of scattered plots, often spread out over large areas and cultivated by unfree tenant farmers.

A distinguishing characteristic in the feudal system was the territorial organization of society. In principle, all plots of land were fiefs. The royal lands were granted by the king to vassals who in turn were bound to serve the monarchy in war. The vassals then enfeoffed under-vassals with parts of the property in a complicated dynamic of duties and services in return. At the base of this system was the large mass of unfree farmers and tenants who supported the entire social structure through their work and their dues.

Feudalism rested on the principle of personal loyalties between lord and vassal, rooted in both the Roman patron/client relationship and in the Germanic connection between chieftain and people. The system entailed both the exploitation of fertile land and the capacity to serve in warfare. The roles of the landlord and the soldier were thus united.[31]

At the top of the feudal pyramid was the king, or the supreme ruler, whose power rested on the right to allot fiefs from the royal lands. It was equally important for the monarchy to be able to reclaim the fief when the loyalty relation ceased. The feudal lords, for their part, had the opposite interest, namely, to ensure that fiefs could be inherited by their descendants. This is the reason why the church became one of the crown's major vassals: because of the oath of celibacy, the clergy had no official heirs and thus had no interest in making land hereditary.

A major flaw in the feudal system was the lack of equilibrium. If all the royal lands were granted as fiefs and could not be reclaimed, then the king lost his position of power. Feudalism did not necessarily lead to chaos, but it did foster fragmentation. Large fiefs were not only self-reliant economically, but also judicially, socially and culturally.

Moreover, a manor's plots of land were scattered geographically and often had shifting boundaries, which made the entire system difficult to administer. Rules, laws and different applications for larger areas were in practice impossible to observe. This was reflected in the absence of a strong central authority in most of the states or state-like territories of the feudal era. Enfeoffment resulted in the almost total fragmentation of the state territory and decentralization of power, but counter-forces were over time able to take advantage of the same system: princes who had amassed a sufficient territorial foundation could effectively establish their control over cohesive territories.[32] The Carolingians, for instance, directly administered a manorial tract around Paris, and from this territorial base were able to conduct a consolidation policy that eventually resulted in the Frankish major power under Charlemagne.[33]

Cities and markets

The dissolution of the Roman Empire during the Great Migrations had resulted in the fragmentation of the territory and the loss of central territorial control. The Great-Migration states lacked the stability of the Roman era, and the structures of these kingdoms were contingent on the ability of the king and other leadership to forcibly consolidate the people and protect their territory against outside threats. The possibility of building cohesive territorial states was counteracted by the feudal system and its closed, vertical organization of society. The central authority in these predominantly agrarian societies remained quite weak.

The transition from Antiquity to the Middle Ages can also be described in economic terms. The Roman Empire was built around maritime trade in the Mediterranean, through a network of cities and markets that culminated in the first and second centuries. The Great-Migration states that followed had been characterized by dwindling foreign trade, dissolution of cities and regional contraction and demarcation. The economic centre in the Mediterranean shifted east, to Byzantium and Asia Minor, which continued to profit from trade with Southeast Asia. Arabic expansion into North Africa in the seventh century confirmed the dissolution of the Mediterranean as a cohesive economic entity. In southwestern Europe, the caliphate of Cordoba evolved into a major economic centre in the tenth century, more powerful than the contemporary Frankish Empire whose communications with the Mediterranean area were dramatically curtailed. The foreign trade of the Islamic world eclipsed Europe's overseas commerce throughout this period. The Carolingian Empire temporarily conducted a more active foreign trade, but the main structures of feudalism remained. Recurring raids from the Vikings in the northwest and the Saracens in the south, typically directed against cities, further confirmed the frailty of western European societies at the time.

In short, the cities that were founded during the Roman era lost much of their significance during the Great Migrations, and were outdone in many respects by Islam, the Saracens and the Vikings. In central Europe, the Hungarians had in the tenth century ravaged many areas but had left most of the cities unscathed.[34] And in Italy, economic ties with Byzantium had never been completely severed, despite the repeated barbaric invasions. Northern Italy's strategic position between the Frankish Empire and Byzantium made it possible for some cities to continue their trade activities. Among these, Venice played a particularly important role from the late tenth century. A link between western and eastern Europe, Venice was the first city in Europe whose economy was based entirely on trade.[35]

The static nature of the feudal system began to dissolve at this time, in connection with an increase in trade and escalating urbanization. Both processes had important consequences for the organization of territory. The growth in trade in the Middle Ages was concentrated in two areas: the Mediterranean, with Italy as the centre, and northwestern Europe, where the focal point was the area between the Rhine and the Seine rivers. The conditions were different in the north and the south. In the Mediterranean world, trade with the Orient played a key role, and cities such as Venice, Amalfi and Naples liberated themselves from Byzantine rule and became important junctions in this highly lucrative east–west trade. The crusades further stimulated commerce, for the Venetians and to a lesser degree also for cities such as Pisa and Genoa. Finally, northern Italian cities like Milan and Florence evolved into early capitalist economic centres, with textiles as their main exports.[36]

Textiles were also an important industry in Flanders and its surrounding areas, the other core region of the trade revolution in Europe. Cities sprang up throughout Flanders, with Bruges as a particularly important commercial centre.[37] During the High Middle Ages, northern Italy and Flanders were linked together by merchants who arrived from the north and the south to attend the fairs in Champagne, east of Paris. Buyers and sellers met at marketplaces, typically in larger cities. Over time, trade expanded to include other parts of the continent, but underdeveloped communications and legal insecurity impeded the full development of foreign trade.[38]

A prerequisite for foreign trade was a structure designed specifically to manage business transactions throughout the areas in question. Beginning in northern Italy, there emerged a system of entrepreneurs who specialized in economic transactions such as currency exchange, granting of credit, contract, insurance and other banking services. In the large commercial cities, capital was gathered that could be lent also for other purposes, for instance to princes needing resources to expand their military forces.

The development of the European cities and the growth in trade during the Middle Ages involved a complicated process that cannot be explained by a simple formula. There was a dividing line between cities that based their livelihood mainly on local trade with agricultural products from the nearby countryside on the one hand, and cities focused on foreign trade on the other. The former type had disappeared already in the early Middle Ages, while the latter, with their network structures, long withstood, and proffered an alternative to, the consolidation of territorial states.[39]

One of the many consequences of foreign trade concerned its impact on territorial organization and control. So long as the merchants themselves were in charge of transporting goods between the producer and the buyer, they had no choice but to unite with one another for protection. In the Italian cities, powerful fleets were built as protection against pirates.[40] Some merchants formed guilds, which were at first loose organizations for joint protection during risky foreign travels, but later evolved into strong bodies that were based in specific cities and had branches abroad.[41] The next step was for the individual commercial cities to join together in leagues. The most well-known example, the German Hanseatic League, at its peak brought together some 200 cities, of which a third were active members.[42]

The European cities during the Middle Ages did not follow a uniform pattern, and their independence varied depending on the power of their superiors. In France, the cities often allied with the monarchy. Some cities were completely outside the reach of the prince's authority, such as the free towns in Germany which were directly under the emperor, whose power base was insufficient to control the cities. Even the territorial princes had only limited power over the cities. In fact, these princes often ended up economically dependent on the cities, rather than the other way around. In Italy, the feudal aristocracy cooperated with, and frequently settled in, the cities.[43]

Around the cities, walls and fortifications served as boundaries to the outside world, and effectively prevented military attacks. As centres for local commerce, the cities had significant influence over the surrounding countryside. The cities did not compete with the territorial princes in regard to land ownership, and there was thus no need for a state apparatus with political control over territory. Nor did the cities have a standing army. If military power was needed, services could be purchased from the princes and mercenaries. Yet in most cases, economic sanctions and the threat of retaliation were sufficient deterrents, and conflicts could be avoided.

The medieval cities brought profound economic, social and cultural change, and ultimately sounded the death knell of feudal society. The cities were centres of innovations. They were economic engines and catalysts for entrepreneurship and societal development. They ushered in the first period of modernization in Europe.

The urban residents identified with their city, rather than with some wider territory, dynasty or ruler. Control over extensive territories was not a prerequisite for commerce, but for merchants, it was imperative that communications over both land and sea involved some safety guarantees. This resulted in alliances with territorial rulers who offered protection in exchange for extraction in the form of taxes and tariffs.[44]

A growing trade network led to the erosion of feudal obstacles to communication, exchange of goods, fixation of prices and payment options. For commercial cities and merchant guilds, control of different markets was more important than ownership of land. Influence over markets could be established through offices and agents in other cities, which continued to emerge at this time. Lübeck, for instance, in the thirteenth century became a key player in trade in the Baltic area, a *primus inter pares* within the Wendish Hanse, and enjoyed a strong position in all economic activity throughout northern Europe. In the High Middle Ages, virtually all of Europe was bound together by a network of cities and city-republics, dominated by a merchant class whose main interest was to secure a maximum of freedom, mobility and access to markets and consumers.

The medieval network of cities long functioned as an alternative to the feudal forms of organization, and in the late Middle Ages as an alternative to the social structures that were based on territorial principalities. Yet in the long run, the principalities succumbed to powerful rivals, and by the end of the medieval era most cities had been integrated into the proto-national states that were emerging in various parts of Europe. Network as an organizing principle fell into abeyance for many years to come.

Emperor and pope: medieval integration projects

During the Great Migrations, the West Roman Empire had been fractured into a number of loosely connected territories, administered according to feudal principles. The imperial structure survived in the east, however, in the form of the Byzantine Empire, while the Arabs during the first centuries after Mohammed established control over the entire southern coast of the Mediterranean, with a European bridgehead on the Iberian peninsula.

The idea of empires was not dead in western Europe, despite extensive fragmentation. The West Frankish Empire, with its Roman, Germanic and Celtic roots, revived notions of imperial grandeur: first the Merovingians, and then the Carolingian dynasty, sought to consolidate the empire. Finally, the Frankish Empire encompassed all western Europe from the Baltic and the North Sea in the north to the Mediterranean in the south. Charlemagne's *imperium christianum*, as it was called, had as its explicit policy to unite the West Christian world under a single government (see Figure 3.4). The deliberate connection to ancient Rome was reflected in the title, *Romanum gubernans imperium*.[45]

The Carolingian Empire had expanded through successful wars, in the south through the establishment of Spanish Marches as defence against the Muslim Moors, in the north through warfare against the Saxons and other Germanic peoples, and in the east against Slavs and Avars. Marches were organized in the northern and eastern border areas as well. These were territories without clear boundaries that functioned as buffer zones against attacks from outside the empire (hence the March of the Danes [Denmark], Nordmark, Ostmark, Steiermark [Styria], among others). It was not easy to maintain such an empire within the framework of a feudal system that rested on personal ties of loyalty, but Charlemagne attempted to build an administrative apparatus based in his immediate court. Direct administration was decentralized, and was conducted in the provinces by counts (*comites*) appointed by the emperor. A certain degree of central control was exercised by the emperor's envoys (*missi*), but this was not sufficient to counteract the growing independence of the feudal aristocracy.[46] The Carolingian Empire was dissolved in the tenth century, after a long period of decay brought about by both external pressures (Arabs and Vikings) and internal conflicts (dynastic, economic and political).

The idea of an overarching European power, which Charlemagne sought to realize in his Western Christian Empire, survived in the eastern part of the Frankish Empire (see Figure 3.5). One of the tribal dukes was appointed German king, albeit with little power outside his own principality. However, the Saxon duke Otto, after having been chosen at a ceremony in Charlemagne's residential city of Aachen, in 962 let himself be crowned emperor in Rome, and declared that he would preserve and renew the Carolingian imperial tradition.[47]

The name given to Otto's creation, the Holy Roman Empire of the German Nation, which did not become official until later in the Middle Ages, is noteworthy.[48] The ancient Roman Empire had been a multi-ethnic state, founded on citizenship rather than language or ethnicity. The new label *sacrum imperium* (holy empire) alluded to Western Christendom in the same manner as Charlemagne had claimed primacy for his Carolingian Empire. The third

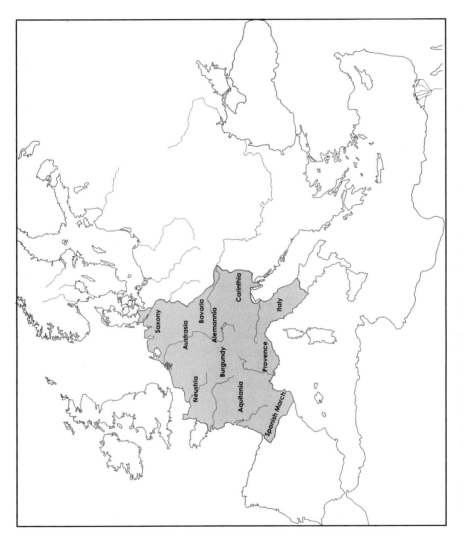

FIGURE 3.4 *The Carolingian Empire in 814*

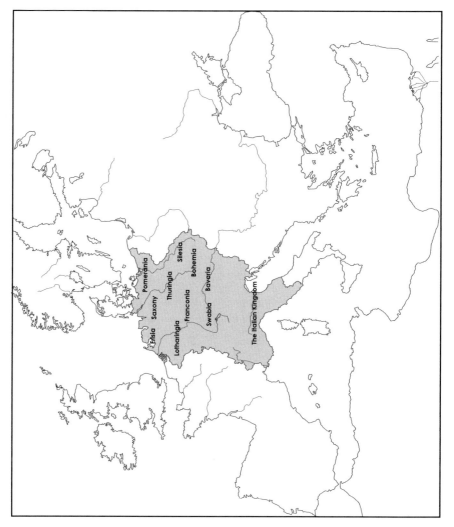

FIGURE 3.5 *The German Empire in the Middle Ages*

qualifier, 'of the German Nation', was added in the late Middle Ages, and implied an ethnic dimension, even if the connotations of the term are difficult to determine today. At any rate, the terminology proved of great symbolic value for the development of a German identity above traditional tribal loyalties.

In the High Middle Ages, the German emperor led a two-front struggle to assert his supremacy – internally against tribal dukes, princes and various strongmen, externally against the Catholic Church and its leadership in Rome. The emperor's relationship to the papacy was complicated, in part because the pope had the privilege of crowning the emperor, and in part because the pope, like the emperor, made claims to universal supremacy. The church and the empire were not solely rivals, however; bishops and abbots were also important actors in the emperor's efforts to crystallize central controls. The fiefs granted to the church were not hereditary, due to the celibacy of the clergy, and thus constituted a freer resource for the emperor than fiefs granted to secular elites. Moreover, the church was not bound to any particular territories and could thus more readily be incorporated into an empire-wide context. During the early years of the empire, the German prelates were an important resource for the feeble imperial authority.

Latent tensions between the emperor and the pope developed into open conflict in the eleventh and twelfth centuries in the so-called struggle over investiture. On paper, the struggle concerned power over religious offices. In reality, however, the conflict had more to do with both parties' claims to universal supremacy – a struggle in keeping with the vertical structures of medieval society.[49] The struggle over investiture ended in a compromise that eroded the power of both parties, while paving the way for the emperor's greatest rivals within the empire, the territorial princes. The central power was thus weakened, and the empire suffered further fragmentation. The feudal structures could not be reconciled with far-reaching territorial integration. The emperors were forced to accept that their power base was limited to their own crownlands and the royal estates.

The German emperors thus did not have a sufficient territorial base to consolidate the state authority. Nor did the electoral college, a loose congregation of Kurfürsten responsible for electing the emperor – the archbishops of Mainz, Trier and Cologne, the count palatine by the Rhine, the margrave of Brandenburg, the duke of Saxony and the king of Bohemia – have a sufficiently strong power base.[50] Being an elector none the less was an important role, and several of the leading electoral families sought to combine their empire-wide influence with a consolidation of their own territory. The independence of the territorial princes was further accentuated after the emperor abdicated, in the so-called Interregnum of 1254–1273. Yet no individual prince was able to amass enough power to counterbalance the remaining electoral collective. During the late Middle Ages, the German imperial power had effectively been nullified, although it continued to exist until the early nineteenth century, when Napoleon formally brought an end to the project.

Historical regions

Regional identity

Throughout the ages, the spatial dimension – territoriality – has played an important role in the development of shared group identities. People have identified both with the territory where they lived, worked, or to which they were otherwise tied, and with people who belonged to the same territory. Shared ways of thinking have been created through social processes, and structures have been built and institutionalized with the territory as a framework.[51]

Such socio-territorial identities are among the most fundamental to the lives of individuals as well as to the history of human society. At times they may strengthen other basic identities, such as class or gender, and in some cases also overshadow, or entirely eliminate, these alternative identity bases. Ethno-territorial identity thus extends both in time and space. Using different terminology, the aforementioned structure can be described as a *region*, understood as a theoretical concept distinct from the everyday use of the term.[52]

The demarcation of regions to some extent has to do with physical-geographic conditions that can prevent contact and communication among groups. In principle, these obstacles are more severe the further back in time we go. The external boundaries of the regions, however, have always been constructed by the inhabitants and are therefore all artificial.[53]

This implies that the significance of boundaries can change. Political decisions and actions – or, as in older times, dynastic shifts – can make older boundaries obsolete. Economic factors can turn existing networks and activities into straitjackets for the region. Technical development can profoundly alter communications. Culture also may change both in content and manifestations, but in general these changes are slow and only perceptible in a *longue durée* perspective.[54]

The development of regional identity is, in other words, a gradual process. The conditions that determine continuity and change differ from case to case. Generally, however, regions that have emerged organically over long periods of time have greater emotional resonance and legitimacy among their inhabitants than regions that are imposed from above, through, for instance, administrative decisions.

The history of Europe has from the outset involved such ethno-territorial processes. Regions with long histories of community and shared cultural experience have considerable potential for political mobilization. The more unique the identity of the region *vis-à-vis* its surroundings, the more effectively the region can be used to mobilize its inhabitants. These historical regions are characterized by a strong connection between people and territory, and have their own institutions, well-developed communications internally, and a sense of cultural affinity.[55]

Historically, evolving regions have played a key role in the history of states as well. A historical region can constitute the territorial base for a state, and correspondingly, the population becomes the governing group within that territory. This is the ideal type for the later nation-state. The historical regions can also constitute a threat or an alternative to territorial states whose boundaries do not coincide with regional identities. The historical region becomes a discernible part of the state territory – an *intra-state region* – or is divided by the state boundary – a *cross-border region*. Frequently, this type of region has a longer history than the state of which the region is a part. A few such regions have for political, military or dynastic reasons been prevented from developing into sovereign states. In other cases, the political will within the region has not been sufficiently strong to achieve statehood. There is thus no linear evolution from historical regions to statehood.

The Roman provinces

A few of Europe's many historical regions have their roots in Antiquity. Starting in the insignificant city-state of Latium, the Romans began a territorial expansion that affected much of the European continent and the entire Mediterranean world. The conquered territories were organized into distinct administrative entities, in some cases entirely new, but quite often adapted to existing entities, typically named after the population. Already during the early Republic, there were several provinces on the Italian peninsula: Latium, Etruria, Campania, Venice, Liguria, Umbria, Apulia and Calabria. Several of these classical names survive in the regional division of present-day Italy.[56]

Outside Italy, the occupied territories were organized as *provinciae*.[57] Vestiges of the Roman division into provinces remain today. When the Romans began to conquer Gaul, inhabited by Celtic peoples, this large area was organized into separate provinces, beginning in the south, the so-called Gallia Narbonensis. The Alps distinguished Gallia Cisalpina from Gallia Transalpina. Under Augustus, the Gallic provinces of Aquitania, Lugdunensis (Lyons) and Belgica became regions under the direct control of the emperor. The Gallic border areas to the Germanic world were divided into two provinces, Germanica Inferior and Germanica Superior. In connection with the Diocletian administrative reforms in the early fourth century, Gaul was united with Spain and Brittany under a common prefecture. This administrative area was dissolved in the late fifth century when the Merovingians founded their own state on West Frankish soil.[58]

Of the Roman provincial divisions, Aquitania survived as a historical region, despite the fact that the area was conquered first by Visigoths and then by the Franks. During the Merovingian era, Aquitania was a duchy, and a kingdom under Charlemagne. By the end of the Middle Ages, the area was integrated into the French state, but the name Guyenne has survived into modern times as a regional designation.[59]

The Roman province Gallia Belgica was dissolved and became part of the Frankish state, but the name was revived in 1830 when the state of Belgium (Belgique) was created. This does not imply a direct continuity, since other identities got the upper hand during the Middle Ages, at the same time as many Roman cities remained, frequently with uninterrupted territorial continuity to the present.[60]

Of the 101 provinces that constituted the Roman Empire after the Diocletian reforms, a few survived only nominally once the administrative division was abolished. Most of them by far were eradicated in name as well. That applied to the Iberian peninsula, for instance, which suffered repeated invasions and prolonged occupations during the Great Migrations. East Rome, the most populated and economically most significant part of the empire, was better able to resist fragmentation.

The Germanic tribal duchies

The world north of Italy and Gaul was known by the Romans as Germania, and was populated mainly by Germanic tribes. The area was never occupied militarily by the Romans, with the exception of the border zone. Sandwiched between the Romans and the Germanic tribes was a belt of Celtic peoples who long served as a buffer. The Germanic world was distinguished by the unusual mobility of its peoples, which became especially apparent during the Great Migrations.

In central Europe, a few centuries BC, various ethnic groups, or 'tribes' emerged. These groups were united by descent, language and culture.[61] Because of their high mobility, territorial identities were probably less developed, while the relationship between the ruler and the people appears to have played an important role both for the solidarity of the group and for the organization of military defence. The tribes, which are better described as tribal leagues, eventually ended up in cohesive territories, either by expansion and amalgamation of core-areas, or by settling into entirely new areas. It was not until these settlements became permanent that the prerequisites for territorially bound identities were created.

When the Carolingian Empire was divided after Charlemagne's death, the East Frankish section eventually gave rise to the German Empire. Since the state authority was weak, the leaders of the tribal leagues, the dukes, were able to maintain their positions. At first, the duke was elected by the leading strata of the tribe, but the position later became hereditary. The power of the dukes rested primarily on their military might. In peacetime, the main responsibility of the tribal dukes was to preserve law and order. Their fortified castles also became fiscal and administrative centres for different regions. Power was thus institutionalized within clearly demarcated territories, giving rise to a particular relationship between ruler, people and territory.[62]

The oldest German duchies, Saxony, Thuringia, Frankia, Swabia, Friesland, Lorraine and Bavaria, were fractured in the early Middle Ages into myriad smaller entities that were constantly changing as a result of feudal and dynastic processes, war and negotiations.[63] The German tribal duchies were not points of departure for any extensive ethno-territorial mobilization, although the symbolic value of the tribal communities has been exploited in various historical contexts up to today. In present-day Germany, Bavaria comes closest to the definition of a historical region, with uninterrupted cultural, territorial and political continuity. In other cases, there have been attempts to establish a link to the embryonic ethno-territoriality of the early Middle Ages, as in the German *Land* of Thüringen. And the name Sachsen (Saxony) recurs in three contemporary *Länder* – Sachsen, Sachsen-Anhalt and Niedersachsen. Apart from that, there are few vestiges of the tribal duchies in today's Federal Republic of Germany, beyond politically neutral symbols for much older regional identities, long since overshadowed by later regional ties.

Developments in what became Germany and France in the early Middle Ages – the eastern and western parts of the Frankish Empire – thus proceeded in totally different directions. In the west, the monarchy was able to successively crystallize its control over the territory and the feudal lords, while the central authority remained weak in the east where territorial fragmentation was the predominant pattern. Lorraine (*Lothari regnum*), the early buffer zone between Germany and France, was subjected to heavy pressures from both the Germans and the French, and remained a bone of contention between the two states. The present French region of Lorraine was created in 1960, but comprises only a small part of Lothar's original realm.[64]

Burgundy, established by the Rhône and the Saône during the Great Migrations, also functioned as a border zone between German and French influence. As a result of external pressures and dynastic shifts, Burgundy was repeatedly partitioned. The name Burgundy therefore designated several different areas. In the west, the duchy of Burgundy became part of France; in the east, the county of Burgundy became an integral part of Germany; and in the south, on Burgundian soil, the short-lived sovereign kingdom of Arelat was formed.[65]

Territorial organization in Europe before 1648

The Peace of Westphalia in 1648, which concluded thirty years of war and destruction in Europe, is generally considered to mark the birth of modern Europe, where sovereign, territorial states are the principal entities and actors in the international system. A glance at the earlier history of Europe, however, indicates that the modern state system dates back further than Westphalia, and that it was in no way self-evident that territorial states would become the main entities in Europe.

Territorial organization can be described on the basis of different premises, with different objectives and different models. In this chapter, we focus on aspects of political organization in territorial and non-territorial terms. Quantitative dimensions such as geographic distance, scope, area and accessibility are important from this perspective, as are qualitative factors that deal with the degree to which the entities in question have been integrated in terms of culture, administration and economics. Another important aspect has to do with the functional efficacy and 'strength' (political, military, economic) of the territorial entities, measured as constancy and time, two of the main variables of history.

From these premises, efforts have been made also to structure the history of Europe on the basis of the size and degree of integration of different territorial projects, and of the existence of alternative modes of organization where control over the territory has not been of decisive importance. The projects that were the largest in area and scope – the Roman Empire, the Carolingian Empire, the Holy Roman Empire of the German Nation and, finally, the papacy – can be placed at the macro-regional level, although none of them encompassed the entire continent of Europe.

At an intermediate level, four other integration projects can be distinguished, namely, the Great-Migration states, the feudal societies, the late medieval territorial principalities and the national churches. These formations were projects only in a general sense. They were the result of deliberate actions and plans as well as random events and coincidences. Nor are these four projects completely distinct from one another; rather, they competed with one another and/or overlapped in time either completely or partially.

Alongside these macro-regional and regional European integration projects, there were other forms of organization that did not rest on the possession of territory. During the transition period between Antiquity and the Middle Ages, in Germanic areas, there existed *tribal confederations*, societies based on the relationship between the tribal leader/king and the people. The rise in trade during the Middle Ages, particularly foreign trade, and the development of *cities* had more profound repercussions. Merchants needed secure bases at home and at their destinations, as well as secure communications, but did not need territories in between.

In light of the distinctions made above, we will attempt to relate these different forms of integration and social projects to the basic model of the territorial field of tension, introduced in Chapter 2 (Figure 2.1). From the perspective of historical change, 'globalization' stands for the evolution toward larger, cohesive entities, while 'regionalization' refers to fragmentation into smaller entities. A region is here understood as smaller than the state of which the region is a part (cross-border regions represent special cases). A union is larger than any individual state. Union, state and region all involve a territorial dimension, while networks lack a territorial base.

This model is not actor-oriented and lacks a temporal dimension. The four spheres exist in a dynamic of constant reciprocal influence, with varying degrees of strength during different periods. The focus of the model is the present: it speaks to the position of today's territorial states in a world that is evolving toward larger entities – globalization – at the same time as states are eroded from within by a conflicting trend of regionalization. The historical overview presented above has shown that the same field of tension was discernible in earlier eras as well.

The first example is the ancient *Roman Empire* (Figure 3.6). In the thousand-year history of Rome, the four spheres clearly emerge as organizational forms of varying importance in different times. The city of Rome and its surrounding province, Latium, constituted the core of a state that in many ways was a prototype for later state-formations with regard to legal system, administration,

GLOBALIZATION

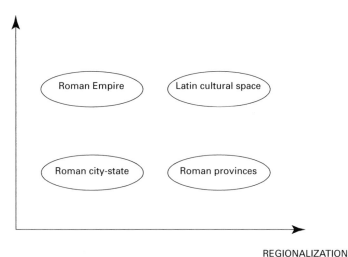

FIGURE 3.6 *The Roman Empire positioned in terms of the territorial field of tension model*

social organization, etc. By systematic conquests, negotiations and treaties, the original city-state was enlarged into an empire, comprising the entire Mediterranean and large parts of central Europe. In principle, the Roman emperors viewed the entire world as a Roman possession.[66] Within the parameters of the empire, various provinces emerged with different forms of government – some under the control of the Roman senate, others subordinated to the emperor. Diverse interests competed with one another: the desire of the Roman, governing elite to crystallize its control over both the empire and the individual provinces, and the efforts of the peripheries to achieve a maximum of autonomy and freedom of action.

The foundations for communications, commerce and cultural exchange were laid within the empire. All this was made possible by the predominance of Latin as the principal means of communication in a world that was ethnically and linguistically disparate. Roads, cities and other aspects of infrastructure were a prerequisite for the different networks that evolved under the Romans, and in part survived after the demise of the ancient world.

The other example is based on Charlemagne's *Imperium Christianum* of the early ninth century (Figure 3.7). Feudalism was the prevalent pattern of social organization under the Carolingians. The feudal structure has traditionally been depicted as a pyramid with a lord (L) at the summit, and a stratum of great vassals (GV) and vassals (V) directly beneath them. Power relations were essentially vertical, and horizontal links were poorly developed or completely non-existent. The feudal power dynamics can also be seen as a network structure with the lord at the centre, with direct ties to the great vassals, who

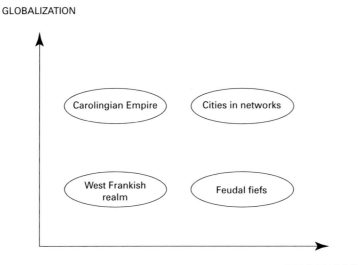

FIGURE 3.7 *The Carolingian Empire positioned in terms of the territorial field of tension model*

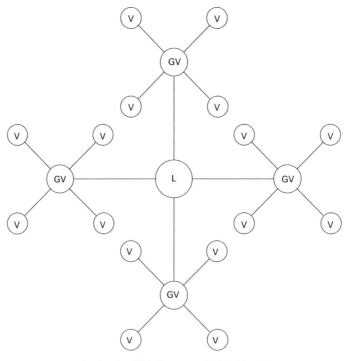

L = Lord   GV = Great vassal   V = Vassal

FIGURE 3.8 *The feudal network*

in turn were connected to their subordinated vassals (Figure 3.8). The position in the network structure depicts centrality and the degree of control/influence.

The Carolingian Empire could not withstand the centrifugal forces, represented mainly by the feudal princes. Charlemagne's efforts to create an administrative network with special envoys (*missi*) lacked a sufficiently strong material base. When the empire dissolved, the West Frankish area became the core of continued state-building.

The medieval cities were not a uniform group. For the majority of these cities, power was originally limited to the local arena. They were rarely more than marketplaces for the surrounding countryside or outgrowths of strategically placed defences. The cities that emerged later on in connection with the growth in trade were in a quite different position. Commerce expanded between the Orient and southern Europe, between southern and middle Europe, and even later between northern and central Europe (the Hanseatic League, for instance). A number of cities became key junctures in this European network, where each individual node had a vested interest in facilitating commercial transactions and protecting transports. It is not surprising that this network constituted a serious challenge to the feudal structures, and, later, to the efforts of the territorial princes to control the entire territory.

The *Holy Roman Empire of the German Nation* is the third grandiose integration project of the Middle Ages (Figure 3.9). Unlike the Carolingian, the German Empire survived for almost a thousand years, from the late tenth to the early

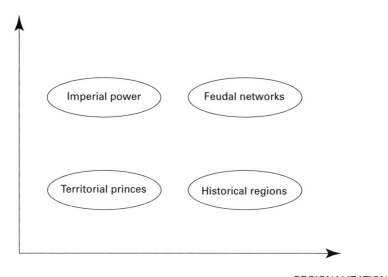

GLOBALIZATION

Imperial power   Feudal networks

Territorial princes   Historical regions

REGIONALIZATION

FIGURE 3.9 *The German medieval empire positioned in terms of the territorial field of tension model*

nineteenth century. The emperors never managed to develop any strong
central authority. Their power base was too weak and the opposition of the
territorial princes too intense.

The German Empire had to compete with the equally grandiose ambitions
of the papacy, which aimed at crystallizing its supremacy not only in the
religious world, but also in the secular arena. The *Catholic Church* is also an
example of a functional network characterized by a common ideology and a
common language, Latin, as unifying elements (Figure 3.10). In keeping with
the terminology of the model, medieval Europe was marked by tensions
between the Catholic Church as a network organization, regional structures
with bishops and dioceses, proto-national states (princes, national churches)
and rival networks (religious orders, monasteries) – not to forget the emerging
cities with their distant trade.

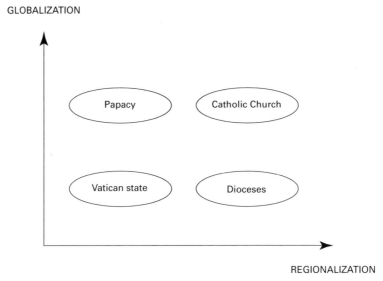

FIGURE 3.10   *The Catholic Church positioned in terms of the territorial field of*
tension model

NOTES

1 Denis de Rougemont, *The Idea of Europe* (New York: Collier–Macmillan, 1966);
Jean-Baptiste Duroselle, *Europe: A History of its Peoples* (London: Viking, 1990).

2 The term 'Europe' appears first in the works of Hesiodus (*c.* 700 BC); see de
Rougemont, *The Idea of Europe*, 30ff. Cf. J.B.F. Kormoos, 'The Geographical Notion of
Europe over the Centuries', in *Europe, Dream – Adventure – Reality*, ed. Hendrik
Brugmans (New York: Greenwood Press, 1987), 85ff.

3 The designation 'Celtic' first appears in sources from the fifth century BC. On the
Celts in history, see, for example, Miranda J. Green, *The Celtic World* (London/New
York: Routledge, 1995).

4 On Indo-Europeanism as a linguistic concept, see J.P. Mallory, *In Search of the Indo-Europeans: Language, Archaeology and Myth* (London: Thames & Hudson, 1989). A different interpretation appears in Colin Renfrew, *Archaeology and Language: The Puzzle of Indo-European Origins* (New York: Cambridge University Press, 1987). A summary of the widespread discussion on the Indo-Europeans is provided by Ernst Wahle in 'Ur- und Frühgeschichte im Mitteleuropäischen Raum', in *Gebhardt: Handbuch der Deutschen Geschichte 1*, 9th edn, ed. Herbert Grundmann (Stuttgart: Klett), 41ff.

5 For a classic study of the problem of migration in history, see Alexander Kulischer and Eugen Kulischer, *Kriegs- und Wanderzüge: Weltgeschichte als Völkerbewegung* (Berlin/Leipzig: Walter de Gruyter, 1932). On Roman contact with the so-called barbarians during the Great Migrations (from approximately the fifth to the seventh centuries), see, for example, Justine D. Randers-Pehrson, *Barbarians and Romans* (Oklahoma: University of Oklahoma Press, 1983).

6 On the Magyar (Hungarian) settlement, see, for example, *A History of Hungary*, eds Peter F. Sugar, Péter Hanák and Tibor Frank (London: Tauris, 1990), 8ff.

7 On the dissemination of the Christian faith in Western Europe, see, for instance, Robert Bartlett, *The Making of Europe: Conquest, Colonization and Cultural Change 950–1350* (London: Penguin, 1993), 5ff. On the Christianization process, see also Hans-Joachim Diesner, 'Zur Rolle der Religion unter besonderer Berücksichtigung des Christentums', in *Die Römer an Rhein und Donau*, eds Rigobert Günther and Helga Köpstein (Vienna: Böhlau, 1975).

8 The two Christian churches parted ways in 1054. The break was the result of diverging interpretations concerning the confession of faith in the creed, the so-called Filioque controversy. See, for instance, Dietrich Ritschl, 'Historical Development and Implications of the Filioque Controversy', in *Spirit of God, Spirit of Christ*, ed. Lukas Vischer (Geneva: WCC, 1981); and Maria-Helene Gamillschegg, *Die Kontroverse um das Filioque* (Würzburg: Augustinus Verlag, 1996).

9 Xavier de Planhol, *Les Fondements géographiques de l'histoire de l'Islam* (Paris: Nouvelle Bibliothèque Scientifique, 1968); Ira Lapidus, *A History of Islamic Societies* (Cambridge: Cambridge University Press, 1988).

10 As for the relation between the older Islamic (Arabic and Berber) philosophy and the ancient Greek worldview, see Taufic Ibrahim and Arthur Sagadeev, *Classical Islamic Philosophy* (Moscow: Progress Publishers, 1990), 115ff especially. See also Thomas F. Glick, *Islamic and Christian Spain in the Early Middle Ages* (Princeton, NJ: Princeton University Press, 1979), especially Chapter 8, 'Science', 248ff.

11 For an overview of the expansion of ancient Rome in the Mediterranean region, see, for example, *Die Römer: Ein enzyklopädisches Sachbuch zur frühen Geschichte Europas*, eds Heinrich Pleticha and Otto Schönberger (Gütersloh, 1977). See also Derek Williams, *The Reach of Rome: A History of the Roman Imperial Frontier, 1st–5th Centuries AD* (London: Constable, 1996). On the Roman expansion northward, see *Die Römer an Rhein und Donau*, ed. Günther and Köpstein.

12 On the Roman taxation of the provinces, see Walter Goffart, *Caput and Colonate* (Toronto: Phoenix, 1974).

13 On the construction of the Roman system of provinces, see *Die Römer*, eds Pleticha and Schönberger, 361ff. For literature on Roman rule and administration, see, for instance, Paul Petit, *La Paix romaine* (Paris: Nouvelle Clio, 1967). For an excellent discussion of the territorial organization in Roman times, see Xavier de Planhol and Paul Claval, *An Historical Geography of France* (Cambridge: Cambridge University Press, 1994).

14 Williams, *The Reach of Rome*.

15 Graham Webster, *The Roman Imperial Army* (London: Adam & Charles, 1969), especially the chapter on 'The Frontier Systems', 47ff; William S. Hanson, 'The Nature and Function of Roman Frontiers', in *Barbarians and Romans in North-West Europe from the Later Republic to Late Antiquity*, eds John C. Barrett et al. (Oxford: BAR, 1989); Randers-Pehrson, *Barbarians and Romans*; Hugh Elton, *Frontiers of the Roman Empire* (London: Batsford, 1996). For older literature on the *limes*, see *Die Römer*, eds Pleticha and Schönberger, 286ff. On the Roman network of roads, which covered some 80,000 kilometers in Trajanus's days, see *Die Römer*, eds Pleticha and Schönberger, 433ff; Raymond Chevallier, *Les Voies romaines* (Paris: Colin, 1972). On the Roman military organization in the frontier areas, see, for example, Fergus G.B. Millar, *The Roman Empire and its Neighbours*, 2nd edn (London: Duckworth, 1981), 104ff.

16 Averil Cameron, *The Mediterranean World in Late Antiquity AD395–600* (London: Fontana, 1993), especially the chapter on 'The Empire, the Barbarians and the Late Roman Army', 33f.

17 The fall of the Roman Empire is among the most widely discussed topics in the discipline of history. For a long time it was believed that the Germanic invasions precipitated the empire's decline. This theory was subsequently replaced by an interpretation that emphasized the expansion of Islam into the southern and western Mediterranean area; see Henri Pirenne, *Mahomet et Charlemagne* (Paris: Félix Alcan, 1937). Later, systematic studies in archaeology yielded yet a new theory, which prevails today. Scholars now highlight internal, rather than external, forces in accounting for the collapse of the state in the late Roman era. See, for instance, Richard Hodges and David Whitehouse, *Mohammed, Charlemagne and the Origins of Europe* (London: Duckworth, 1983); cf. Lars Andersson, 'Pirenne, Bolin och den nya arkeologin', *Scandia*, 55 (1989), 163–83. See also Herwig Wolfram, *The Roman Empire and its Germanic Peoples* (Berkeley, CA: University of California Press, 1997), 301ff.

18 Lucien Musset, *The Germanic Invasions: The Making of Europe AD 400–600* (University Park, PA: Pennsylvania State University Press, 1975); Williams, *The Reach of Rome*.

19 The idea that peoples who are specifically named in early sources constituted clearly demarcated ethnic groups has been questioned by modern scholarship. Research now emphasizes the importance of the community over the importance of ethnic descent; see 'Der Begriff Völkerwanderung', in *Der Grosse Ploetz: Auszug der Geschichte* (Freiburg: Verlag Ploetz, 1980), 320. The problems associated with indiscriminately employing ethnic criteria to descriptions of realities in pre-history and early history are discussed in Thomas Wallerström, 'On Ethnicity as a Methodological Problem in Historical Archaeology', in *Visions of the Past: Trends and Traditions in Swedish Medieval Archaeology*, eds Hans Andersson et al. (Stockholm: Central Board of National Antiquities, 1997).

20 See Denis Sinor, 'The Hun Period', in *Cambridge History of Early Inner Asia*, ed. D. Sinor (Cambridge: Cambridge University Press, 1990), 177ff; Edvard A. Thomson, *The Huns* (Oxford: Blackwell, 1996). On the Alans, see Bernhard S. Bachrach, *A History of the Alans in the West* (Minneapolis: Berna, 1973).

21 Randers-Pehrson, *Barbarians and Romans*; Barrett et al. (eds), *Barbarians and Romans in North-West Europe*.

22 Planhol and Claval, *An Historical Geography*, 94.

23 On the Ostrogoths in Italy, see Heinz Löwe, 'Deutschland im fränkishen Reich', in *Gebhardt: Handbuch der Deutschen Geschichte 1*, 9th edn, ed. Herbert Grundmann (Stuttgart: Klett, 1970), 97ff. See also Herwig Wolfram, *History of the Goths* (Berkeley, CA: University of California Press, 1988).

24 On the Visigoths in Spain, see Bernhard F. Reilly, *The Medieval Spains* (Cambridge: Cambridge University Press, 1993), Chapters 1–2.

25 On the Vandals, see Frank M. Clover, *The Late Roman West and the Vandals* (Aldershot: Variorum, 1993).

26 Paul-Marie Duval, *Gallien: Leben und Kultur in römischer Zeit* (Stuttgart: Reclam, 1979); Fustel de Coulanges, *La Gaule romaine*, revised edn (Paris: Editions de Fallois, 1994), 95ff especially.

27 Wolfgang H. Fritze, *Frühzeit zwischen Ostsee und Donau* (Berlin: Duncker and Humbolt, 1982).

28 On the Great-Migration states, see Löwe, 'Deutschland im fränkishen Reich', 95ff. For a new perspective on the Lombard kingdom in Italy, see Dick Harrison, *The Early State and the Towns: Forms of Integration in Lombard Italy AD 568–774* (Lund: Lund University Press, 1993).

29 On the Merovingians, see *Lexikon des Mittelalters*, vol. 6 (Munich: Artemis, 1977–1997), 543; *Dictionary of the Middle Ages*, vol. 8 (New York: Charles Scribner's Sons, 1982–1989), 277ff. A comprehensive overview of existing literature on the subject appears in Löwe, 'Deutschland im fränkischen Reich', 107ff.

30 For a characterization of the medieval feudal system, see Aron J. Gurevitj, *Feodalismens uppkomst i Västeuropa* (Stockholm: Tiden, 1979). On the concept 'feudalism', see Otto Brunner, 'Feudalismus: Ein Beitrag zur Begriffsgeschichte', in *Neue Wege der Verfassungs- und Sozialgeschichte* (Göttingen: Vandenhoeck & Ruprecht, 1968). On the spreading and characteristics of the enfeoffment system in different parts of Europe, see *Lexikon des Mittelalters*, vol. 5, especially 1807ff.

31 Guy Fourquin, *Lordship and Feudalism in the Middle Ages* (London: Allen & Unwin, 1976). On the economic foundations of the medieval feudal system, see, for instance, Michel Postan (ed.), *The Agrarian Life of the Middle Ages: Cambridge Economic History of Europe 1* (Cambridge: Cambridge University Press, 1966). On specifically legal aspects of enfeoffment, see B. Diestelkamp, 'Lehen', in *Lexikon des Mittelalters*, vol. 5, especially 1807.

32 Löwe, 'Deutschland im fränkishen Reich', 111ff, 119ff.

33 Planhol and Claval, *An Historical Geography*, 245ff.

34 Robert H. Bautier, *The Economic Development of Medieval Europe* (London: Variorum, 1971), 58ff.

35 Ibid., 65ff.

36 N.G.J. Pounds, *An Economic History of Medieval Europe* (London: Longman, 1994); Robert S. Lopez, *The Commercial Revolution of the Middle Ages* (Cambridge: Cambridge University Press, 1971); Bautier, *Economic Development of Medieval Europe*; Daniel Waley, *The Italian City-Republics* (London: Longman, 1988); Hendrik Spruyt, *The Sovereign State and Its Competitors* (Princeton, NJ: Princeton University Press, 1994), 130–50.

37 David Nicholas, *Medieval Flanders* (London: Longman, 1992).

38 Robert H. Bautier, *Sur l'histoire économique de la France médiévale: la route, le fleuve, la foire* (London: Variorum, 1991); Bautier, *Economic Development of Medieval Europe*, 110ff; see also *Lexikon des Mittelalters*, vol. 2, 1685ff and references especially.

39 E. Whiting Fox, *History in Geographic Perspective: The Other France* (New York: W.W. Norton, 1971).

40 Giovanni Tabacco, *The Struggle for Power in Medieval Italy: Structures of Political Rule* (Cambridge: Cambridge University Press, 1989); Waley, *The Italian City-Republics*.

41 Norbert Ohler, *The Medieval Traveller* (Woodbridge: Boydell Press, 1989), 59ff especially.

42 See, for instance, Phillippe Dollinger, *Die Hanse*, 3rd edn (Stuttgart: Kröner, 1981).

For an account of the number of Hanseatic cities, see ibid., 570f; Spruyt, *The Sovereign State*, 109–29.

43 There is an extensive body of literature on the medieval cities of Europe. See, for instance, Edith Ennen, *Die europäische Stadt des Mittelalters* (Göttingen: Vandenhoeck & Ruprecht, 1972). On the relationship of the cities to the imperial power and the principalities, see, for example, Fritz Rörig, *The Medieval Town* (Berkeley, CA: University of California Press, 1975), 72ff.

44 Charles Tilly, *The Formation of National States in Western Europe* (Princeton: Princeton University Press, 1975); Charles Tilly and Wim P. Blockmans (eds), *Cities and the Rise of States in Europe AD 1000 to 1800* (Boulder, CO: Westview, 1994). Concerning 'protection' and 'extraction', see Charles Tilly, 'War Making and State Making as Organized Crime', in *Bringing the State Back In*, ed. Peter B. Evans et al. (Cambridge: Cambridge University Press, 1985).

45 Louis Halphen, *Charlemagne et l'empire carolingien* (Paris: Albin Michel, 1947); on titular issues, see Grundmann (ed.), *Gebhardt: Handbuch der Deutschen Geschichte 1*.

46 Concerning the institution of royal envoys (*missi dominici*), see, for instance, François L. Ganshof, *The Carolingians and the Frankish Monarchy: Studies in Carolingian History* (London: Longman, 1971), 23.

47 On the founding of the German empire, see, for example, Helmut Beumann, 'Das Kaisertum Ottos des Grossen', *Historische Zeitschrift* 195 (1962), 529ff; Helmut Beumann, 'Die Bedeutung des Kaisertums für die Entstehung der deuschen Nation in Spiegel der Beziehungen von Reich und Herrscher', in *Aspekte der Nationenbildung im Mittelalter*, eds Helmut Beumann and Werner Schröder (Sigmaringen: Thorbecke, 1978).

48 Beumann, 'Das Kaisertum Ottos des Grossen'; Helmut Beumann, 'Der deutsche König als "Romanorum Rex"', *Sitzungsberichte* XVIII:2 (Frankfurt am Main: Johann Wolfgang Goethe-Universität, 1981).

49 On the struggle over investiture, see *Lexikon des Mittelalters*, vol. 5, 479f and references; see also Gerd Tellenbach, *The Church in Western Europe from the Tenth to the Early Twelfth Century* (Cambridge: Cambridge University Press, 1993).

50 On the system of electors, see E. Schubert in *Lexikon des Mittelalters*, vol. 5, 1581f.

51 On territorial identity see Rune Johansson, 'The Impact of Imagination', in *Regions in Central Europe: The Legacy of History*, ed. Sven Tägil (London: Hurst & Co., 1999).

52 Paul Claval, 'The Region as a Geographical, Economic and Cultural Concept', *International Social Science Journal* 112 (1987), 159ff; cf. David Grigg, 'The Logic of Regional Systems', in *The Conceptual Revolution in Geography*, ed. Wayne Davies (London: University of London Press, 1972).

53 On boundaries, see Sven Tägil, Kristian Gerner, Göran Henriksson, Rune Johansson, Ingmar Oldberg and Kim Salomon, *Studying Boundary Conflicts: A Theoretical Framework* (Stockholm: Esselte, 1977), especially Appendix, 150ff. See also Sven Tägil, 'The Question of Border Regions in Western Europe: An Historical Background', in *Frontier Regions in Western Europe*, ed. Malcolm Anderson (London: Frank Cass, 1983).

54 Tägil et al., *Studying Boundary Conflicts*, 121ff.

55 On historical regions, see Tägil (ed.), *Regions in Central Europe*.

56 On the Roman administrative divisions, see Petit, *La paix romaine*, 134ff. On the provinces, see also Andrew W. Lintott, 'What was the Imperium Romanum?', *Greece and Rome*, 28 (1981), 53ff; W.T. Arnold, *The Roman System of Provincial Administration to the Accession of Constantine the Great* (Chicago: Ares Publishers, 1974). On Gaul, see de Coulanges, *La Gaule romaine*.

57 Arnold, *The Roman System*.

58 Duval, *Gallien*.

59 On the emergence of Aquitaine, see Michel Rouche, *L'Aquitaine des Wisigoths aux Arabes: Naissance d'une région* (Paris: Touzot, 1979). See also George T. Beech, 'Aquitaine', in *Medieval France: An Encyclopedia*, eds William W. Keebler and Grover A. Zinn (New York: Garland, 1995).

60 On Belgium, see, for instance, Horst Lademacher, *Geschichte der Niederlande: Politik – Verfassung – Wirtschaft* (Darmstadt: Wissenschaftlishes Buchgesellschaft, 1983). On Belgian pre-history, see Jean Stengers, 'La formation de la frontière linguistique en Belgique', *Collection Latomus*, XLI (Brussels: Latomus, 1959).

61 On the concept of 'Stem', see Grundmann (ed.), *Gebhardt: Handbuch der Deutschen Geschichte 1*, 701ff and references. Cf. also note 19 above.

62 See Sven Tägil, 'The German Stem Duchies', in Tägil (ed.), *Regions in Central Europe*.

63 On the earliest tribal duchies, see Grundmann (ed.), *Gebhardt: Handbuch der Deutschen Geschichte 1*, 135ff, 212ff, 220ff and 747ff.

64 On Lorraine, see R. Thomas McDonald, 'Lorraine', in *Medieval France: An Encyclopedia*, eds William W. Kebler and A. Zinn Grover (New York: Garland, 1995), 560f. On the current regional division, see Michel Parisse (ed.), *Historie de la Lorraine* (Toulouse: Privat, 1978), 467f.

65 The name 'Burgundy' has been applied to several different areas and principalities. See K.F. Werner, 'Zum Burgund-Begriff', in *Lexikon des Mittelalters*, vol. 2, 1062. On the duchy of Burgundy, see the Bibliography in *Lexikon des Mittelalters*, vol. 2, 1085ff.

66 Lintott, 'What was the Imperium Romanum?', 53f.

4

The Emergent State

While all forms of organization, from hunter–gatherer tribes to empires and states, occupy a certain space, they are predicated on and defined by territorial parameters to varying degrees. The modern state is an archetypically territorial entity, and the division of the world into mutually exclusive territorial states is the overriding organizational aspect of the current political map.

Territory, *population*, *authority* and *recognition* are essential aspects of statehood, according to most definitions. A state is generally understood as an organization, which claims ultimate authority over the population within a well-defined territory. In order to participate in international relations, it must also be recognized by other states. The state needs external authorization to be the ultimate authority claimant; this is not an attribute of the state but is attributed to the state by other state rulers.[1] In modern times, statehood has been denied to 'uncivilized' societies during the age of imperialism, to republicans during the Napoleonic wars, and to socialist revolutionaries in the twentieth century.[2]

Sovereign states, interacting in an anarchic environment, are the stuff of international politics, according to the (neo)realist school which has dominated the academic study of international relations for half a century. Current theorists and practitioners of *Realpolitik* have tended to view states as generic and universalized organizations. Yet critics of the (neo)realist paradigm have demonstrated the variable and contingent nature of states. Sovereign statehood is but one particular form of territorial practice, which displays considerable variance across time and space. The traditional state of, say, the seventeenth century differed from the modern state in several respects. 'Even in this century,' argue Yale Ferguson and Richard Mansbach, 'state forms have been hard to distinguish from empires (e.g., the Soviet Union), tribal conglomerates (e.g., Rwanda and Kenya), religious movements (e.g., Iran of the mullahs), cities (e.g., Singapore), or even coteries of families (e.g., El Salvador).' They characterize the world as a 'living museum' where earlier political forms and ideas are preserved behind the facade of a modern state system.[3]

The constituent elements of statehood should thus be examined, not as constants, as is so often done, but as variables. In this chapter we shall first look for medieval precedents of the modern state and the principle of sovereignty.

The Treaty of Westphalia of 1648 is generally seen as the birthdate of the modern state. What were the alternatives to territorial states around that time? And why did sovereign states, rather than any of the alternatives, become the predominant way of organizing domestic and international politics? After addressing these questions, we conclude by discussing the concept of sovereignty, the foundation of statehood. Our perspective throughout the chapter is that state and sovereignty are 'mutually constitutive and constantly undergoing change and transformation'.[4]

State and sovereignty before 1648

In modern history, from the end of the fifteenth century and especially since the Peace of Westphalia in 1648, the sovereign territorial state has been the principal actor in the international system. Both the concept and the terminology are far older, however, and change has not followed any uniform pattern. Some of the present-day states of Europe have a continuity that can be traced back to the early Middle Ages, while others are significantly later constructions. Throughout history, states have emerged, have been transformed in both form and content, and frequently have dissolved and merged into new units.

The fundamental characteristics of the modern state – sovereignty, state government, state territory and people – had precursors in the medieval pre-modern state. The terminology was, of course, different. 'State' (from the Latin *status*) as an overarching label did not develop until the eleventh or twelfth centuries, first in southern Europe and far later in Germanic-speaking areas.[5] The term 'sovereignty' is derived from the medieval Latin word *superanus* (twelfth century), and does not exist in classical Latin. Sovereignty, which in our time is inherently linked to statehood, had no place in a world of feudal states or in the German states of the late Middle Ages: neither the German territorial princes nor the German emperor were sovereign in the modern sense.[6]

Even though there were references during the Middle Ages to an abstract *summum imperium*, the ultimate authority generally rested with a specific ruler or a dynasty, not with any abstractly construed state. However, medieval practice was not unambiguous in this aspect either. While in the fifteenth century Machiavelli could make a distinction between republics and principalities with respect to Italy, the Holy Roman Empire was a bewildering patchwork of cities, princes, ecclesiastical authorities and other feudal remnants.

From dynasties to states and nations

The most common form of political rule during the Middle Ages was the monarchy.[7] The king was in principle the highest representative of power and control within the state territory. Dynastic politics and redistribution of estates entailed constant, and often radical, revisions of territorial boundaries. In fact, it was not until after the Middle Ages that the kingdoms obtained a more definitive territorial demarcation and continuity.

The consolidation of the monarchic territorial states followed varying chronologies from case to case. To a considerable extent, the variance had to do with material resources. Without the necessary means, it would have been impossible to effectively institutionalize the administration, the law and the defence of the land to secure the independence of the state. Of decisive importance were stable revenues from taxation, which required a functioning system for tax collection.[8] The position and extension of the territory were also significant. In central Europe, feudal fragmentation had progressed so far that the German emperor never succeeded in gathering sufficient resources to balance the power of the electoral college. What the different German princes had in common was their ambition to curtail the authority of the emperor, since no individual prince was powerful enough to single-handedly challenge the imperial dynasty that held nominal power.[9]

None the less, a single prince, Charles V of Habsburg, was able to create a great European empire that stretched from the North Sea and the Baltic to the Mediterranean, by combining territories under his direct control – the Austrian hereditary lands – with his formal role as German emperor. Charles V's domains included the kingdoms of Spain, Sardinia, Sicily and Naples. This territorially fragmented empire, which was largely the result of dynastic transactions, was again dissolved into its constituent parts, even before a permanent, empire-wide administration had been established.[10]

The medieval perception of territory was closely tied to the ruler's, or the dynasty's claims and rights. For the majority of people, an abstraction such as the 'state' had little significance. Their identity was bound to more immediate environments and tangible realities, such as their family, kin-group and local community. As institutions based on the state and its territory were created, the state gradually became relevant not only for the elites but also for ordinary people.[11] As a rule, state-building was a dynamic process, frequently spanning several generations. At times, however, change occurred quite rapidly, particularly during times of war and other international upheavals. Over time, both the state and the state territory entered into the individual's self-perception.[12]

The consolidation of the territorial state in the late Middle Ages was accompanied by an ever-stronger monarchy with the financial means to establish institutions and strengthen military capabilities. This was particularly apparent in southwestern, western and northern Europe. The importance of territorial control was illustrated by the single-minded policies of the French kings throughout the Middle Ages to constantly add new areas to the royal domains, which originally were of rather modest scope. More and more administrative competencies were subordinated to the royal council, the *Curia Regis*. Only in the mid-sixteenth century, however, did the French kings exercise complete control over the entire state territory.[13]

Spain is another of Europe's oldest states, with boundaries that have remained almost unchanged since the state was founded in 1516. The Spanish state is the outcome of a long series of earlier integration projects: the Roman, the Visigoth during the Great Migrations, the Moorish (712–1492), the competing Castilian and Catalonian projects (1035–1492 and 1140–1410 respectively), and the empire that was created through the merger of Castile and Aragon towards the end of the Middle Ages.[14]

Several of these integration projects were successful inasmuch as the central authority temporarily enjoyed a powerful position, while the influence of the regions declined correspondingly. Regional differentiation was none the less apparent from the early Middle Ages, particularly at times when two or more integration projects competed with each other.

England and Scotland also have long histories of state- and nation-building. In 1603, a personal union joined the formally equal kingdoms of Scotland and England. About a century later, in 1707, a British state was created, whereupon the separate English and Scottish parliaments were dissolved and replaced by a common parliament, which in practice was dominated by the English. The British state-formation, which included England, Scotland and Wales, had a shared monarchy and parliament. Other than that, few common institutions were developed. It was significant that the state territory during the fifteenth century became permanently delimited to the British isles, when all continental possessions (with the exception of Calais) were lost, mainly to France, which in turn could cement its own territorial boundaries.[15]

Similarly, the state-formations of northern Europe were characterized by remarkable continuity, although they lagged behind central Europe in their cultural development. The Danish kingdom was consolidated in the late tenth century, the Norwegian and the Swedish somewhat later. State-building occurred through the fusion of smaller ethno-regional entities. Sweden, for instance, emerged when the Sveas and the Geats joined into a single kingdom in the eleventh century. By the end of the Middle Ages, Denmark, Norway and Sweden had achieved a sufficient degree of consolidation, institution-alization and external demarcation to be characterized as proto-modern states. Attempts to forge a common Nordic state in the fifteenth century, the Kalmar Union, failed due to elite opposition, especially in Sweden. The Nordic states thereafter evolved in separate directions. The territorial core-areas remained intact, but the external boundaries continued to be unstable for several centuries.[16]

In eastern Europe, states based on a powerful dynasty emerged in the late Middle Ages. Poland, under King Kasimir (the House of Piast), Bohemia under King Charles IV (the House of Luxemburg) and Hungary under King Louis (the House of Anjou) – all three kings had the epithet 'the Great' – could be characterized as regional great powers. Poland was enlarged territorially after a series of victories against the Teutonic Order states. Through a union with Lithuania in 1388, Poland became Europe's largest territorial state, stretching from the Baltic to the Black Sea. Towards the end of the Middle Ages, the region became increasingly unstable, partly as a result of the Ottoman expansion into the Balkans and southeastern Europe.[17]

The consolidation of the territorial state with reasonably fixed external boundaries, institutionalized exercise of power and some kind of cultural foundation was thus primarily a west European phenomenon, while central Europe (the German Empire, Burgundy) and Italy remained fragmented and unstable, as did many of the less developed parts of eastern Europe.

Inadequate communications made it difficult to maintain control over large, far-flung territories. In the absence of roads, the waterways played a key role. Neither the Danish–British empire of Canute the Great nor the various Baltic projects – Hanseatic, Danish and Swedish – were sustainable alternatives to clearly demarcated territorial states. The ancient Roman Empire remained unmatched in its scope until the colonial expansions of the nineteenth century made possible the creation of manageable global empires.

The medieval state-building process is far too complicated to capture in a simple formula. So far, we have focused mainly on territorial demarcation, monarchy as a form of government and the institutionalization of common organs. Nation-formation also deserves some attention in this context. The state territory can be perceived by the population as their exclusive possession and be an important part of the people's self-perception. The longer the territory has been intact and been institutionalized, the more likely it is that a territorially based identity will crystallize among the population.

The identification of individuals with other members of the group also takes time to develop. In modern states, national identities play an important role. Indeed, state-building and nation-building have often been parallel processes, particularly after the emergence of nationalism as a sort of superideology in Europe in the past two centuries. Many scholars argue that national identity is the direct result of deliberate propaganda and indoctrination. In their view, the modern nation-state is an artificial construction, developed in connection with the modernization and industrialization processes during the latter half of the nineteenth century.

Against this background, the state-formations of previous eras seem to diverge from the modern state-building process in a fundamental way.[18] National identity shared by the broader strata of society did not exist in the states that were formed during the Middle Ages. Yet the contemporary perception of nationhood cannot be regarded as a mere construction. Even imagined communities may have roots far back in history,[19] although the nineteenth-century principle of nationality – that the boundaries of the state and nation should coincide – fundamentally altered the basis for territorial organization.[20]

In retrospect, the outcome of the medieval state-building process appears contingent rather than the result of rational policies and circumstances. How, for instance, could the French kings, despite unfavourable circumstances, succeed in establishing a territorially cohesive state, while the German emperor failed? Why did there not emerge a single Nordic state, but three separate nation-states? Why did Spain become a seemingly cohesive state, while Italy remained plagued by fragmentation (with the exception of the development of the Two Sicilies in the south)?

There is no monocausal answer to these questions. Even though each case was unique, it is clear that the emergence of a strong territorial state required a clearly demarcated territory with fixed boundaries and internal controls. In France, the kings were able to overcome feudal fragmentation through systematic acquisitions of territory from the feudal aristocracy and lesser princes, but also by waging successful wars against the English, who had substantial possessions on the continent.

In other places, such as Germany, the particularist structures proved too strong. Similarly, in Italy the large commercial cities with their powerful bourgeoisie had enough resources to maintain their independence. As well, the monarchy in the border area between France and Germany lost the struggle over sovereignty. Burgundy, rich in resources, never became a lasting principality or a sovereign territorial state. Instead, sovereignty came to be exercised by the Swiss confederation in the southern parts of the region, and by the Netherlands in the northern parts. Both state-formations were finally confirmed by the Peace of Westphalia in 1648, which signalled the birth of the modern European state.

The sovereign state and its alternatives

The European origin of the modern state system should be emphasized; 'the story of the formation of the modern state is in part the story of the formation of Europe, and vice versa'.[21] In fact, for a long time the legitimacy and recognition of states did not extend beyond Europe. For centuries few non-European polities were recognized as sovereign states and admitted as members of the state system. It could be argued that the development of a state system contributed greatly to catapulting Europe ahead of other continents during the modern era. Only with decolonization after the Second World War did the state system become global. And still today many states in the third world remain 'quasi-states', insofar as they are granted juridical sovereignty while lacking the empirical hallmarks of European state sovereignty.[22]

The conventional view is that the sovereign state is the result of the Treaty of Westphalia of 1648. The peace agreement that brought to an end the Thirty Years War has generally been regarded as a major turning point in history, a decisive break with the medieval past. It 'serves as a crucial demarcation between an era still dominated by competing claims to religious universalism and hierarchical authority and an era of secular competition and co-operation among autonomous political communities.'[23] The current international system of sovereign states is therefore often referred to as the Westphalian system. In fact, Westphalia has become 'an icon for international relations scholars'.[24] Recently, scholars have questioned the conventional view of Westphalia, arguing that Westphalia was neither the beginning of the sovereign state nor the end of all medieval remnants: 'political entities with exclusive control over a well-defined territory existed well before the Peace, and feudal and universal institutions, which were eventually extinguished, continued well after it'.[25]

However, the Peace of Westphalia may serve as a useful indicator of a broader transition process. In searching for alternatives to the sovereign, territorial state, we need then to look first at the organizational forms that existed in medieval Europe before Westphalia; second, at the organizational forms that coexisted with the state at the time of Westphalia but were eventually displaced.

In medieval Europe political authority was layered and overlapping. Authority over territory was neither exclusive nor discrete, and occupants of a particular territory were subject to a multitude of authorities. The medieval system has been characterized as 'a heteronomous structure of territorial rights and claims', that is, 'a quintessential system of segmental territorial rule . . . that had none of the connotations of territorial exclusiveness conveyed by the modern concept of sovereignty'.[26] Jurisdictions overlapped; church, lords, kings, emperors, and towns could simultaneously make rival claims to authority and jurisdiction. The result was a patchwork of overlapping, incomplete and tangled authority claims and a system of plural allegiances. There were no clear demarcations between private and public authority, between domestic and international politics, or between the political and economic sphere.

The medieval system, in short, was essentially non-territorial, insofar as territoriality was not the defining characteristic of organization. Political rule was not premised on territorial delimitation.[27] Feudalism, the church and the Holy Roman Empire represent three different organizational forms in the Middle Ages, which lacked territorial fixity and exclusiveness.

The organizational principles of feudalism and universal rule, whether by the church or through empire, were fundamentally at odds with the logic of sovereign territoriality, and with the Peace of Westphalia these modes of organization lost legitimacy. However, the territorial state had yet to prove itself in competition with various organizational forms that were the result of fundamental realignments in Europe. How and why did the sovereign state, over time, become the predominant mode of political organization?

The origins and explanations of state prevalence

Scholars who have pursued this question tend to agree on the historical contingency of the state. The modern state is not the result of any unilinear, inevitable historical process.[28] Nor were states created by design. Only rarely did European rulers have coherent plans or models of state formation, and no one designed the components of modern states, such as treasuries, courts and central administrations.[29] Rather, the state can be seen as 'the precarious result of a rare historical conjunction, closely linked to particular circumstances'.[30] Hence, in tracing the origin of the sovereign state, we have to rely on 'theories of historical contingency' and 'steer a narrow road between randomness and teleology'.[31]

Moreover, researchers concur that cities or city-states were the main remaining competitors of the sovereign state, once universalist empire, Roman theocracy and feudalism lost ground. Cities have historically been associated with the accumulation of capital, in contrast to other entities that have relied primarily on coercion and domination. Coercion-intensive paths were followed in those parts of Europe where there were few cities, little concentrated capital and thin trade routes, such as Russia and the Nordic countries.[32] The city-states of northern Italy and Flanders, on the other hand, epitomize capitalist trajectories. Medieval Venice is a case in point:

> Through all the conquest, Venetian commercial interests reigned supreme. The city's leading families were merchants and bankers, the city's governing council represented the leading families, the doge came from that same patriciate, the city's military forces drew on its own population, and its military and diplomatic policies promoted the establishment of commercial monopolies, protection for its merchants, and channeling of trade through Venice rather than the creation of a territorial empire.[33]

Not only cities or city-states competed with the emergent territorial states at the time of the Westphalian Treaty, but also city-leagues. Since they were non-territorial in character, city-leagues, such as the Hanseatic League, were antithetical to the sovereign state. They were not only non-contiguous, but lacked borders altogether. They were functionally rather than geographically integrated. The Hanseatic League could raise troops and equip large fleets. Yet it had no centralized legal system, although it included a variety of legal codes at the municipal level.

In addition to agreeing about the historical contingency of the state and about its chief competitors, researchers also tend to concur that it was far-reaching environmental changes that made medieval modes of organization obsolete and brought about the predominance of one organizational form, the state.

However, there is no consensus as to what environmental changes were most important in accounting for the prevalence of states. Was it changes in the domestic or in the international environment that were decisive? And did these changes primarily concern coercion or economic exchange? This is where researchers disagree, at least in terms of emphasis. Yet there seems to be a fair amount of agreement that it is the nexus of internal and external pressures on the one hand, and of economic exchange and coercion on the other, that may explain the eventual triumph of the territorial states as well as the varied trajectories of states. While according primacy to different parts of this nexus, researchers seem to concur that these factors are interrelated and intertwined. Our point of departure, therefore, is that the evolution and advantages of the sovereign state can be epitomized in the twin dimensions of internal–external and economic exchange–coercion (cf. Figure 4.1).

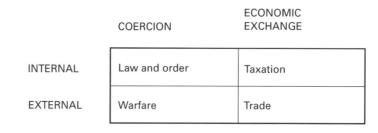

FIGURE 4.1 *Dimensions of the emergent state*

The argument, in short, is that states proved more effective than cities or city-leagues in either waging war, trading with other units, keeping order within their realm, or extracting resources from its subjects – or a combination of these factors. It is probably fair to say that explanations focusing on external rather than domestic factors occupy a predominant position in contemporary academia, so let us start there.

Those emphasizing coercion argue that because of their advantage in translating their resources into success in war, states superseded empires, cities and city-leagues as the predominant European political entities. The existing units may have started in very different positions concerning the distribution of concentrated capital and coercion, to recall Charles Tilly's distinction, but 'military competition eventually drove them all in the same general direction'.[34]

One may speak of a 'merger of the military with the commercial spirit' in medieval Europe: 'Moving amidst a warlike, violence-prone society, European merchants had a choice between attracting and arming enough followers to defend themselves, or, alternatively, offering a portion of their goods to local potentates as a price for safe passage'.[35] In the city-states of northern Italy, military contracts developed – *condotta* in Italian; hence the professional soldiers were called condottieri, contractors. Soldiers became salaried (etymologically, the word 'soldier' means a person who fights 'for pay') and did not have to rely on raiding as before, while enough citizens concluded that taxes were preferable to being plundered.[36]

The advantages of the Italian city-states, which rested on efficient tax collection, debt-funding, professional military management, and successful trading and warfare around the Mediterranean, were eclipsed by the gun-powder revolution. When cannons were introduced in naval warfare toward the end of the fifteenth century, Mediterranean galleys, built for speed, became extremely vulnerable. 'The impact of a cannonade on lightly constructed ships was as catastrophic as the initial impact of the same guns on castle walls; and its effect lasted much longer, since no technical riposte to the supremacy of heavy-gunned ships at sea was discovered until twentieth-century airplanes and submarines came along'.[37] This entailed far-ranging changes in war and statecraft, favouring the larger states north of the Alps, especially France and the Habsburg empire, which had the scale to absorb the increased costs.

The invention and diffusion of firearms had already tipped the military advantage toward rulers who could afford to cast cannons and build new, stronger fortresses. Now mobile siege artillery, along with trained, disciplined infantry came into use, at the same time as sailing vessels carrying big guns came to predominate in naval warfare. This entailed a power shift from the Mediterranean city-states to those units which had followed a middle course between coercive and capitalist trajectories, where there was a coincidence of coercive centres and centres of capital. The British Isles as well as France, Prussia and Spain illustrate this trajectory of 'capitalized coercion'.[38] From the seventeenth century onward the capitalized coercion form proved more effective in war, and therefore provided a compelling model for other types of states.

The reliance on mass conscription, initiated during the wars of the French Revolution and Empire, represents another turning point. Previously, rulers had considered the raising of armies from their own population costly and politically risky and had preferred mercenary armies. With the *levée en masse*, 'the character of war changed, and the relationship between warmaking and civilian politics altered fundamentally'.[39] In combination with the British industrial revolution, which facilitated the industrialization of warfare, this produced a new turning-point in warfare and state formation, which reinforced the advantage of the larger transalpine states.

As warfare and the preparation for war became increasingly costly, states became dependent on taxation and the availability of credit. The state's extractive claims compelled rulers to strike bargains with individuals and groups, which produced rights, privileges, and protective institutions that had not existed before. Later, ordinary people were granted political rights and social programmes in exchange for their service as soldiers. Thus, while it was the expansion of military force that drove the process of state formation in the first place, the non-military activities of the state gradually grew, so that military expenditure declined as a share of most state budgets. Military organization eventually moved from a dominant segment of the state structure to a more subordinated position.

Another way to account for the ultimate success of the state is to point to the economic transformation of medieval Europe, in particular the expansion of trade. While acknowledging that states emerged from the interplay of market forces and military activity, proponents of this perspective argue that the ability to wage war is an intervening variable, determined by the efficacy of particular institutional arrangements.[40] The ability to make credible commitments in international treaties and to provide benefits to its subjects through trade is then seen as the decisive advantage of the state over its competitors.

The alternative success story reads something like this. In response to economic changes in the late Middle Ages – rising agricultural production, monetarization of the economy and expanding trade – three new modes of organization emerged: the sovereign state, the city-league and the city-state. A new social group, the burghers, emerged with new sources of revenue and power, which did not fit the old feudal order. The burghers sought political allies, and depending on the nature of coalitions, there were different institutional outcomes. Of these, the state proved to be more effective and more efficient than its competitors in terms of being able to keep its promises in economic exchanges. Decentralized organization in combination with mutual distrust between the cities entailed cheating and unreliability in their external relations. At the same time, the Hanseatic League, the major remaining city-league, suffered from its non-territorial logic of organization, along with the fact that it had difficulties binding all its members to external agreements. Significantly, the Hanse was never allowed to be an equal participant at the Peace of Westphalia and was dissolved some twenty years later.

The much smaller city-states, by contrast, were recognized without objection at the Peace of Westphalia and survived much longer. The continued existence of many small German principalities is the most obvious example. Unlike city-leagues, they were territorial units and were therefore more compatible with a system of sovereign states. And city-states behaved similarly to states in international affairs. Some of them, in fact, converted themselves into miniature states. However, in the long run they proved to be less competitive than the sovereign states, and by the end of the eighteenth century the city-states were replaced by sovereign states.

The lack of standardization of measures, weights, coinage and legal systems among city-states and city-leagues made them less competitive than the centralized sovereign state when trade expanded in the late Middle Ages.[41] The refusal among the emerging sovereign states to recognize the Hanseatic League, while recognizing or at least tolerating city-states, spelled the death of the League and the survival of city-states into the nineteenth century. Finally, when city-states in the end proved to be less successful than the territorial states, the inhabitants of city-states looked for alternative models of rule. The sovereign state became the preferred form that was copied universally.

While explanations of the emergence and prevalence of the state tend to emphasize its comparative advantages in handling external relations, be it warfare or trade or a combination of both, factors relating to the internal organization of states also figure in most accounts. The nexus of warfare and taxation has already been alluded to above. And taxation is part of the picture of economic and political change in Europe. Edmund Burke argued that 'the revenue of the state is the state'.[42] Taxation illustrates how states relate to societies and to the external political and economic system. External changes, especially new military technologies, pressurized states to find sources of taxation; John Hobson speaks of 'geofiscal cycles', referring to 'the pressures of international military activity, measured by the *fiscal costs* of war and war preparation'.[43] In his perspective, strong states were those that had a close embedded relationship with society, whereas weak states sought to gain despotic power over society through repression. Strong states tended to rely on income taxes and free trade, whereas weak states preferred indirect taxes and tariff protectionism.[44]

Related to taxation was the creation of a body of laws and the policing of society. Controlling the principal means of coercion within its territory was crucial not only to its ability to collect taxes but also to its mobilization of the state's resources externally. The success of the state, in short, hinged on its ability to 'successfully uphold a claim to monopoly of the legitimate use of physical force in the enforcement of its order'.[45] In short, the interplay of economic forces and coercion, internally as well as externally, may account for the rise of the territorial state. Let us turn, next, to an examination of the sovereignty principle, which over the centuries has been so central to statehood and has contributed to disabling possible contenders to the state.

Sovereignty

Sovereignty has been defined as 'the institutionalization of public authority within mutually exclusive jurisdictional domains',[46] or as 'a set of institutionalized authority claims'.[47] The key words in these and other definitions are *institution* and *authority claims*. First, they reflect an understanding of sovereignty as an institution that defines and empowers the state rather than as an attribute of states. Sovereignty, as Stephen Krasner has pointed out, is firmly institutionalized in terms of vertical depth and horizontal linkage.[48] Vertical depth refers to the extent to which an institution defines individual actors. Under sovereignty, individuals are to a great extent defined through their citizenship, as inscribed in their passports. Horizontal linkage refers to the number of links institutional practices has with other practices, to the number of changes that would have to be made if a particular institution were altered. Several practices are inextricably linked with sovereignty, such as diplomacy, the practice of levying duties on merchandise when it passes a borderline, immigration control, or, for that matter, Olympic games. All would be meaningless, or at least would have to be fundamentally altered, in the absence of sovereignty.

As for the second component of the cited definitions of sovereignty, the state claims authority over its territory and its population. The territorial authority claims underlying state sovereignty rest on notions of property rights. Both in terms of the origin of the sovereignty concept and its evolution as a social construct, one can make an analogy with Roman private law, which grants a property holder the right to exclude others and to use and convey his property freely. The exclusionary character of the Roman institution of property was transferred to the state's relation to its territory and resources. Thus, sovereignty became the international equivalent of private property rights domestically. They can be seen as analogous concepts, insofar as ownership entails the exclusion of others and gives rise to a system of social relations among 'possessive individualists'. At the same time, exclusive ownership, under Roman law as well as the institution of sovereignty, carries with it responsibilities and obligations. Ownership is subject to limits on its use and disposition, which may change over time.[49]

Thus, littoral states came to claim authority beyond their land territory via the concept of territorial waters. Property rights also extended 'to the centre of the earth' to cover mining.[50] In the first years of the twentieth century, when manned flight seemed a possibility but no aircraft had yet crossed national boundaries, jurists engaged in an instructive discussion of the application of sovereignty to airspace as well. The parallel with territorial waters was noted, 'with the sole difference that the sea of air abuts upon the sovereignty beneath in a vertical instead of horizontal direction'.[51] Proponents of state sovereignty in the air pointed out that activities in the airspace above a state were far more dangerous to a state than activities in the adjoining sea; hence, 'as long as the law of gravity prevails, a State must have unfettered control over air vessels passing above its territories, in order to protect itself and to carry on its administration'.[52] The analogy with territorial waters suggested that a lower zone of territorial airspace might be established, just as state sovereignty had been extended to adjacent waters. And just as the sea beyond the territorial waters was free, so one could conceive of a higher zone of free airspace above a certain agreed altitude. A common principle was that the territorial zone should reach as high as the state could exercise its authority. In the case of territorial waters, borders were originally determined by the range of cannons; the territorial airspace might, by analogy, extend as far as the range of artillery. For example, a 1,500 metre limit was suggested.[53] Eventually, states have come to claim sovereignty in the entire airspace, leaving outer space as a global common, along with the high seas. With the extension of territory to surrounding waters and airspace, borders can no longer be seen as simple lines but rather as spheres.[54]

As for the state's authority claims over the population within its territory, the institution of sovereignty imparts to the state 'meta-political' authority. That is, states claim and are recognized as having the authority to define what is political in the first place and thus subject to state coercion. 'With sovereignty, states do not simply have ultimate authority over things political; they have the authority to relegate activities, issues, and practices to the economic, social, cultural, and scientific realms of authority or to the state's own realm – the political'.[55]

The authority deriving from sovereignty should not be confused with control. Authority refers to the claim to exclusive right to make rules, whereas control refers to the state's ability to enforce that claim. Control can be achieved through the use of brute force; but if authority is effective, force or compulsion need not be used.[56] While the state's claim to ultimate political authority has been recognized for three-and-a-half centuries, state control has varied greatly across time, regions and issue-areas.[57]

Variable sovereignty

Sovereignty is usually understood as an absolute concept but, as we have seen, a discussion of the definition of sovereignty reveals its variable nature. Moreover, sovereignty is a multidimensional institution, with variation over time and space in these various dimensions. Let us look at some basic dimensions of sovereignty that have been identified by analysts.

One can, for instance, make a distinction between the 'constitutive' and 'functional' dimensions of sovereignty.[58] The state's claim to ultimate authority in a particular political space represents the constitutive dimension. Territorial segmentation and the monopolization of violence within the political space are central features of current authority claims. The functional dimension, on the other hand, delineates the range of activities over which the state can legitimately exercise its authority (extensiveness). Within this range, which may vary across issue-areas, between states and over time, the degree to which state authority penetrates society (intensiveness) may vary. For example, the authority claims of today's industrialized states are far more extensive and intensive than those of medieval or nineteenth-century states, as states have included more and more in the political realm and increasingly have intruded into formerly 'private' aspects of people's lives.

Another basic distinction can be made between the internal and external aspects of the constitutive dimension of sovereignty. In addition to establishing the state's exclusive authority – and the non-intervention of other states – within its territory, sovereignty defines the international obligations and activities of states; what states are, or are not, allowed to do in the international arena. Sovereignty can be understood as a framing concept, a *parergon*; in the same way that a frame relates to a work of art and its background, sovereignty places phenomena in the classes of domestic politics and international politics, yet cannot itself be a member of either class.[59] With sovereignty, political authority is inextricably linked with territory. Political authority is limited to the people and resources found within geographical boundaries: 'Sovereignty delineates authority according not to functions but to geography.'[60]

Expanding on the distinction between internal and external aspects of sovereignty, Stephen Krasner has suggested that the term sovereignty is commonly used in four different ways, which he labels domestic sovereignty, interdependence sovereignty, international legal sovereignty and Westphalian sovereignty.[61] *Domestic sovereignty* refers to the structure of authority within a state and its effectiveness. This is the dimension that preoccupied early theorists of sovereignty, like Jean Bodin and Thomas Hobbes, who wanted to provide an intellectual rationale for a final and absolute source of political authority. Authority structures may vary considerably – authority may be concentrated in the hands of one entity or divided among several institutions; the structure may be unitary or federal – without this affecting the other dimensions of sovereignty. *Interdependence sovereignty* denotes the ability of a government to regulate movements of people, goods, money and ideas across its borders. It concerns control rather than authority. *International legal sovereignty* refers to whether or not a state is recognized by other states and thus concerns status and legitimacy rather than control. *Westphalian sovereignty*, finally, concerns the autonomy of domestic authority structures – specifically, the absence of external influences. Actually, the norm of non-intervention in internal affairs is not a heritage of the Treaty of Westphalia but was articulated only towards the end of the eighteenth century; yet it has become associated with the so-called Westphalian model. Westphalian sovereignty, argues Krasner, has always been a myth or 'organized hypocrisy'.[62]

The main point of this classification, apart from pointing to the variation across time and space in the four dimensions of sovereignty, is to 'unbundle' sovereignty, to show that its different components can exist independently of each other. For instance, the effectiveness of political authorities within their own borders (domestic sovereignty) or their ability to control transnational flows (interdependence sovereignty) may vary without influencing international legal or Westphalian sovereignty.

From yet another perspective one may look at the variation in the practices or instruments of sovereignty. Today we tend to take for granted that the military and the diplomatic corps are principal instruments of sovereign states. Sovereignty is associated with 'direct control of the means of internal and external violence'.[63] However, as Janice Thomson has demonstrated, it was only a little more than a century ago that states monopolized the exercise of coercion beyond their borders. For several centuries, mercenaries set the European standard of military performance.[64] Mercenaries were still common in the European armies of the seventeenth and eighteenth centuries. For instance, less than 10 per cent of Gustavus Adolphus's army was Swedish in 1632. The share of foreigners in the eighteenth-century armies of the major European powers ranged from some 20 to nearly 70 per cent. Swiss soldiers and officers served in the Prussian, French, British, Austrian and Dutch armies; and Polish nobles served in the Prussian, Austrian, Swedish and Russian armies.[65]

Similarly, European sea power long had a quasi-private character. Privateering, a sort of state-sponsored piracy, was a legitimate practice for nearly six centuries. And semi-sovereign mercantile companies were the creations of seventeenth-century Europe. The Dutch and British East India Companies are examples in point. In addition to their economic privileges, they could raise armies or navies, build forts, wage war and make treaties. The mercantile companies thrived for nearly three centuries.

Moreover, diplomacy, like warfare, was 'marketized and internationalized' well into the nineteenth century. In the seventeenth and eighteenth centuries diplomats were, by and large, 'parts of a social order which transcended national boundaries' and felt themselves 'part of an aristocratic international to which national feeling was hardly more than a vulgar plebeian prejudice'.[66] Diplomats could easily change from one monarchical employer to another. Thus, among the ministers and advisers brought to the Congress of Vienna in 1815 by the Russian Tsar Alexander I were two Germans, one Greek, one Corsican, one Swiss, one Pole – and one Russian.[67] In short, diplomats – who, along with soldiers, can be seen as principal instruments in the exercise of sovereignty – were only recently brought under strict state control.

Thus far we have defined sovereignty in terms of institutionalized authority claims and have discussed the multidimensional character and variability of sovereignty. In conclusion, let us consider the institutionalization process.

What are some of the milestones or turning points in the evolution of sovereignty? One major transformation in the institutionalization of sovereignty occurred as the concept came to be identified with the territory of the state and state institutions, rather than the person of the monarch.[68] In economist jargon, the state turned from a private to a public good.

With the advent of nineteenth-century nationalism, the link between sovereign authority and a defined population, rather than territory, came to the fore. With nationalism, the state was reconceptualized as an entity providing identity and security. Thus, nationalism 'fed directly into the sovereign territorial ideal, and at the same time it gave states that approximated the nation-state ideal a powerful new basis of legitimacy'.[69]

The argument has been made that understandings of sovereignty tend to be redefined in the wake of major political upheavals, such as war. One study of the aftermaths of the Napoleonic Wars, the First and Second World Wars and the Cold War identifies cyclical changes between 'state sovereignty', which emphasizes sovereign authority over a defined territory, and 'national sovereignty', which stresses sovereign authority over a defined population.[70]

Whereas the victorious states after the Napoleonic Wars favoured dynastic claims of territory over national claims by newly liberated peoples throughout Europe, the end of the First World War led to new state formations based on the principle of national self-determination. The victorious allies in the Second World War, on the other hand, had fought against expansionist nationalism and established the priority of the integrity of established state borders over the integrity of national or nationalist groups. After the end of the Cold War, finally, there are indications of a swing away from state sovereignty toward national legitimation of sovereignty. The reunification of Germany and the breakup of the Soviet Union into new states along national lines are cases in point.

In summary, sovereignty has proved to be a powerful institution that conditions the thinking and behaviour of actors in world politics. The rules and norms associated with the institution of sovereignty are obviously consequential, yet they are not absolutely constraining. 'Despite the existence of widespread and widely accepted rules associating sovereignty with non-intervention, constitutional independence, and the need for territory, entities have been established that compromise or defy these norms'.[71] Recent European examples include Belarus and the Ukraine, which became original members of the United Nations even though they were part of the Soviet Union; Andorra, which enjoys the status of a sovereign state even though France and Spain control its security affairs and retain the right to nominate two of the four members of its Constitutional Court; and Bosnia, which gained recognition as a state only after extensive intervention in its internal affairs and after the Dayton Accords had established internal arrangements including two and possibly three quasi-sovereign entities.

Sovereignty, as we have seen, can be regarded as a social construct, subject to changing interpretations.[72] In our treatment of the concept we have emphasized its variable character. Conceiving of sovereignty as 'caught up in an endless process of becoming' has its advantages and disadvantages. The major disadvantage is that 'because it is so subject to change, achieving clarity on the concept of sovereignty is extremely difficult'.[73] One advantage is that it forces us to ask pertinent questions about the future of sovereignty, as we will do in the next chapter.

NOTES

1 Janice E. Thomson, *Mercenaries, Pirates and Sovereigns: State-Building and Extraterritorial Violence in Early Modern Europe* (Princeton, NJ: Princeton University Press, 1994), 17.

2 Cynthia Weber and Thomas J. Bierstecker, 'Reconstructing the Analysis of Sovereignty: Concluding Reflections and Directions for Future Research', in *State Sovereignty as Social Construct*, eds Thomas J. Bierstecker and Cynthia Weber (Cambridge: Cambridge University Press, 1996), 279.

3 Yale H. Ferguson and Richard W. Mansbach, 'Political Space and Westphalian States in a World of "Polities": Beyond Inside/Outside', *Global Governance*, 2 (1996), 282.

4 Thomas J. Bierstecker and Cynthia Weber, 'The Social Construction of State Sovereignty', in Bierstecker and Weber (eds), *State Sovereignty as Social Construct*, 11.

5 On the concept of statehood during the Middle Ages, see Werner Conze, 'Staat und Souveränität', in *Geschichtliche Grundbegriffe 6*, eds Otto Brunner and Werner Conze (Stuttgart: Klett–Cotta, 1990).

6 On the concept of sovereignty during the Middle Ages, see, for example, Diethelm Klippel in *Lexikon des Mittelalters*, vol. 6 (Munich: Artemis/Lexma, 1977–1997).

7 On the Medieval monarchy, see Thomas Renna, 'Theories of Kingship', *Dictionary of the Middle Ages*, vol. 7, (New York: Charles Scribner's Sons, 1986), 259–71; Benjamin Arnold, *Princes and Territories in Medieval Germany* (Cambridge: Cambridge University Press, 1991).

8 John B. Henneman, *Royal Taxation in Fourteenth Century France*, 2 vols. (Philadelphia: American Philosophical Society, 1971/1976).

9 W.T. Arnold, *The Roman System of Provincial Administration to the Accession of Constantine the Great* (Chicago: Ares Publishers, 1974), 40ff.

10 For a classic study on the international role of the Habsburgs, see Adam Wandruszka, *Das Haus Habsburg: Die Geschichte einer europäischen Dynastie* (Vienna: Herder, 1978), especially the chapter on 'Die Habsburgische Weltmacht', 104ff. See also Jean Bérenger, *A History of the Habsburg Empire, 1273–1700* (London: Longman, 1994).

11 Anssi Paasi, *The Institutionalization of Regions: Theory and Comparative Case Studies* (Joensuu: Joensuun Yliopisto, 1986); Anssi Paasi, 'The Institutionalization of Regions: A Theoretical Framework for Understanding of the Emergence of Regions and the Constitution of Regional Identity', *Fennia*, 164 (1986): 105–46.

12 Robert D. Sack, *Human Territoriality: Its Theory and History* (Cambridge: Cambridge University Press, 1986); Torsten Malmberg, *Human Territoriality* (The Hague: Mouton, 1980); Marcelo Rivano-Fischer, 'Human Territoriality', *Psychological Research Bulletin* 1987:6; Rune Johansson, 'The Impact of Imagination', in *Regions in Central Europe: The Legacy of History*, ed. Sven Tägil (London: Hurst & Co., 1999). Concerning the concept 'nation' during the Middle Ages, see Helmut Beumann and Werner Schröder (eds), *Aspekte der Nationenbildung im Mittelalter* (Sigmaringen: Thorbecke, 1978).

13 Xavier de Planhol and Paul Claval, *An Historical Geography of France* (Cambridge: Cambridge University Press, 1994); Hendrik Spruyt, *The Sovereign State and Its Competitors* (Princeton, NJ: Princeton University Press, 1994), 77–108. See also Karl Bosl, 'Staat, Gesellschaft, Wirtschaft im deutschen Mittelalter', in *Gebhardt: Handbuch der Deutschen Geschichte 1*, 9th edn, ed. Herbert Grundmann (Stuttgart: Klett, 1970), 712 with references.

14 Martin Martinez y Riqué, 'Spanien: kastilianskt imperium eller nationalstat i vardande?', in *Europa – Historiens återkomst*, 3rd edn, ed. Sven Tägil (Hedemora: Gidlunds, 1998); Bernhard F. Reilly, *The Medieval Spains* (Cambridge: Cambridge University Press, 1993).

15 On state and nation in the British isles, see, for instance, Robin Frame, *The Political Development of the British Isles 1100–1400* (Oxford: Oxford University Press, 1990). On Scotland see also G.W.S. Barrow, *The Kingdom of the Scots* (London: Arnold, 1973); on Ireland, see Dáibhí O. Cróinín, *Early Medieval Ireland: 400–1200* (London: Longman, 1995).

16 Birgit Sawyer and Peter Sawyer, *Medieval Scandinavia* (Minneapolis: University of Minnesota Press, 1993).

17 Oscar Halecki and A. Polonsky, *A History of Poland*, 3rd edn (London: Dent, 1992); Ferdinand Seibt, *Karl IV: Ein Kaiser in Europa 1346–1378* (Munich: Süddeutscher Verlag, 1978); Peter F. Sugar, Péter Hanák and Tibor Frank (eds) *A History of Hungary* (London: Tauris, 1990).

18 See, for example, Eric B. Hobsbawm, *Nations and Nationalism since 1780: Programme, Myth, Reality* (Cambridge: Cambridge University Press, 1990).

19 Anthony D. Smith, *Nations and Nationalism in a Global Era* (Oxford: Blackwell, 1995); Liah Greenfeld, *Nationalism: Five Roads to Modernity* (Cambridge, MA: Harvard University Press, 1993).

20 Øyvind Østerud, *Nasjonenes selvbestemmelsesrett* (Oslo: Universitetsforlaget, 1984).

21 David Held, *Democracy and the Global Order* (Stanford, CA: Stanford University Press, 1995), 31.

22 See Robert Jackson, *Quasi-States: Sovereignty, International Relations and the Third World* (Cambridge: Cambridge University Press, 1990).

23 R.B.J. Walker, *Inside/Outside: International Relations as Political Theory* (Cambridge: Cambridge University Press, 1993), 90.

24 Stephen D. Krasner, 'Westphalia and All That', in *Ideas and Foreign Policy: Beliefs, Institutions, and Political Change*, eds Judith Goldstein and Robert O. Keohane (Ithaca, NY: Cornell University Press, 1993), 235.

25 Ibid.

26 John G. Ruggie, *Constructing the World Polity: Essays on International Institutionalization* (London and New York: Routledge, 1998), 147.

27 Spruyt, *Sovereign State*, 35.

28 Cf. Charles Tilly, *Coercion, Capital, and European States, AD 990–1992*, rev. edn (Oxford: Blackwell, 1992), 21; Spruyt, *Sovereign State*, 18–21.

29 Tilly, *Coercion, Capital*, 25–7.

30 Jean-Marie Guéhenno, *The End of the Nation-State* (Minneapolis, MN: University of Minnesota Press, 1995), xii.

31 Tilly, *Coercion, Capital*, xi, 33.

32 Ibid., 16–33.

33 Ibid., 145.

34 Ibid., 190–1.

35 William H. McNeill, *The Pursuit of Power* (Chicago: University of Chicago Press, 1982), 64.

36 Ibid., 78.

37 Ibid., 100.

38 Tilly, *Coercion, Capital*, 76.

39 Ibid., 83.

40 Ibid., 30.

41 Ibid., 159–63.

42 Quoted in John Hobson, *The Wealth of States: A Comparative Sociology of International Economic and Political Change* (Cambridge: Cambridge University Press, 1997), 5.

43 Ibid., 199. Emphasis in original.

44 Ibid., 10, 210.

45 Max Weber, as quoted in Thomson, *Mercenaries, Pirates and Sovereigns*, 7.

46 Ruggie, *Constructing the World Polity*, 147.

47 Thomson, *Mercenaries, Pirates and Sovereigns*, 14.

48 Stephen D. Krasner, 'Sovereignty: An Institutional Perspective', *Comparative Political Studies*, 21 (1988), 66–94.

49 Cf. Friedrich Kratochwil, 'Sovereignty as *Dominium*: Is There a Right of Humanitarian Intervention?' in *Beyond Westphalia? State Sovereignty and International Intervention*, eds Gene M. Lyons and Michael Mastanduno (Baltimore, MD: Johns Hopkins University Press, 1995); Ruggie, *Constructing the World Polity*, 147–50.

50 H. Erle Richards, *Sovereignty over the Air* (Oxford: Clarendon Press, 1912), 12–13.

51 Arthur K. Kuhn, 'The Beginnings of an Aerial Law', *American Journal of International Law*, 4 (1910), 112.

52 Richards, *Sovereignty over the Air*, 8.

53 J.F. Lycklama à Nijeholt, *Air Sovereignty* (The Hague: Martinus Nijhoff, 1910), 11–14.

54 For a detailed analysis of the nature of frontiers in the modern world, see Malcolm Anderson, *Frontiers: Territory and State Formation in the Modern World* (Cambridge: Polity Press, 1996).

55 Janice E. Thomson, 'State Sovereignty in International Relations: Bridging the Gap Between Theory and Empirical Research', *International Studies Quarterly*, 39 (1995), 214.

56 Stephen D. Krasner, 'Problematic Sovereignty' (paper presented at the Annual Convention of the American Political Science Association, Boston, MA, September 1998), 6.

57 Thomson, 'State Sovereignty', 214, 223.

58 Thomson, *Mercenaries, Pirates and Sovereigns*, 14–16; Thomson, 'State Sovereignty', 224.

59 Jens Bartelson, *A Genealogy of Sovereignty* (Cambridge: Cambridge University Press, 1995), 51.

60 Thomson, 'State Sovereignty', 227.

61 Krasner, 'Problematic Sovereignty'.

62 Ibid., 20.

63 Anthony Giddens, *A Contemporary Critique of Historical Materialism*, vol. 2, *The Nation-State and Violence* (Berkeley / Los Angeles, CA: University of California Press, 1985), 121.

64 Thomson, *Mercenaries, Pirates and Sovereigns*; cf. Tilly, *Coercion, Capital*, 83–4.

65 Thomson, *Mercenaries, Pirates and Sovereigns*, 29–30.

66 M.S. Anderson, as quoted in G.R. Berridge, *Diplomacy: Theory and Practice* (London: Prentice Hall/Harvester Wheatsheaf, 1995), 12.

67 Hans J. Morgenthau, *Politics Among Nations: The Struggle for Power and Peace*, 3rd edn. (New York, Alfred A. Knopf, 1966), 245–7.

68 John Agnew, 'The Territorial Trap: The Geographical Assumptions of International Relations Theory', *Review of International Political Economy*, 1 (1994), 61.

69 Alexander B. Murphy, 'The Sovereign State System as Political-Territorial Ideal: Historical and Contemporary Considerations', in Bierstecker and Weber (eds), *State Sovereignty as Social Construct*, 97.

70 J. Samuel Barkin and Bruce Cronin, 'The State and the Nation: Changing Norms and the Rules of Sovereignty in International Relations', *International Organization*, 48 (1994), 107–30.

71 Krasner, 'Problematic Sovereignty', 2.

72 Cf. Bierstecker and Weber, 'Social Construction of State Sovereignty'; Barkin and Cronin, 'State and Nation', 109.

73 James N. Rosenau, *Along the Domestic–Foreign Frontier: Exploring Governance in a Turbulent World* (Cambridge: Cambridge University Press, 1997), 218.

5

The Resilient State

Stripped of its variable elements, the institution of sovereignty underlies a conception of the state as (a) an organization with far-reaching authority claims but with varying control; (b) situated at the international/national vortex with 'dual anchorage' enabling it to exercise power both domestically and internationally;[1] (c) an entity whose control is based primarily on coercion and economic exchange, domestically (policing/taxation) as well as internationally (warfare/trade); and (d) an entity which has legal personality and is to be seen as an actor in its own right, and not merely a reflection of societal and economic interests.

Having explored the origins and prevalence of the state, we inevitably encounter the question: Why has the state persisted through more than three centuries? One straightforward answer is that the state has proven adaptable to environmental change, and therefore no alternative viable entity has emerged to contest and replace states. A fuller answer involves addressing the problem of *legitimacy*. The extensive authority claims of the sovereign state need to be recognized by internal and external actors. Externally, the sovereign state has been legitimated by various diplomatic practices, international law and, more recently, international organizations. The internal legitimation of the state into the present period has centred around two value-laden concepts: *nation* and *democracy*. Let us therefore briefly consider the ideals of the nation-state and the democratic state in turn, with a view to their legitimating function.

The nation-state

The historical function of nationalism, it has been said, 'has been to achieve the coincidence of state and civil society through the creation of the nation-state'.[2] The essence of nationalism is political particularism:

> *Particularism*, because nationalism identifies a 'people,' distinct from others; *political*, because it requires that this particularism receive political expression, in and through a state. For nationalism, the state is the political expression and guardian of a community that exists anterior to its state, but that exists best when it has its own state.[3]

The nation-state, then, represents 'a marriage of culture and politics';[4] it implies a congruence of the functional system of state institutions and the ethos or cultural system, embodying sentiments of community and solidarity that sustain the state.[5] It rests on a 'normative nationalist principle', which holds that cultural unity between rulers and ruled is mandatory.[6]

The co-definition of nation and state has gained wide currency, as alluded to in Chapter 1. Moreover, 'few historicopolitical concepts are used . . . with greater nonchalance than the term *nation-state*'.[7] To add some clarity, one might distinguish between nation-states, part-nation-states, multi-nation-states, and state-nations.[8] A *nation-state* is the result of a development where the nation precedes the state and where the state reflects the national political ambitions. European examples include Germany and Italy. *Part-nation-states* are those where the nation in political power is simultaneously ruling in another state or other states. One obvious European example was East and West Germany during the Cold War, and to a certain extent also Germany and Austria. *Multi-nation-states* encompass within their borders two or several nations. The Soviet Union was an example of 'imperial' multi-nation-states, whereas Switzerland remains an example of a 'federative' one. In *state-nations*, finally, state-building precedes nation-building. Relatively new countries with massive immigration, such as the United States and Australia, are prominent illustrations. In Europe, France may serve as an example.

At any rate, reflection on nationalism as a force legitimating the state requires that the two concepts 'state' and 'nation' be kept apart which, in turn, calls for a definition of 'nation'. This is easier said than done. There are no objective criteria by which one can define what is and what is not a nation. Nations are not objective facts, although nationalists tend to present them as such. They are 'imagined communities', to employ Benedict Anderson's much-used phrase.[9] They rest on a sense of community, which may have various foundations. Thus there have existed and exist many types of nations and nationalism. Tom Nairn's characterization of nationalism as 'the modern Janus' is to the point.[10] The Janus face of nationalism looks simultaneously in different directions, and therefore is perhaps best understood in terms of a series of dichotomies.

INTERNAL/EXTERNAL DIMENSION Nationalism is both inward- and outward-looking. In the words of one caustic characterization, a nation is 'a society united by a common error as to its origin and a common aversion to its neighbors'.[11] The internal sense of community is facilitated by the existence of other nationalities that can be considered inferior to, or at least less normal than, one's own nation. The distinction between 'us' and 'them' is central to national sentiments. In other words, nationalism is at the same time integrative and conflictual.

HISTORY/FUTURE Nationalism looks backwards as well as forwards; it entails visions of the past as well as the future. It capitalizes on historical memories and myths while mobilizing for future development. Past glories or injustices are adduced in preparation for a better future. Thus, paradoxically, nationalism is both a remnant of the pre-modern in modernity and one of the constitutive features of this very modernity.[12]

IDEOLOGICAL/PRIMORDIAL NATURE   On the one hand, nationalism is frequently viewed as a philosophical idea or doctrine advocating national self-fulfilment. Thus, Elie Kedourie treats nationalism as an ideology born in Europe in the early nineteenth century, whose ideas – elevation and idealization of the state, justified violence in the name of progress, national self-determination and a universal history through which nations emerge – were originally formulated by German romantic philosophers, such as Herder, Fichte, Schelling, Schiller and Schleiermacher.[13] On the other hand, nationalism can be seen as a natural, primordial phenomenon, as an extension of kinship. Nationalism, in this view, is the natural expression of ethnic or cultural identity. Of course, it is not a question of either/or: to be effective as an ideology, nationalism must resonate in primordial human sentiments.

UNIVERSALISM/PARTICULARISM   The French Revolution is commonly singled out as a seminal event in the history of modern nationalism. This may seem paradoxical, as the revolution was fought in the name of universal principles concerning the rights of man. The concept of *citizenship* epitomizes the paradox. To be a citizen means, on the one hand, not being simply a subject but being born to freedom; on the other hand, citizenship is always tied to a particular state. Thus, the French Revolution turned subjects of the king into citizens of the French nation. Modern citizenship, accordingly, is a combination of universalism and particularism. Rather than denying ethical universalism, nationalism represents a particularistic way of construing it.[14]

ETHNIC/CIVIC FOUNDATION   The 'ethnic-genealogical' conception of nationalism, which rests on a sense of affiliation and solidarity with the ethnic community into which one is born and socialized, is often contrasted with the 'civic-territorial' conception, which rests on loyalty to the state expressed in terms of citizenship rights and obligations. This dichotomy reappears under several different labels. The differentiation in German between *Gemeinschaft* and *Gesellschaft*, or between *Kulturnation* and *Staatsnation*, similarly refers to the ethnic/civic foundation of nations. The difference is sometimes illustrated by reference to the origins of the German (ethnic) nation and the French (civic) nation, and between the German principle of *ius sanguinis* and the French *jus soli*, respectively. Yet it could be argued that both conceptions exist side by side in modern national states.[15]

   The fact that 'nation' and 'nationalism' can take various shapes and mean different things to different people may represent a problem for analysts in search of generalizable truths, but makes it a powerful legitimating force in the political realm. A lot of different things can be legitimated in the name of the nation. Once created, nations and nation-ness 'became "modular," capable of being transplanted, with varying degrees of self-consciousness, to a great variety of social terrains, to merge and be merged with a correspondingly wide array of political and ideological constellations'.[16]

For the state, this has proved to be a mixed blessing. The idea of national self-determination 'at once grounds and yet threatens to undermine' the modern state.[17] On the one hand, it has fostered the coincidence of nationalist sentiments and state boundaries. On the other hand, it has stimulated divergent and oppositional nationalisms in many parts of the world. At any rate, the principle of national self-determination gained prominence after the First World War through President Wilson's Fourteen Points. The legitimacy of national self-determination was enhanced after the Second World War; since it 'has been so closely associated with the decolonization movement, the justice of which is more or less taken to be self-evident, it has provided a strong moral foundation for the ethnonationalist cause that has an immediate appeal to liberal sentiments'.[18]

In Europe, in particular, nationalism has primarily been a lever which state governments have used to mobilize popular energies and resources in support of their objectives. It was only after the Westphalian state came into existence that nationalism became a significant political force. In that sense, 'nationalism depends on, and is parasitic upon, the modern state'.[19] At the same time, the banner of nationalism was shouldered by governments, which mobilized popular support around an ensemble of symbols and myths, marking political identity. The state increasingly became the main vehicle for mass education and the transmission of culture. To be effective as legitimating instruments, these symbols and myths somehow had to resonate among the population. The vocabulary of nationalism typically refers to kinship and home which 'denote something to which one is naturally tied'.[20]

Several factors contributed to the rise of nationalism as a principle legitimating the state in Europe. Ernest Gellner, for example, emphasizes the functional connections between nationalism and industrialization.[21] The industrial society requires a single communicative code. A homogeneous culture in the form of language and symbols is crucial for industrial society to work properly. National education and national media become important instruments underpinning the nation-state. In fact, Gellner considers the monopoly of legitimate education more central to the industrial state than the monopoly of legitimate violence.[22] Adrian Hastings, who dates the birth of European nations to the late Middle Ages, emphasizes the role of the vernacular translations of the Bible in creating written languages (German in 1466, Italian in 1471, Catalan in 1478, English in 1535, and so on).[23] Benedict Anderson points to a combination of factors accounting for the creation and legitimacy of 'imagined communities of nationality': the territorialization of religious faith, the decline of antique kingship, the interaction between capitalism and print, the development of vernacular languages-of-state, and changing conceptions of state.[24]

In sum, there may be several reasons why nationalism has become such a powerful legitimating instrument of the state. Yet few states live up to the ideals of a nation-state. The social boundaries of culturally cohesive nation-groups and the political boundaries of given states seldom coincide. According to one estimate, only some 2–3 per cent of today's states would qualify as nation-states in a strict sense.[25] The breakup of Yugoslavia as well as Basque, Corsican or Northern Irish nationalisms represent brusque reminders that the nation-state remains an ideal even on the European continent.

Does this mean that nationalism is retreating as a legitimating instrument for states? Several observers would answer in the affirmative. Eric Hobsbawm, for instance, argues that the high-water mark of nationalism was between 1918 and 1950 and that its role today is negative and divisive.[26] The kind of small nations envisaged by separatists and nationalists have little prospects of surviving in today's and tomorrow's world. Far from being the motivating force it once was, nationalism is now at most a complicating factor or catalyst for other developments. Similarly, Mathew Horsman and Andrew Marshall claim that the principal motors of change have outgrown nationalism. 'There is nothing national about capitalism, industrialism, warfare or technology,' they reason: 'Each has developed within national frameworks, but that is no longer necessary nor even desired.' Nationalism, in their view, is turning into tribalism.[27]

The Janus face of nationalism precludes a definite answer to the question. Suffice it to note that nationalism as a legitimating force is increasingly called into question, and that this is something to take into account when assessing the position and prospects of the territorial state, as we shall do later in this chapter. Now let us turn to another, more recent legitimating instrument of the state: democracy.

The democratic state

The sovereign state was originally the domain of rulers who claimed extensive powers for themselves. Notions of 'popular sovereignty' can be traced back to Locke and Rousseau.[28] However, 'from classical antiquity to the seventeenth century, democracy, when it was considered at all, was largely associated with the gathering of citizens in assemblies and public meeting places'.[29] Only by the early nineteenth century did notions of representative democracy shift the terms of reference from small states and cities to become the legitimating creed of nation-states. And by the end of the century democratic states were evolving in Europe. The consolidation of representative democracy is largely a twentieth-century phenomenon.

The creation of the League of Nations after the First World War represented an effort, led by US President Woodrow Wilson, to legitimate a system of sovereign states on the twin pillars of democracy and national self-determination. To Wilson, 'national self-determination ranked as an essential corollary of democracy. Just as the people had the right to govern themselves within the national system, so the nations had a right to govern themselves within the global system'.[30] Sovereignty was thereby converted into 'a symbol of liberty in international relations, comparable to democracy as a symbol of domestic freedom'.[31] In short, nationalism and the aspirations to democracy and personal freedom are part of the same social, intellectual and moral revolution, even if the 'other' side of the Janus face of nationalism tends to pervert democratic values.[32] The nation-state has come to be seen as the primary 'container' of democratic politics, and the modern *demos* is understood in terms of a nation within a delimited territory.[33]

At any rate, it is really only after the end of the Cold War that 'democracy has become the fundamental standard of political legitimacy' worldwide. In the mid-1970s, still 'more than two-thirds of all states could reasonably be called authoritarian. This percentage has fallen dramatically; less than a third of all states are now authoritarian, and the number of democracies is growing rapidly.'[34] The democratization of formerly authoritarian states and the seemingly universal acceptance of democratic ideas have impelled some observers to proclaim 'the end of history': liberal democracy, in this view, constitutes the end point of a directional historical process and the final form of government.[35] Moreover, the compelling idea of 'democratic peace', the notion that democratic states do not wage war against each other, has reinforced the common impression that democracy has become the principal legitimating force of the state at the turn of the century.[36]

Yet the striking paradox is that 'more and more nations and groups are championing the idea of democracy; but they are doing so at just that moment when the very efficacy of democracy as a national form of political organization appears open to question'.[37] In part, the problems of contemporary democracy have internal sources. However, decreasing popular participation and growing mistrust of politicians, which are familiar parts of the European political landscape and which can be construed as a legitimation crisis, have external sources as well. As a result of economic interdependence and globalization, the economic manoeuvrability and autonomy of democratically elected governments is increasingly constrained by sources of unelected and unrepresentative economic power.[38] Thus, 'governments may have no direct role in vital decisions which affect the very security or welfare of their citizens whilst equally the consequences of government decisions may have serious impacts extending well beyond their own territorial jurisdiction.'[39]

The lack of congruence between rulers and ruled raises important questions of accountability: can the government be held accountable on the very issues which affect the daily lives of those it purports to represent? 'In a world where transnational actors and forces cut across the boundaries of national communities in diverse ways, and where powerful states make decisions not just for their peoples but for others as well, the questions of who should be accountable to whom, and on what basis, do not easily resolve themselves.'[40]

At issue is the habitual conception of constituencies, representation and political participation in terms of territorial state boundaries. What is the 'relevant community' to deal with 'interdependence issues' that transcend state boundaries, such as acid rain, the use of non-renewable resources, AIDS, or the instability of global financial markets? To whom do decision-makers have to justify their decisions, and to whom should they be accountable? Whose consent is necessary, and whose participation is justified?[41]

In sum, whereas nationalism today may have a more corroding than unifying effect on states, democracy has become the prevalent legitimating creed. At the same time, democracy faces a number of serious challenges which in effect represent challenges to the sovereign state itself. It is to these challenges that we now turn.

Challenges to the sovereign state

Today the sovereign state presents a puzzling paradox. On the one hand, we can observe 'the virtually universal recognition of territorial sovereignty as the organizing principle of international politics'. On the other hand, there is an equally clear 'tendency toward erosion of the exclusivity associated with the traditional notion of territoriality'.[42] This has given rise to a lively debate concerning the persistence or obsolescence of the territorial state. Instead of arguing either that the state is here to stay or that it has no future, we will try to identify some of the principal challenges to the state as a territorial and sovereign unit. Specifically, we will discuss technological, economic, ecological and demographic challenges as well as changing identifications. After that, we will examine how the state has adjusted to these extraneous changes and consider problems of governance in the world of today and tomorrow.

The technological challenge

The accelerating pace of technological change is perhaps the foremost characteristic of the contemporary era. As Susan Strange notes:

> No one under the age of thirty or thirty-five today needs convincing that, just in their own lifetime, the pace of technological change has been getting faster and faster. The technically unsophisticated worlds of business, government and education of even the 1960s would be unrecognisable to them. No fax, no personal computers, no accessible copiers, no mobile phones, no video shops, no DNA tests, no cable TV, no satellite networks connecting distant markets, twenty-four hours a day. The world in which their grandparents grew up in the 1930s or 1940s is as alien to them as that of the Middle Ages.[43]

While we are used to viewing technological development as an enabling factor, it can also represent challenges to the territorial state. The first such challenge came from weapons technology. John Herz was one of the earliest scholars to analyse how nuclear weapons undermined the previously impermeable territorial state as a unit of protection. Previous innovations in military technology, such as the 'gunpowder revolution' of the later Middle Ages in Europe, had rendered particular power units, such as castles or walled cities, obsolete. But whereas these changes had usually led to an extension of the realm of a defensible entity, such as from city-states to territorial states, nuclear technology seemed to have a more fundamental effect. It seemed to presage the end of territoriality. 'The power of protection, on which political authority was based in the past, seems to be in jeopardy for any imaginable entity'.[44] While nuclear realities have indeed changed the premises of international politics in many ways, few analysts would today ascribe to nuclear weapons such revolutionary effects. In fact, Herz himself later became doubtful of his earlier predictions and, in a later work, argued that the nuclear age had instead issued in 'new territoriality' and 'the unavailability of force'.[45]

Today the focus is more on the new challenges stemming from recent developments in the technology of communications which have compressed time and space in unprecedented ways.

> The ability to exploit the potential of geo-stationary orbit and the electro-magnetic spectrum, coupled with the development and application of micro-electronics, has produced systems of communication which are both instantaneous in effect and global in scope. Moreover, the cost of such systems has declined significantly over the past twenty-five years, while new developments such as the use of broadband fibre-optics have greatly expanded capacity, permitting massive increases in the volume of communications.[46]

Speed and mobility have become overriding qualities. Whereas the rapidly advancing communication technologies may enhance the ability of states to control or repress their citizens, they are inherently transnational in nature. By facilitating direct, worldwide links between individuals and groups, they render the state permeable to information flows from all corners of the world. No longer can the state control what its citizens read, hear or view. Even more important, new communication technologies have contributed to profound economic changes, such as the development of global production strategies and the integration of financial markets. This combination of technological and economic change may represent the most formidable challenge to the state.

The economic challenge

Intertwined with the changes in communication technology, dramatic shifts have occurred in the organization of economic activity. Globalized and globalizing markets have accentuated the contrast between 'bounded' political systems and 'unbounded' economic exchanges.[47] Several factors interact to diminish the state's earlier control over economic activity. Whereas the growth of the 'welfare state' was possible only while capital was relatively immobile beyond state borders,[48] financial markets have today become deregulated and globalized, making maximum use of cutting-edge information technology. Every day some 1,500 billion dollars are traded in the financial market, a sum about forty times the value of traded goods and exceeding the reserves of the major central banks. State currencies are vulnerable to the vagaries of the financial market, where the actors are largely beyond state control. Moreover, the speed of decisions in the financial market contrasts with the inertia of government decision-making.

While the globalization of finance is most conspicuous and far-reaching today, the globalization of production proceeds apace. According to one estimate, more than half of the world's goods and services are produced according to strategies that involve planning, design, production and marketing on a global scale.[49] Multinational corporations (MNCs) account for about 30 per cent of world output, 70 per cent of world trade and 80 per cent of international investment.[50] In some respects, the leading MNCs are larger economic entities than many states. For instance, if General Motors were a country, it would have the world's twentieth largest economy. A list of the top hundred economic actors in the world (measured in sales figures and GNP, respectively) would include a roughly equal number of states and MNCs.[51] In some markets, especially those at the forefront of technological change, the dominance of MNCs is striking. Thus, half of the world market in semi-conductor production is shared between 10 US and Japanese MNCs, and the market share of the top 21 firms is 70 per cent.[52]

One important aspect of this development is the loss of state control of economic activity. The global presence and mobility of major MNCs provide them with an effective 'exit option' – they are able to evade taxes, tariffs and other forms of state controls by moving the affected functions to another country with more favourable conditions. International trade has traditionally been administered by the state, via bilateral trade agreements or multilateral arrangements, such as the General Agreement on Tariffs and Trade (GATT). Today, well over a quarter of trade across state boundaries is intra-firm trade.[53]

The contrast between globalized economies and territorially bound states is at the core of an ongoing debate between 'transformationalists', who envisage a radical break with the past, and 'sceptics', who emphasize continuities rather than discontinuities and foresee continued state centrality.[54] Transformationalists argue that the globalization trend compromises the institution of sovereign statehood by rendering territorial boundaries increasingly porous, reducing government control and constraining the scope for autonomous action. Susan Strange, for one, draws the conclusion that we are witnessing a power shift away from states towards world markets, which represents 'probably the biggest change in the international political economy to take place in the last half of the twentieth century'.[55]

[T]he authority of the governments of all states, large and small, strong and weak, has been weakened as a result of technological and financial change and of the accelerating integration of national economies into one single global market economy. Their failure to manage the national economy, to maintain employment and sustain economic growth, to avoid imbalances of payments with other states, to control the rate of interest and the exchange rate is not a matter of technical incompetence, nor moral turpitude nor political maladroitness. It is neither in any direct sense their fault, nor the fault of others. None of these failures can be blamed on other countries or on other governments. They are, simply, the victims of the market economy.[56]

The ecological challenge

The state-centric conception of the world emphasizes the division into separate, independent communities with sovereign authority, delineated clearly in time and space. The emergent ecological view of the world, by contrast, conceives of a physical and social totality, a single community of humans and other species, ultimately dependent on the physical environment; the 'biosphere', not the 'sovereign domain', then becomes the relevant vantage point.[57] Growing attention to ecological problems challenges the sovereign state. 'First, the principle of sovereignty is an impediment to action designed to ameliorate critical ecological dilemmas. Secondly, it is itself a major contributing cause of the environmental problems which confront humanity.'[58]

On the one hand, sovereign states are ill-suited to handle the transnational issues or 'global indivisibilities'[59] of environmental degradation. Like economic globalization, ecological globalization takes different forms. One can, for example, make a distinction between transboundary pollution, environmental interdependence and the degradation of the environmental commons.[60] The fact that Sweden receives acid depositions from its Scandinavian neighbours as well as from Germany, Britain and the Baltic states is an example of transboundary pollution. Greenhouse emissions leading to altered climatic patterns epitomize environmental interdependence. The commons are those elements of the environment that are simultaneously used by several states while under the effective jurisdiction of no one, such as the atmosphere or the high seas. In neither of these problem areas can individual states provide effective solutions.

On the other hand, 'the theory and practice of sovereignty geographically insulates the state from the global effects of its actions'.[61] Decisions, which can be defended as legitimate sovereign choices within the state's domain, may contribute to global environmental degradation. The continuation of certain state practices, such as the reliance on the use of armed force, threatens devastating impacts. In several respects, then, the emergence of ecological problems and paradigms challenges the territorial state.

The demographic challenge

The state's claim to power over the citizens within its territory rests on the assumption of a well-defined and rather immobile population. Nationalism furthermore presupposes a homogeneous population. Hence, the ability to control frontier crossings and the right to refuse entry to aliens are regarded as essential attributes of sovereignty. However, checking every individual who crosses a state boundary is becoming increasingly difficult and costly.

Advances in high-speed transport have fuelled a graphic surge in the number of travellers, commuters, migrants and refugees. In 1960 there were 70 million international tourists; by 1995 there were nearly 500 million.[62] Inexorable population growth in combination with increasing amounts of information impel people from the poor 'south' to move to the rich 'north'. Wars, famines, political persecution and human rights violations generate refugee flows. The number of refugees and displaced persons rose from 17 million in 1991 to a record 27 million in 1995. Even with a decrease to 21.5 million by early 1999, refugees at that time still represented one out of every 280 persons on earth.[63] While tourism is predominantly a phenomenon of rich countries and refugees of poor countries, the dramatic increase in mobility contributes to the porousness and permeability of the state. Loyalty to a particular state can no longer be taken for granted, and the notion of the state as a home is undermined by the increasing number of people in 'a generalized condition of homelessness'.[64]

Changing identifications

The revolution in information technology along with greater mobility have facilitated the emergence of new social movements operating in, and receiving their impetus from, a larger transnational space sometimes labelled 'civil society'. At the same time as nationalism, once a powerful instrument of the sovereign state, has proven to be a two-edged sword, these social movements – be they environmental, anti-nuclear, feminist, cultural or religious – offer alternative loyalties and identities. They suggest a new model of citizenship which embraces the principle of 'duties beyond borders'.[65] While less tangible than the other challenges, the tendency among individuals to define their identities in other than territorial or national terms – such as profession, religion, generation or gender – tends to erode the state's monopoly on loyalty and identification.

Threatened sovereignty?

Does the combination of technological, economic, ecological, demographic and identification challenges to the state represent a more fundamental threat to the institution of sovereignty as well? How do the outlined changes affect the state's authority claims? The state's claim to ultimate power over its *territory* is challenged by transboundary issues like environmental protection and AIDS as well as the presence of foreign capital and corporations. Moreover, the value of territory may have diminished as a result of technological and economic changes. The successful states of today, such as the United States and Japan, owe their success not to the possession of territory but to their key role in global markets and their character as global business civilizations.

Similarly, the state's exclusive power over its *population* is called into question by recent developments. Multiple identities and loyalties erode the state's claim to speak on behalf of all its citizens, and the lack of ability to solve transboundary problems threatens the legitimacy of the state. In addition, there have been less tangible, but equally important, value shifts which challenge the state's claim to ultimate authority over its population. The increasing acceptance of human rights as an international value, and of intervention on human rights grounds, represents one such value change, which challenges the state's authority claim. After the end of the Cold War, democratic values seem to have achieved similar international status. It has become established practice for external actors – be they the United Nations, regional international organizations, individual interested governments, non-governmental organizations (NGOs) or international personalities – to monitor domestic elections in new democracies. On the European continent, elections in Russia and other countries of the former Soviet empire have thus become not just local but global events. Only a few years ago such practices would have been regarded as serious encroachments on sovereignty.[66]

If we return to the distinction between domestic, interdependence, international legal and Westphalian sovereignty, introduced in the previous chapter, we can note that the outlined challenges to the state have primarily affected *interdependence sovereignty*. They add up to a markedly reduced ability by contemporary states to control and regulate the flow of goods, persons, pollutants, diseases and ideas across territorial boundaries. It may be argued that decreasing interdependence sovereignty does not necessarily imply a loss of domestic sovereignty; increases in transnational flows have not undermined state control or hampered national policy agendas – in fact, the level of government spending in industrialized countries has continued to increase during the process of globalization.[67] Yet, to the extent that citizens perceive that a significant part of their welfare depends on these transnational flows rather than government policies, the authority of the state is increasingly called into question. Similarly, interdependence sovereignty is not directly related to Westphalian sovereignty. Yet, in practice, the loss of interdependence sovereignty 'has prompted states to enter into agreements (an exercise of international legal sovereignty) to create international institutions some of which have compromised their Westphalian sovereignty by establishing external authority structures'.[68] We shall return to this problem in Chapter 7 on the European Union. In sum, the erosion of interdependence sovereignty tends to challenge the other dimensions of state sovereignty as well.

State responses

How has the state reacted to the challenges outlined in the previous section? This is an important question to pose, since so much of the debate about the future of the sovereign state is framed in terms of its either prevailing or disappearing. 'In idealizing the territorial state we cannot see a world in which its role and meaning change,' one researcher admonishes.[69] In this section we will look at some ideas as to how the role of the state has changed in response to the multiple challenges it is facing. Specifically, we will pay heed to the partly overlapping notions of the trading state, the competition state and the virtual state.

In the 1980s, Richard Rosecrance envisioned the rise of the *'trading state'*, which he saw as an ideal type in contradistinction to the traditional territorial state.[70] The trading state follows a different logic from the territorial state. Trading states do not base their wealth and security on the possession and conquest of land. Territorial size is of little significance, as the examples of Singapore and Hong Kong demonstrate. Trading states strive to be different from other states and to find a niche where they have comparative advantages, whereas territorial states strive to be functionally similar. Interdependence rather than sovereignty is the cornerstone of the trading state's existence. By entering into trade relations and increasing mutual dependencies, trading states raise the costs of military conquest and thus become less prone to wage war against each other.

It is significant that the former warring states, Germany and Japan, have drawn the lessons of defeat in the Second World War and have become leading trading states, argues Rosecrance. The crumbling of the Soviet Union can also be seen as a symbolic expression of the defeat of the old-fashioned territorial state with a heavy emphasis on military defence; and the conclusion in 1995 of the Uruguay Round and the creation of the World Trade Organization can be regarded as another sign of the ascendancy of the trading state. In more differentiated terms, Europe can be seen as part of the 'liberal core' of industrialized states, where the trading-state logic prevails; the 'realist periphery' of developing states, on the other hand, lacks absolute deterrents to war as well as shared norms concerning democracy and markets, which makes old-style balance-of-power politics the norm.[71]

Another, compatible argument is that the *'competition state'* is taking the place of the welfare state, especially in the industrialized core.[72] It is its capacity to promote a relatively favourable investment climate for transnational capital that is decisive for a state's standing. Adherents of this perspective maintain that 'competition for world market shares has replaced competition for territory as the name of the game between states'.[73] Factors of importance in this competition can be human capital, infrastructure, support for research and development, basic public services to assure a good quality of life for transnationally mobile firms and sectors, and a public policy environment favourable to investment and profit-making.

Taxation is one core state function that is affected by this competition. As most traditional sources of taxation have become highly mobile and increasingly tend to seek lower rates of taxation, competition among states will create a downward movement of taxes generally. For example, the international mobility of capital represents a considerable constraint on the state's assertion of its rights to tax businesses.[74] Especially in Europe, with its high-speed transport and geographical proximity of states, taxes on consumption and highly educated workforces face this kind of competition and downward pressure, while taxes on real estate and uneducated labour do not.

A more recent conceptualization envisages the emergence of the '*virtual state*' as the successor of the trading state.[75] It rests on the argument that states are today downsizing, in functional if not in territorial terms. The virtual state, which downsizes its territorially based production capability and becomes reliant on mobile factors of production, is the analogue of the virtual corporation, 'an entity with research, development, design, marketing, financing, legal, and other headquarters functions, but few or no manu-facturing facilities: a company with a head but no body'.[76] The function of the state is in the process of redefinition, as production by domestic industries increasingly takes place abroad and territory becomes less valuable than technology, knowledge and direct investment. Like the virtual corporation, the virtual state formulates overall strategy and invests in human capital rather than amassing expensive production capacity. The virtual state becomes a 'negotiating entity' which 'depends as much or more on economic access abroad as it does on economic control at home'.[77] Analogous to the corporate world, the political world may increasingly become divided into 'head' and 'body' nations.[78]

Kuwait during the 1990–91 occupation by Iraq may serve as one illustration. Kuwait was an example of the virtual state, insofar as its status was as strongly tied to its foreign stockholdings, bank accounts, real estate holdings and financial networks as it was to its territory. Therefore, the Kuwaiti government was able to perform many of its usual functions in exile. Iraq occupied Kuwait's state territory and destroyed the oil wells, the physical source of wealth, but failed to capture the virtual state.[79] Perhaps even more to the point, major states like the United States and Japan, which today rely as much on global economic access as on domestic economic control, in several respects seem to be moving in the direction of 'virtual states'.

The common denominator of these different conceptualizations of the changing role of the state is the notion that it is gradually turning into a mediator between political and economic spheres and between domestic and international activities, rather than being the omnipotent authority internally, and exclusive agent externally, of a well-defined territory and population, as the traditional sovereignty principle prescribes. Sovereignty, in the contemporary perspective, refers primarily to a certain legal authority that states can use as a lever in bargaining along the domestic–international frontier.

> Rather than connoting the exercise of supremacy within a given territory, sovereignty provides the state with a legal grip on an aspect of a transnational process, whether involving multinational investment, the world's ecology, or the movement of migrants, drug dealers, and terrorists. *Sovereignty is less a territorially defined barrier than a bargaining resource for a politics characterized by complex transnational networks.*[80]

We shall return to a discussion of transnational networks in the next chapter. But, in conclusion, let us take a brief look at the implications of this changing role of the state for our view of the international system in general and the European political order in particular.

Governance without government?

To summarize, territorial state boundaries no longer always coincide with spheres of authority. There are widespread feelings that the state is losing its previous control over territory and population and command over outcomes. To play on words, the state seems to be 'in a bit of a state'.[81] Traditional 'governmentality', to use Foucault's pun,[82] is giving way to notions of 'ungovernance' – the idea that the diffusion of authority away from states 'has left a yawning hole of non-authority'.[83]

Various types of 'non-state authority' vie with the state. It might be useful to imagine 'a continuum between one extreme in which non-state authority sustains and reinforces the authority of the state, and, at the other extreme, a non-state authority which contests and challenges, or threatens to supplant that of the state'.[84] In other words, one may distinguish between 'sovereignty-bound' and 'sovereignty-free' actors.[85] Close to the state-supporting or sovereignty-bound extreme we find the international bureaucracies of intergovernmental organizations (IGOs) and transnational insurance conglomerates. Somewhere between the two extremes we can locate transnational corporation and cartels, various non-governmental organizations (NGOs) and transborder regions. And at the other, state-threatening or sovereignty-free extreme, we find secessionist groups as well as transnational criminal organizations or mafias and terrorist organizations.

These are by no means toothless organizations that are, or can readily be, subordinated to state authority. Criminal and terrorist organizations challenge the state's claim to a monopoly on violence and are, in that respect, reminiscent of the pirates and privateers of yesteryear (even to the extent that criminal and terrorist violence can be either 'marketized' or state-sponsored). The other organizational forms challenge the state's claims to exclusive authority over its territory and population. They all demonstrate that the institution of sovereignty today obscures multi-layered practices of authority and influence.

Whereas the international system of sovereign states has traditionally been described as anarchy, the term 'global governance' has in recent years gained wide adherence as an effort to capture the complex global patterns of authority that have emerged in the wake of 'the organizational explosion of our times'.[86] Admittedly, it remains a fuzzy concept which defies unequivocal definition. Global governance has been characterized as 'the sum of the many ways individuals and institutions, public and private, manage their common affairs', which includes 'formal institutions and regimes empowered to enforce compliance, as well as informal arrangements that people and institutions either have agreed to or perceive to be in their interest'.[87] It is conceived 'to include systems of rule at all levels of human activity – from the family to the international organization – in which the pursuit of goals through the exercise of control has transnational repercussions'.[88] Global governance is essentially 'governance without government'.[89] We shall return to the governance concept in our discussion of the nature of the European Union in Chapter 7.

At any rate, the notion of governance implies an international order that is based neither on anarchy nor on hierarchy. Moreover, it suggests a multi-layered rather than state-centric organizational map. It is with this in mind that we now turn in the following chapters to considering alternative ways of organizing European space.

NOTES

1 The expression 'dual anchorage' is taken from John Hobson, *The Wealth of States: A Comparative Sociology of International Economic and Political Change* (Cambridge: Cambridge University Press, 1997), 12.

2 Joseph A. Camilleri and Jim Falk, *The End of Sovereignty? The Politics of a Shrinking and Fragmenting World* (Aldershot: Edward Elgar, 1992), 27.

3 Sanjay Seth, 'Nationalism in/and Modernity', in *The State in Transition: Reimagining Political Space*, eds Joseph A. Camilleri, Anthony P. Jarvis and Albert J. Paolini (Boulder, CO: Lynne Rienner, 1995), 48.

4 Camilleri and Falk, *The End of Sovereignty?*, 27.

5 Irmline Veit-Brause, 'Rethinking the State of the Nation', in Camilleri et al. (eds), *The State in Transition*, 59.

6 Stephanie Lawson, 'The Authentic State: History and Tradition in the Ideology of Ethnonationalism', in Camilleri et al. (eds), *The State in Transition*, 82.

7 Veit-Brause, 'Rethinking the State of the Nation', 61.

8 Rune Johansson, Ralf Rönnquist and Sven Tägil, 'Territorialstaten i kris? Integration och uppsplittring i Europa', in *Europa – Historiens återkomst*, 3rd edn, ed. Sven Tägil (Hedemora: Gidlunds, 1998), 21–3.

9 Benedict Anderson, *Imagined Communities: Reflections on the Origin and Spread of Nationalism*, revised edn (London/New York: Verso, 1991).

10 Tom Nairn, *The Break-up of Britain: Crisis and Neo-Nationalism* (London: New Left Books, 1977).

11 J.S. Huxley and A.C. Haddon, *We Europeans* (New York: Harper and Row, 1935), 5; as quoted in Otto Klineberg, *The Human Dimension in International Relations* (New York: Holt, Rinehart and Winston, 1964), 54.

12 Patrik Hall, *The Social Construction of Nationalism* (Lund: Lund University Press, 1998), 23.

13 Elie Kedourie, *Nationalism* (London: Hutchinson, 1960).

14 Seth, 'Nationalism in/and Modernity', 50.

15 Anthony D. Smith, *The Ethnic Origins of Nations* (Oxford: Blackwell, 1986), 145.

16 Anderson, *Imagined Communities*, 4.

17 Seth, 'Nationalism in/and Modernity', 56.

18 Lawson, 'The Authentic State', 79.

19 Seth, 'Nationalism in/and Modernity', 49.

20 Anderson, *Imagined Communities*, 143.

21 Ernest Gellner, *Nations and Nationalism* (Oxford: Blackwell, 1983).

22 Ibid., 34.

23 Adrian Hastings, *The Construction of Nationhood: Ethnicity, Religion and Nationalism* (Cambridge: Cambridge University Press, 1997).

24 Anderson, *Imagined Communities*.

25 Veit-Brause, 'Rethinking the State of the Nation', 62.

26 Eric J. Hobsbawm, *Nations and Nationalism since 1780: Programme, Myth, Reality* (Cambridge: Cambridge University Press, 1990).

27 Mathew Horsman and Andrew Marshall, *After the Nation-State: Citizens, Tribalism and the New World Disorder* (London: Harper Collins, 1995), 182.

28 David Held, *Democracy and the Global Order* (Stanford, CA: Stanford University Press, 1995), 42–6.

29 Ibid., 11.

30 Inis L. Claude, Jr., *Swords into Plowshares: The Problems and Progress of International Organization*, 3rd edn (New York: Random House, 1964), 47.

31 Ibid., 48.

32 Seth, 'Nationalism in/and Modernity', 52.

33 Anthony McGrew, 'Globalization and Territorial Democracy: An Introduction', in *The Transformation of Democracy?*, ed. Anthony McGrew (Cambridge: Polity Press, 1997), 5.

34 David Held, 'Democracy and Globalization', *Global Governance*, 3 (1997), 251.

35 Francis Fukuyama, *The End of History and the Last Man* (New York: The Free Press, 1992).

36 For influential formulations of the 'democratic peace' thesis, see Michael Doyle, 'Liberalism and World Politics', *American Political Science Review*, 80 (1986), 1151–69; Bruce Russett, *Grasping the Democratic Peace: Principles for a Post-Cold War World* (Princeton, NJ: Princeton University Press, 1993).

37 Held, 'Democracy and Globalization', 251.

38 Ibid., 257.

39 Anthony McGrew, 'Democracy Beyond Borders? Globalization and the Reconstruction of Democratic Theory and Practice', in McGrew (ed.), *The Transformation of Democracy?*, 237.

40 Held, 'Democracy and Globalization', 261.

41 Cf. ibid., 262; Held, *Democracy and the Global Order*, 18.

42 Friedrich Kratochwil, 'Of Systems, Boundaries, and Territoriality: An Inquiry into the Formation of the State System', *World Politics*, 39 (1986), 27.

43 Susan Strange, *The Retreat of the State: The Diffusion of Power in the World Economy* (Cambridge: Cambridge University Press, 1996), 7.

44 John H. Herz, *International Politics in the Atomic Age* (New York: Columbia University Press, 1962), 13.

45 John H. Herz, *The Nation-State and the Crisis of World Politics* (New York: David McKay, 1976), 226–52.

46 Charlotte Bretherton, 'Introduction: Global Politics in the 1990s', in *Global Politics: An Introduction*, ed. Charlotte Bretherton and Geoffrey Ponton (Oxford: Blackwell, 1996), 4.

47 Kratochwil, 'Of Systems, Boundaries, and Territoriality', 43.

48 Cf. John Agnew, 'The Territorial Trap: The Geographical Assumptions of International Relations Theory', *Review of International Political Economy*, 1 (1994), 70.

49 John Stopford and Susan Strange, *Rival States, Rival Firms: Competition for World Market Shares* (Cambridge: Cambridge University Press, 1991), 4.

50 McGrew, 'Globalization and Territorial Democracy', 6; Held, 'Democracy and Globalization', 256.

51 Cf. Horsman and Marshall, *After the Nation-State*, 201.

52 Chris Mulhearn, 'Change and Development in the Global Economy', in Bretherton and Ponton (eds), *Global Politics*, 185.

53 Strange, *Retreat of the State*, 48.

54 McGrew, 'Globalization and Territorial Democracy', 9.

55 Strange, *Retreat of the State*, 43.

56 Ibid., 14.

57 Cf. Camilleri and Falk, *The End of Sovereignty?*, 172, 192.

58 Ibid., 179.

59 The term is taken from James A.Caporaso, 'International Relations Theory and Multilateralism: The Search for Foundations', *International Organization* 46 (1992), 599–632.

60 David Goldblatt, 'Liberal Democracy and the Globalization of Environmental Risks', in McGrew (ed.), *Transformation of Democracy?*, 78–9.

61 Camilleri and Falk, *The End of Sovereignty?*, 185.

62 McGrew, 'Globalization and Territorial Democracy', 6.

63 The information is taken from the homepage of UNHCR (United Nations High Commissioner for Refugees), www.unhcr.ch.

64 Agnew, 'The Territorial Trap', 75.

65 See Andrew Linklater, 'Citizenship and Sovereignty in the Post-Westphalian State', *European Journal of International Relations*, 2 (1996), 77–103.

66 See James N. Rosenau, *Along the Domestic–Foreign Frontier: Exploring Governance in a Turbulent World* (Cambridge: Cambridge University Press, 1997), 254–71.

67 Stephen D. Krasner, 'Problematic Sovereignty' (paper presented at the Annual Convention of the American Political Science Association, Boston, MA, September 1998), 9.

68 Ibid., 10.

69 Agnew, 'The Territorial Trap', 77.

70 Richard Rosecrance, *The Rise of the Trading State* (New York: Basic Books, 1986).

71 See James G. Goldgeier and Michael McFaul, 'A Tale of Two Worlds: Core and Periphery in the Post-Cold War Era', *International Organization*, 46 (1992), 467–91.

72 See, for example, Philip Cerny, *The Changing Architecture of Politics: Structure, Agency, and the Future of the State* (London: Sage, 1990); Philip Cerny, 'Globalization and the Changing Logic of Collective Action', *International Organization*, 49 (1995), 595–625.

73 Strange, *Retreat of the State*, 73.

74 Ibid., 62.

75 Richard Rosecrance, 'The Rise of the Virtual State', *Foreign Affairs*, 75 (1996), 45–61.

76 Ibid., 51.

77 Ibid., 52.

78 Ibid., 53.

79 Cf. Alexander B. Murphy, 'The Sovereign State System as Political-Territorial Ideal: Historical and Contemporary Considerations', in *State Sovereignty as Social Construct*, ed. Thomas J. Bierstecker and Cynthia Weber (Cambridge: Cambridge University Press, 1996), 109; Agnew, 'The Territorial Trap', 71–2.

80 Robert. O. Keohane, 'Hobbes's Dilemma and Institutional Change in World Politics: Sovereignty in International Society', in *Whose World Order?: Uneven Globalization and the End of the Cold War*, ed. Hans-Henrik Holm and Georg Sørensen (Boulder, CO: Westview Press, 1995), 177 (emphasis in original).

81 R.B.J. Walker, 'From International Relations to World Politics', in Camilleri et al. (eds), *The State in Transition*, 21.

82 See Michel Foucault, 'Governmentality', in *The Foucault Effect: Studies in Governmentality*, eds L. Martin, H. Gutman and P. Hutton (Amherst, MA: University of Massachusetts Press, 1991). The term 'governmentality' figures centrally in Thom Kuehls, *Beyond Sovereign Territory* (Minneapolis: University of Minnesota Press, 1996).

83 Strange, *Retreat of the State*, 14.

84 Ibid., 92.

85 These are the terms used in James N. Rosenau, *Turbulence in World Politics* (London: Harvester Wheatsheaf, 1990).

86 James N. Rosenau, 'Governance in the Twenty-first Century', *Global Governance*, 1 (1995), 16.

87 *Our Global Neighbourhood: The Report of the Commission on Global Governance* (Oxford/New York: Oxford University Press, 1995), 2.

88 Rosenau, 'Governance in the Twenty-first Century', 13.

89 James N. Rosenau and Ernst-Otto Czempiel (eds), *Governance Without Government: Order and Change in Word Politics* (Cambridge: Cambridge University Press, 1992).

6

Transcending Space

There is today a growing tension between the power that controls the territory, and interests tied to networks. The networks of firms and science, to name two areas crucial for our future welfare, have broken free from traditional political and social perimeters. The territorial overlap between industrial, scientific and political interests has been disrupted. Territory, long the principal domain of political power and democracy, no longer coincides with new, growing problem areas that are closely linked to technological change, new forms of production, and emerging modes of resource exploitation. Unemployment, economic imbalance and environmental decay are examples of such new problems. In addition, there is a tension between rapid and slow processes, between 'tenacious' and 'brittle' structures within technology, economics and politics.

The network concept

As mentioned, territory is understood as a contiguous part of the earth's surface. The territory is distinguished from its environment by a boundary, and the boundary marks the difference between inside and outside, between belonging and exclusion. Moreover, the term territory is used to designate a 'political space', or 'power sphere'. *Networks* depict the geographic space as points (nodes) connected by lines (links). The network discriminates between nodes that are tied to the net and those that are not. As discussed in Chapter 2, the significant difference between the two concepts becomes apparent when important networks become autonomous in relation to territories to which democratic controls are confined.

In Chapter 2, we distinguished between three types of networks: physical, institutional and socio-cultural. Transportation networks belong to the physical dimension, while firms and other organizations are institutional networks. Social and cultural nets unite individuals and thus also knowledge areas and social environments. Like intertwined nervous systems, they transmit ideas and impulses. Examples include kin-groups and other social relations that tie individuals to each other in various types of communities of interests, collaboration and shared knowledge.

Transportation networks can be mapped. Organizational and social nets, however, are often far more difficult to depict in concrete terms, although they may be well-developed and discernible also to outside observers. Hotel and retail chains, monastic orders and the Salvation Army belong to these categories. But many influential networks are relatively invisible and anonymous to outsiders. The Italian Mafia, for instance, emerged as an imperceptible network in territories that were always under the control of other power centres. Drug cartels and so-called underground organizations weave worldwide nets that national police forces attempt to break, usually to little avail. In business and science, there is a mixture of well-known and less visible relations that transcend physical boundaries. In these worlds, it seems that the significance of *informal* contacts is growing at the expense of *formal* ties.

Figures 6.1–6.4 outline the attributes of a few stylized networks. Figure 6.1 shows a network with few links. The degree of connectivity is low. There exists one central node to which all other nodes are tied. All contacts must be made either in or via the central node. Examples of such networks are modern transportation systems. By way of comparison, the connectivity in Figure 6.2 is higher than in the first example. The distinction between centre and periphery is less apparent. In Figure 6.3, connectivity is complete. Each node is directly connected to all other nodes. An organization that follows this pattern is usually called 'flat'.

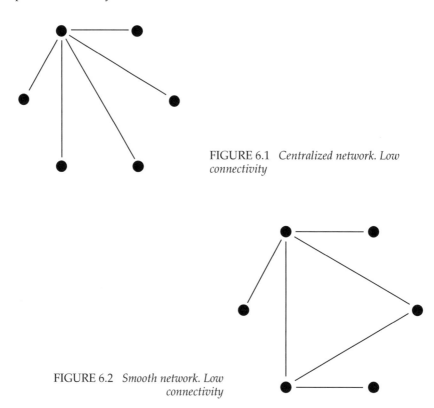

FIGURE 6.1 *Centralized network. Low connectivity*

FIGURE 6.2 *Smooth network. Low connectivity*

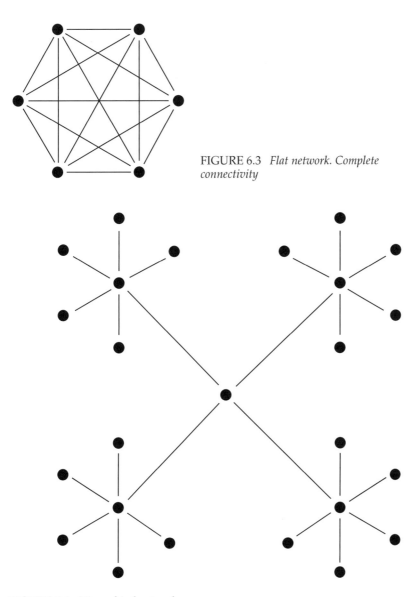

FIGURE 6.3 *Flat network. Complete connectivity*

FIGURE 6.4 *Hierarchical network*

These simple examples indicate that total connectivity can exist only in smaller networks. Only small organizations can be entirely flat. The number of possible bilateral communication channels within an organization increases with size. Two persons need only one channel for their mutual contact. Four individuals require six such channels, and six persons need 30 (see Figure 6.3). In an egalitarian network with 100 nodes, 4,950 links are needed, and one with 1,000 nodes requires 499,500 links. The result is that large networks often exhibit hierarchic forms, such as in Figure 6.4. This applies to the majority of physical networks, with telecommunications as a notable exception. It applies to all major institutional networks as well. When social networks grow, certain nodes become more strategic and influential than others.

Theoretical challenges

Manuel Castells has coined the term *network society* to describe the world at the dawn of the new millennium. His conception draws attention to the fact that many of society's major functions are organized as networks. 'Networks constitute the new social morphology of our societies, and the diffusion of networking logic substantially modifies the operation and outcomes in processes of production, experience, power and culture'.[1]

The revolution in information technology is a principal prerequisite for the rise of the network society. Castells draws a parallel with the invention of the alphabet in Greece around 700 BC, which laid the foundation for a written language, abstract thought and modern science. In the same way that the 'alphabetic mind' prompted a qualitative transformation of human communication, today's integration of various modes of communication into an interactive network is seen as a technological change of similar historic dimensions.[2]

The term network has become prevalent in many different fields of science. In fact, it has been argued that 'network' is replacing the 'atom' as a general symbol of science. Whereas the atom represents simplicity, regularity and closure, network stands for complexity, flexibility and openness.[3] Similarly, the network concept poses a series of challenges against traditional perceptions within geography, economics and political science. For geographers, conventional understandings of distance, accessibility and range are dissolved. Space can no longer be assumed to be continuous. Distance in space and time can no longer be correlated in the same manner as before. Accessibility and reachability are no longer contingent on one's physical location on a surface, but on one's position in relation to different nodal networks. In the geographic context, there thus exists an important difference between *territorial proximity* (physical proximity, closeness and contiguity) and *proximity in networks*. Well-developed transportation and communication systems allow access to, and contacts between, cities and structures that may be far from one another physically. Persons who queue in the same line may be entirely anonymous to one another, while at the same time feeling closeness and affinity to friends who live far away and whom they see only infrequently.

The morphology of networks also involves a new view of *markets*. Within business administration and economics, the network concept is used to describe a form of organization *within* the firm and to characterize the interaction *between* the firm and its environment. Studies of the relationship between supplier and consumer have, for instance, identified networks in the interaction between the firms and their environment. In neo-classical economic models, the market is generally assumed to include a multitude of actors, who act independently of one another. Network models of business administration, however, chart bonds of trust between firms and customers. Such ties are enduring and have been developed in order to reduce uncertainty, and thereby also transaction costs.[4]

The network concept has made its way into political science as well. It has challenged the traditional way of treating political organization. First, network analysis replaces the conventional 'closed-system' view of self-contained organizational units with an 'open-system' perspective. Secondly, it chooses interaction between different organizations as the unit of analysis. And thirdly, it focuses on 'informal organization' rather than formal relations of authority within and between units. Network analysis was first applied to national political systems. More recently transnational, issue-based networks have caught the attention of researchers.[5] Today, as we shall see in Chapter 7, the European Union has become a prominent focal point of network analysis.

In political science the network concept has been used primarily in a loose, metaphorical way.[6] Also, in the political realm network can be either an analytical or an operative concept. In the latter case, network is conceived of as an instrument through which actors act to realize their objectives jointly and 'networking' is seen as a strategy.[7]

The term *policy network* has been coined by political scientists. A policy network can be described by its actors, their linkages and its boundary. It includes a relatively stable set of public and private organizational actors within a given issue-area, linked through communication and the exchange of information, expertise and other policy resources. The boundary of a given policy network is not primarily determined by formal institutions but results from a process of mutual recognition.[8]

There is a confusing variety of understandings and applications of the policy network concept. At one level, researchers differ with respect to method-ological orientation, preferring quantitative or qualitative approaches. At another level, a distinction can be made between an 'interest mediation school' and a 'governance school'.[9] The interest mediation school conceives policy networks as a generic concept and an analytical tool which applies to all kinds of relationships between interest groups and the state, between public and private actors. For the governance school, on the other hand, policy networks characterize a special form of public–private interaction. In an increasingly complex and dynamic environment, where hierarchical coordination is becoming increasingly difficult, governance becomes feasible only within policy networks. The term policy network, then, signals a change in the structure of political organization rather than just representing a new analytical tool.

One of the main advantages of networks over formal organizations is that they allow informal interorganizational coordination which avoids problems associated with hierarchy and representation, while facilitating the development of trust and frank exchanges of information.[10] The informality of networks rests on the personal relationships that develop as a result of frequent interaction. Networks link elites; presence or absence in networks is therefore a critical source of power and domination. While individual network participants are agents of organizations, it is also a crucial feature of networks that interorganizational relations are strengthened by interpersonal links.[11] Networks, in short, imply personal contacts within the context of organizational contacts.

Policy networks are generally described as *non-hierarchical*, but the degree of hierarchy or non-hierarchy may vary. A network rests on links between interdependent actors. It represents a 'flat' or 'horizontal' organizational form in contrast to vertical ones based on hierarchic authority. Networks are sometimes located between hierarchies and markets.[12] Markets presuppose a large number of autonomous actors with little interdependence; hierarchies consist of chains of subordination where superordinate actors are dependent on the performance of subordinate ones who have little autonomy. Networks, by contrast, rest on the coexistence of autonomy and interdependence. Even in pluralist and decentralized polities, 'the number of actors is not large enough to constitute a "political market"'.[13] Networks, in other words, remain the only alternative to hierarchies in the political realm.

The republic of the learned

One prominent and early European example of network structure can be found in the sphere of higher learning and research. The first educational institutions after Antiquity were the cathedral schools and the schools attached to monasteries. The main purpose of this *archipelago of religious schools* was originally the education of priests. Under the auspices of the church, an educational system evolved that was autonomous *vis-à-vis* the political powers of the time. The religious schools laid the foundation for the creation, in the Middle Ages, of universities that were largely independent of the dynastic states. Thus, the 'republic of the learned', a kingdom without territory, was born.[14]

A network of universities

The university of Bologna, founded in 1088, is generally considered to be the oldest in Europe, although the claim has been contested. The university in Paris is believed to be somewhat younger. The two institutions set the pattern for later medieval universities. In Bologna, students, united in 'nations' or fraternities – *universitas* in Latin – were responsible for appointing and removing professors. In Paris, the teachers created *universitas magistrorum*. Masters and courses were organized into faculties, where uniform norms and quality controls were developed. To the outside world, this was reflected in standardized course contents and in the certificates, diplomas and insignia that the universities conferred. Proceeding from this common organizational basis, the universities built autonomous networks.

Over time, the universities became the most enduring monuments of medieval culture in Europe, alongside the cathedrals. The manner in which the universities spread is in keeping with geographic theories of the diffusion of innovations. At first, new universities were offshoots of older ones in their immediate vicinity, but eventually they began to emerge in more remote areas. New centres, in turn, became springboards for secondary propagations. The university in Padua was created when students and teachers from Bologna moved out. Oxford University was established in the late twelfth century as a scion of Paris. In the thirteenth and fourteenth centuries, the academic archipelago grew denser within the Romance language area. Germanic and Slavic areas became part of the network in the late fourteenth century, with universities in Prague, Vienna, Cologne, Erfurt, Heidelberg and Cracow. When the University of Rostock was established, the continental network had reached the Baltic Sea. The Nordic region received its first university in 1477, in Uppsala.[15]

The different units in the academic archipelago were linked together through extensive intellectual traffic. Students from different parts of Europe went to prestigious universities with well-known instructors. In a sense, students migrated in the same manner as journeymen, artists and musicians, scarcely aware of the boundaries they traversed on their paths. Professors frequently moved between different universities, contributing to the creation of an academic community in constant transition. Latin, the common language, made possible this mobility and facilitated the emergence of the network. Few persons had Latin as their native tongue. Those who learned the language became part of a bilingual intelligentsia. The development of the printing press provided scholars with a new medium that brought continuity and stability to research and teaching. Books had a permanent form that could be reproduced, if at first in limited editions. Few people could read, and the university was for a long time a literate oasis in a vast desert of illiteracy. The educated sector became the mediators between the vernacular and Latin. According to one estimate, 77 per cent of all books published before 1500 were written in Latin.[16]

During the Reformation, the growing power and territorial ambitions of the monarchy altered the role and position of the universities. In the Nordic area, ties between institutions of higher learning and the Catholic Church were completely severed. Many of the channels that brought Roman influence to northern Europe were thereby closed. The Germanic language areas, the Protestant and Reformed parts of Europe, gained influence at the expense of the Romance, Catholic areas. When integrated territorial states began to emerge in the sixteenth and seventeenth centuries, higher education was given a new role. Scholarship became closely linked to the formation of the new states in France, Britain, Denmark–Norway and Sweden–Finland. The Bible was translated into national languages, and libraries became national.

From national to international academia

When scholars – particularly scientists, engineers, and those in the medical profession – travelled abroad in the eighteenth century, it was often in the true spirit of mercantilism, to obtain knowledge and competencies to the benefit of their own country. The nineteenth century was an age of nationalism. Higher education and research primarily served the nation. Throughout Europe, state-run secondary schools and various vocational schools were opened. Specialized colleges were established alongside the older universities, to make possible the study of specific vocations in addition to pure research. All public careers, and the overwhelming majority of employment opportunities within business and industry, were framed within national boundaries. The 50 millions who emigrated from Europe to America during this time were almost all landless peasants or servants who lacked a formal education.

The great breakthrough of science, now entirely in the service of the state, occurred during the Second World War. The warring countries enlisted the universities and the research departments of firms to help the government conduct total war. In Germany, prominent engineers and scientists were summoned to barbed-wire-fenced research camps to build new weapons. In the United States, experts in various fields were brought together in secret laboratories. Research results that in peacetime probably would have taken several decades were produced within a few years. Entire cities were built with the sole purpose of fostering applied research and development.

After the war, research and university education increased dramatically both in scope and in general importance. In earlier times, higher learning belonged to an exclusive elite. Today, between a third and half of any age group in the industrialized world obtain a degree. Research and higher education are considered essential to the cultural, technological and economic advancement of individual states. The quality of the population's education is an important determinant of the international competitiveness of states and firms. Higher education and research are also important forces behind regional development. In several countries, the foundation of new universities and colleges has been used as a political instrument for regional mobilization.

The expansion and significance of research are still treated primarily as a national concern. At the same time, research and development are today conducted in international networks outside the control of individual states, although governments still finance significant shares. Research has transcended national parameters and takes place within network structures that in many respects echo the patterns of medieval Europe. In an archipelago of institutes of higher learning and research centres, different places are bound to each other through a net of cross-border relations, and the academic world is today part of an unprecedented communication system.

The formal cooperation between institutes of higher learning and research has increased significantly. Every university and college today has an international secretariat. As recently as a few years ago, most had only a few agreements with foreign schools; today, they tend to have hundreds. These agreements cover cooperation in various areas, including the exchange of students. Growing numbers of agreements and research grants are today administered by the European Union. The situation best resembles a jungle of formal relations, whose assembled significance is difficult to estimate. Even more importantly, informal spheres of activity are emerging in the shade of these formal, centrally directed forms of cooperation. Informal contacts between scholars multiply, and projects involving several research institutions from different countries become increasingly common. Supported by the revolution in information technology and telecommunications, these informal modes of collaboration leave their mark on publication patterns and a growing number of international workshops, symposia and conferences. Scholars are among today's most arduous travellers.[17]

Books remain the emblem of scholarly communication. Books can be stored, they can be distributed, and they can be read by many. They can be reread, in their entirety or in parts. They facilitate evaluation, reflection, control and critique. Scholars gain recognition largely through their written works. Never before have so many academic publications appeared as today, most of them in English, the *lingua franca* of our era. Bibliometric studies have come into fashion. There are today large indexes of scholarly citations within different disciplines. These indicate that scientific information circulates quite freely across national boundaries, yet in surprisingly closed disciplinary circles. They also show that different authors, and thus different research environments, have at various times exercised a dominating influence within a certain subject area. Joint authorship has increased greatly in recent years.[18]

Scholars have traditionally been among the most active correspondents. Until around 1970, the exchange of letters was a principal means for mapping the foreign contacts of individual scholars. New telecommunications – telephone, fax and electronic mail – have subsequently replaced written correspondence. These various means of contact fill a supportive function. Face-to-face contacts, letters and telecommunications complement each other. Conversations and meetings have always been, remain and will continue to be the most important medium for exchanging information within the academic world. Historically, knowledge could only be shared and passed on to subsequent generations by word of mouth. Socrates left us no written works. Plato was prolific, but it was primarily through dialogue that knowledge spread among the students of the *Akademia* in the fourth century BC. Over time, the written word became a means of protecting information from oblivion.

The significance of the spoken word today lies in the deeper implications of 'talking together'. Technological channels cannot convey the many different impressions conveyed in face-to-face contacts. Whereas all existing forms of media filter information, direct conversations permit dialogue with immediate responses. Through debate and discussion, ideas and arguments can be tested without delay. Studies suggest that scholars today devote more than half of their work-time to conversation. The number of international conferences as well as the number of participants keep growing. The relevance of social communication and the need for face-to-face encounters have not diminished in the building of contemporary academic networks.

Stateless firms

For at least 400 years, it has been taken for granted that the economy is a matter of national concern. This view dates back to mercantilism, formulated at a time when economists were preoccupied with the rivalries between the great powers of Europe, namely, Portugal, Spain, France, the Netherlands and England. Mercantilism considered states not only as political and military powers, but also as economic 'beings' that contend with other territorial units to generate well-being and prosperity for their citizens. Adam Smith outlined the theoretical framework of this perspective as early as 1776.[19]

Since then, economic theory has closely followed the development of the modern nation-state and the welfare state. In classical and neo-classical theory, the world is characterized by territorial order and a significant degree of predictability. International competition is synonymous with foreign trade. The exchanged products presumedly emanate from firms that are firmly embedded within the boundaries of their home country. Gross national product, national balance of trade, national growth, national prosperity and national savings are seen as meaningful measures.

When individual firms began to open branches and start production abroad, the economic order started to erode. Today, industrial production, based on science and technology, is no longer confined by state territories. The trend is not new *per se*. According to the Finnish philosopher Georg Henrik von Wright, for instance, industry sought to transcend the boundaries of the state already in the infancy of industrialism. Raw materials had to be imported, finished products had to be exported. From the outset, there was thus a conflict between the political system engendered by the territorial states, and the forms of production organized by firms.

In the nineteenth century, this tension remained latent as states expanded their territories. von Wright views colonialism as an attempt by states to adapt their territories to the growing spheres of interest of business. Not only great powers such as Great Britain, France and Germany, but also smaller countries such as Belgium and the Netherlands, grew into empires. During colonialism, business and the state coexisted in a sort of territorial mutual understanding. Competition between large firms over foreign markets and resources paralleled the power struggles between states. The territorial harmony between economic and political interests was disrupted fundamentally when the colonial system was dissolved, and the states withdrew into the shell of the motherland. The tension was not fully exposed during the two world wars and their problematic repercussions.[20]

Regardless of whether one agrees with this rendition of history, it is clear that the technological–industrial and the political spheres are no longer compatible. The conflict has grown for decades and became a tangible problem in the 1970s and 1980s. Large firms continue to break out of traditional political and social frames, following the trend set long ago by science and cultural life. It is no longer only a question of adapting to expanding markets and remote natural resources. Through foreign branches, mergers, acquisitions, strategic alliances and cooperative agreements, a tangle of new cross-border networks emerges, with varying ownership and wavering patriotic loyalty. Today's stateless organizations can only to a limited degree be controlled and influenced within territorially demarcated national decision-making systems. Through new strategies for collaboration and specialization within networks, firms can also exploit the comparative advantages of several countries.

A Swedish example

What, then, is the extent of these autonomous networks that transcend national boundaries? Let us limit the perspective to transnational corporations, that is, firms and conglomerates with activities in several different countries simultaneously. According to the 1993 World Investment Report published by the United Nations, 37,000 transnational corporations control a third of the world's privately owned means of production. These are large firms, representing not only manufacturing but also trade and services.

The extent of cross-border activity varies with the physical size of states. Large countries with significant domestic markets can contain wide networks within their borders. Conversely, in small countries, expanding firms tend to develop a foreign base early. Sweden, a small, economically advanced country provides an illustrative example. Of the 37,000 firms listed by the United Nations, 3,500 are Swedish. This means that Sweden is the motherland of as many transnational corporations as Japan, nearly twice as many as France and more than ten times as many as Italy.[21] In terms of transcending national boundaries, Swedish business must be characterized as unique, especially taking its limited size into consideration. Soon, 'Swedish' industry will offer as many employment opportunities abroad as at home.

In 1994, Sweden's twenty largest corporations, in their various branches worldwide, together turned over twice the value of all Swedish exports, or half of the country's total GNP. These corporations in 1994 had 775,000 employees, more than the total number of industrial workers within Sweden. The firms listed in Table 6.1 represent manufacturing, forestry, pharmaceutics and construction.[22]

As mentioned, cross-border business networks are not entirely new. They have evolved since the end of the nineteenth century. Whereas previously the foreign activity of firms was surpassed by domestic activity, the foreign–domestic ratio has lately been reversed, as reflected in the last three columns in Table 6.1.

If we take cross-shareholding into account, efforts to depict cross-border business networks become quite complex. Many Swedish firms that are active abroad are owned in part by foreign shareholders. A third of the stock of the thirty largest Swedish firms was estimated to be in foreign hands in 1995. More than half of Ericsson's shares, and nearly half of Astra's shares, were owned by foreigners, for instance.[23]

The establishment of transnational networks beyond state control usually proceeds through a series of steps. The first phase involves penetration of

TABLE 6.1 *The twenty largest manufacturing firms with a home base in Sweden*

Firm	Turnover 1994 (billion SEK)	Number employees 1994 (1000s)	% of which abroad 1980	% of which abroad 1990	% of which abroad 1994
1 Asea Brown Boveri, ABB	230	207	25	85	80
2 Volvo	156	74	28	32	69
3 Electrolux	108	109	60	82	85
4 Ericsson	83	74	58	56	—
5 Tetra Laval	63	37	—	—	92
6 Stora	49	27	12	68	86
7 Svenska Cellulosa, SCA	34	24	32	65	92
8 Svenska Kullagerfabriken, SKF	33	40	81	90	94
9 Skanska	32	29	—	—	81
10 Astra	29	14	—	—	95
Total 1–10	*817*	*635*			
11 Axel Johnsson Group	28	11	—	—	—
12 Pharmacia	26	19	—	—	94
13 Sandvik	25	29	—	—	90
14 Atlas Copco	21	18	68	80	97
15 MoDo	20	11	—	23	92
16 Trelleborg	20	12	—	—	93
17 Saab	19	7	—	—	94
18 Assi Domän	17	12	—	53	93
19 Avesta Sheffield	17	8	—	—	96
20 NCC	17	13	—	—	89
Total 1–20	*1,027*	*775*			

Source: see text, note 22

foreign markets, without establishing a physical presence abroad. In later stages, the firm opens branches abroad. With regard to ownership and the functions transferred abroad, different levels of internationalization can be distinguished. At a first level, the firm establishes, or increases, production in its branches abroad. A second level involves transferring marketing, management and research units to foreign countries. At a third level, it is no longer possible to define the ownership of the corporation unequivocally in geographic terms. Fourth and finally, headquarters and the central management of the firm are transferred. The corporation has thus effectively changed its nationality or may be labelled stateless.[24]

Returning to Table 6.1, it is questionable whether all of the listed examples can be called Swedish. Asea Brown Boveri (ABB) was registered as a Swiss firm, but over 50 per cent of the company was owned by Asea, which was registered in Sweden.[25] In this sense, Asea Brown Boveri was a stateless firm, although it preferred to describe itself as 'multidomestic'. SKF, a ball-bearing manufacturer, liked to depict itself as a 'truly international company'. In 1991, it was active in over 130 countries. SKF had 100 factories spread throughout nineteen countries for the production of its goods. Sales were conducted from 100 offices via 8,000 distributors based in fifty countries. Even the Swedish forest industry, dependent on natural resources and predominant in Swedish exports, had moved a large share of its operations abroad.[26]

So far, our discussion has centred on autonomous networks that solidify as a result of ownership conditions and organizational regulations, that is, through the creation of transnational corporations and conglomerates. In addition, there are more informal economic networks that nevertheless prove to be enduring and influential. Such networks include horizontal and vertical integration between subcontractors, service companies and sites of assembly, collaborating in extensive production systems. The true scope of such complexes is difficult to estimate. Parts of them exist within the confines of national and regional boundaries, but the trend today is towards complex transnational networks.

The future of the national economy

This development raises the question whether economic policies can be pursued within national perimeters in the future. Several scholars have addressed this question, including Robert Reich in his notable book *The Work of Nations*.[27] By the early twentieth century, he argues, economic nationalism had been established in much of the world. For citizens in the United States, Great Britain, Germany, France, Italy, Japan and several other developed countries, their personal welfare was linked directly to the economic wealth of their homeland. Around 1950, there were obvious connections between the success of large firms, the national economy and the standard of living of individual citizens. Since then, production, in particular the major portion controlled by large corporations, has lost much of its national identity. National flagships have been replaced by cosmopolitan firms and stateless conglomerates. Business has developed a net that spans the globe, in which money and information circulate relatively freely. These nets are virtually unencumbered by geographic boundaries; they can don whatever national garb seems most comfortable at any given moment.

At the same time, it becomes ever more difficult to determine the origin of a product. Finished goods may include components and labour from widely different locations. A common combination for 'American' products is that the financial coordination is located in the United States, while the design of the product takes place in Italy and Germany. High-tech components are obtained from Japan, less advanced ones from Taiwan and Singapore. Computer services are provided by Ireland or Barbados. British firms handle advertising and marketing.

In his book Reich links the concept of nation to the population, and highlights knowledge and human skill as the most important resources for the future. On the horizon looms a society where prosperity is contingent on education and skilled labour to an unprecedented degree. It is foreseeable that prosperity in the future will increase only for the most educated sectors of society, while less educated citizens will experience a decline in their standard of living. This implies the emergence of a 'dual', fractured society characterized by dramatic inequalities and contrasts between social groups and between geographic areas.

As will be discussed in Chapter 9, such a scenario will engender significant geographic redistributions of economic activity and prosperity. Businesses might in the future develop primarily in areas that offer coveted human resources, such as university towns and major cities. The duality may be manifested in other ways as well. There may emerge a mobile group of educated persons with residences in different parts of the world, who choose their location depending on where the most attractive opportunities are at any given point in time. They may constitute the 'cavalry' of the future, accompanied by a new 'infantry', a group characterized by low levels of education and few possibilities to improve their standard of living.

Regardless of how the dual society will be configured, it will incorporate significant social and geographic differentiation. Thus far, the political issues of redistribution and reallocation raised by such inequalities have been handled in a national context. As George Soros has noted, economic globalization has significantly weakened the state's ability to provide welfare for its citizens, since capital can avoid taxation far more easily than can labour.[28] In short, the emergence of autonomous economic networks accentuates the eroding omnipotence and changing role of the state, delineated in Chapter 5.

NOTES

1 Manuel Castells, *The Rise of the Network Society* (Oxford: Blackwell, 1996), 469.

2 Ibid., 327–8.

3 Kevin Kelly, quoted in ibid., 61–61n.

4 Håkan Håkansson, *Corporate Technological Behaviour: Co-Operation and Network* (London: Routledge, 1989); Bo Malmberg, 'The Effects of External Ownership', Geografiska regionstudier Nr 24 (Uppsala: Department of Human Geography, 1990); Paul R. Christensen, Heikki Eskelinen, Bo Forsström, Leif Lindmark and Eirik Vetne, 'Firms in Networks: Concepts, Spatial Impacts and Policy Implications', in *Networks and Regional Development*, ed. Sven Illeris and Leif Jacobsen, NordREFO 1990: 1 (Copenhagen and Stockholm: Nordiska institutet för regionalpolitisk forskning, 1990); Björn Axelsson and Geoffrey Easton (eds), *Industrial Networks: A New View of Reality* (London/New York: Routledge, 1992). See also Chapter 4 in Castells, *The Rise of the Network Society*.

5 See, for example, Christer Jönsson, 'Interorganization Theory and International Organization', *International Studies Quarterly*, 30 (1986), 39–57; Peter M. Haas (ed.), *Knowledge, Power, and International Policy Coordination* (Boston, MA: MIT Press, 1992); Leon Gordenker, Roger A. Coate, Christer Jönsson and Peter Söderholm, *International Cooperation in Response to AIDS* (London: Pinter, 1995); Margaret Keck and Kathryn Sikkink, *Activists beyond Borders: Advocacy Networks in International Politics* (Ithaca, NY: Cornell University Press, 1998).

6 Frans van Waarden, 'Dimensions and Types of Policy Networks', *European Journal of Political Research*, 21 (1992), 30.

7 Kenneth Hanf and Laurence J. O'Toole Jr, 'Revisiting Old Friends: Networks, Implementation Structures and the Management of Inter-Organizational Relations', *European Journal of Political Research*, 21 (1992), 171.

8 Grant Jordan and Klaus Schubert, 'A Preliminary Ordering of Policy Network Labels', *European Journal of Political Research*, 21 (1992), 12.

9 Tanja A. Börzel, 'What's So Special about Policy Networks: An Exploration of the Concept and Its Usefulness in Studying European Governance', *European Integration Online Papers* 1 (1997) [http://eiop.or.at/eiop/texte/1997-016a.htm].

10 Cf. Donald Chisholm, *Coordination Without Hierarchy: Informal Structures in Multiorganizational Systems* (Berkeley, CA: University of California Press, 1989).

11 Cf. David Marsh and R.A.W. Rhodes, 'Policy Communities and Issue Networks: Beyond Typology', in *Policy Networks in British Government*, eds David Marsh and R.A.W. Rhodes (Oxford: Clarendon Press, 1992), 261–2.

12 See, for example, Jennifer Frances, Jeremy Mitchell, Rosalind Levaçiç and Grahame Thompson, 'Introduction', in *Markets, Hierarchies and Networks: The Coordination of Social Life*, eds Grahame Thompson, Jennifer Frances, Rosalind Levaçiç and Jeremy Mitchell (London: Sage, 1991).

13 Volker Schneider, 'The Structure of Policy Networks: A Comparison of the "Chemicals Control" and "Telecommunications" Policy Domains in Germany', *European Journal of Political Research*, 21 (1992), 112.

14 Sverker Sörlin, *De lärdas republik: Om vetenskapens internationella tendenser* (Malmoe: Liber-Hermods, 1994).

15 The development of the university in Europe as a geographic process of innovation has been described by Kerstin Cederlund in a series of maps that are included in, for instance, *Sweden in the World: National Atlas of Sweden* (Stockholm: Almqvist & Wiksell, 1993). See also Anne Buttimer, *The Wake of Erasmus* (Lund: Lund University Press, 1989).

16 The figures are obtained from Benedict Anderson, *Imagined Communities: Reflections on the Origin and Spread of Nationalism*, rev. edn (London/New York: Verso, 1991).

17 See Kerstin Cederlund, 'Universitetet i internationella nätverk', Rapporter och notiser 140 (Lund: Department of Social and Economic Geography Lund University, 1995).

18 As examples of the use of bibliometric studies, see Olle Persson, 'Informell kommunikation bland forskare och tekniker', Research Report No. 56 (Umeå: Department of Sociology, University of Umeå, 1980); Olle Persson, 'Svensk kunskapsimport – några indikatorer', Inforsk Papers on Communication Studies No. 19 (Umeå: Department of Sociology, University of Umeå, 1983); Tor Nørretranders and Tor Haaland, 'Dansk dynamit: Dansk forsknings internationale status vurderet ud fra bibliometriske indikatorer', Forskningspolitik 8 (Copenhagen: Forskningspolitisk råd, 1990).

19 Adam Smith, *An Inquiry into the Nature and Causes of the Wealth of Nations* (London: W. Strahan and T. Cadell, 1776). (Later editions have been published under the title *The Wealth of Nations*.)

20 Georg Henrik von Wright, *Myten om framsteget* (Stockholm: Bonniers, 1993).

21 *World Investment Report* (Geneva: UNCTAD, 1993).

22 The material has been compiled by Ulf Erlandsson and appears in *Sweden in the World*. Additions have subsequently been made. The figures were obtained from the

annual reports of the corporations as well as sundry other compilations. The figures at times may vary depending on the source, but not to such an extent that the variation significantly affects the conclusions.

23 The gaps in Table 6.1 reflect the fact that the firms that were registered in 1994 did not have the same form and scope in 1980 and 1990, with mergers and acquisitions, names and ownership changed. The statistics on foreign ownership of Swedish companies are obtained from 'Börsen på väg ut ur Sverige', *Dagens Nyheter*, 6 August 1995.

24 For a more detailed discussion of the different theories within the subject area, and of the different arguments used to support the gradual internationalization of the firm, see, for example, Kjell Nordström, *The Internationalization Process of the Firm: Searching for New Patterns and Explanations* (Stockholm: Institute of International Business, 1991); Bertil Ohlin, Per-Ove Hesselbom and Per Magnus Wijkman (eds), *The International Allocation of Economic Activity* (London: Macmillan, 1977).

25 *Långtidsutredningen 1995*, SOU 1995: 4 (Stockholm: Fritzes, 1995), 114.

26 Jan-Evert Nilsson, 'Svensk massa- och pappersindustri i förändring', Industridepartementet Ds 1991: 35 (Stockholm: Department of Industry, 1991).

27 Robert B. Reich, *The Work of Nations: Preparing Ourselves for 21st-century Capitalism* (New York: Alfred A. Knopf, 1991).

28 George Soros, 'Kapitalismen går mot sammanbrott', *Dagens Nyheter*, 23 December 1997.

7

Towards an Ever Closer Union?

As we have seen, the state has come to be perceived as the natural entity since 1648, and the nation-state as its desirable manifestation in our century. However, in a longer historical perspective empires or unions of state-like entities have been more prominent. An argument can be made that 'laminated polyethnic empires' have been the norm for civilized governance throughout history, whereas ethnically uniform states have proved to be marginal and ephemeral.[1] The question then arises, whether the European nation-states of recent centuries may in the long run be supplanted by larger units, and whether the European Union is the harbinger of such a development. Before addressing questions formulated in the present and future tense, about the nature and prospects of the European Union, let us look back and search for possible precedents of today's efforts at uniting Europe.

Europe as a political project before 1648

In contemporary debates concerning the European Union and its expansion, proponents of an 'ever closer union' are inclined to characterize European integration as a political design with deep historical roots. A long-term perspective, however, does not lend unequivocal support to such a rendering of history. Neither during Antiquity nor in the Middle Ages was Europe an evident option, either as a territorial basis or as a common framework for political integration. The ancient Greeks did not perceive themselves as part of Europe. The focal point of Alexander the Great's empire lay further east, and the Romans were interested primarily in the Mediterranean region, not the European continent.

Under Charlemagne, around 800, the term Europe came into use as a label for the Carolingian realm, and thus designated not the continent, but the West Christian parts of Europe.[2] In the Middle Ages, however, the boundaries of this European core-area were extended northward through Germany to Scandinavia, and eastward to Poland, Bohemia–Moravia and Hungary. The West Christian foundation for a shared identity was also reinforced by the perceived threat from Islam in the south and by the rivalry with the Orthodox Church in the east.[3]

The medieval German emperors depicted their projects as a plan for European integration in quite a different way from the Carolingian monarchy. The German project, too, rested on a West Christian basis, concentrated in the East Frankish parts of the empire. Like the Roman popes, the German emperors claimed to be the highest authority in all West Christian territory, but neither claimant had the resources to outmanoeuvre his rival. To substantiate its territorial claims, the papacy produced a forged document 'proving' that in the fourth century, upon moving his residence from Rome to Byzantium, Emperor Constantine the Great had granted the pope political supremacy over all of western Europe. The deed of gift played a key role in the papacy's claims not only to religious, but to secular authority as well. Although the deed was revealed as a forgery in the late Middle Ages, the papacy continued to refer to it until the end of the eighteenth century.[4] By that time, the pope's secular authority had been reduced dramatically, not only in northern Europe, which was Protestant since the sixteenth century, but also in Catholic southern Europe.

Nor was the other major European project in the Middle Ages, the German Empire, particularly effective. This effort to unite Europe was wrecked not so much by the emperor's struggle against the pope, but by competition from the increasingly powerful territorial princes. The idea of an integrated western Europe lost its political relevance in the seventeenth and eighteenth centuries, when the emerging territorial states, based on dynastic politics, were considered the natural heirs to the large medieval imperial projects. Some of these West European states were instead able to build colonial empires outside Europe, in connection with the commercial expansion that introduced the modern era.

All of the medieval integration projects in Europe failed to resist the preponderant forces of fragmentation. The Roman Empire dissolved and was partitioned during the Great Migrations. The Carolingian Empire was unable to overcome the rigid structures of feudalism. The German emperor never gained control over the territorial princes and commercial cities, and the power of the papacy was eroded by the growing autonomy of the national churches and the secession of reformers from the Catholic community.

From Napoleon to Hitler: uniting Europe by force

In the years around 1800, Napoleon delivered the death blow to the ailing German empire and crowned himself emperor of a new domain, imbued with French values and governed regionally by members of his own family. Napoleon's project was short-lived, however, as newly aroused nationalist sentiments made the people unwilling to accept French dominance. Instead of transnational unity, the principle of national self-determination and the nation-state became prevalent ideologies and organizational forms.[5]

The Napoleonic empire (see Figure 7.1) can also be seen as another manifestation of traditional French expansionism, which aimed at enlarging

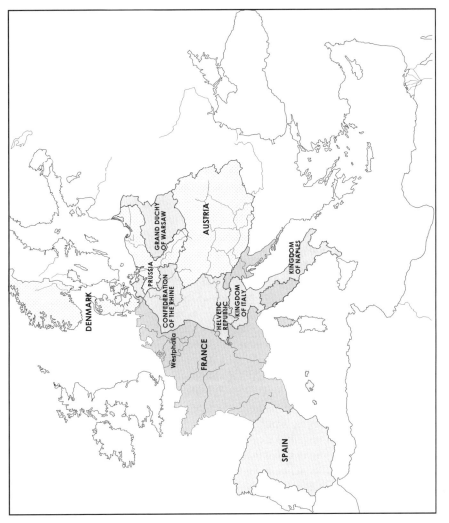

FIGURE 7.1   *The empire of Napoleon in 1812 (including satellite and allied states)*

France at the expense of her neighbours and was reflected, for instance, in the policies of Louis XIV. In Napoleon's Europe, there was no room for either Great Britain or Russia, let alone a union of independent territorial states.[6]

After the fall of Napoleon, it became clear that the medieval idea of a European community on a Christian foundation was not entirely defunct. The monarchies that had defeated Napoleon assumed a leading role in the reconstruction of Europe. In 1815, the Holy Alliance, the initiative of the Russian Tsar Alexander I, brought together European great powers of different religious denominations: the Orthodox tsar, the Catholic Austrian emperor and the Lutheran Prussian king. These were eventually joined in the Alliance by several other monarchs. Each ostensibly represented a 'Christian nation'.[7]

The Holy Alliance primarily had symbolic importance, as an expression of a common interest in preventing the recurrence of a devastating war in Europe. In practical terms, periodic great power conferences came to manage the new security system of Europe, based on a balance of power between the major European powers. In these, Great Britain, Prussia, Russia, Austria and, with certain initial restrictions, France were the leading actors. This 'Concert of Europe' provided an ideological context in which various security problems could be resolved in accordance with the interests of the great powers (for instance, in Italy, Spain and Portugal). However, it was eventually overshadowed by the rising tide of nationalism throughout Europe.[8] In the late nineteenth century, the balance of power structures evolved into complicated alliance systems that eventually proved incapable of preventing the outbreak of the First World War in 1914.

The European dilemma – to achieve stability and security within the framework of a disparate state system – seemed unsolvable in the first half of the twentieth century. The First World War resulted in the dissolution of four imperial creations: the German, the Russian, the Habsburg and the Ottoman.[9] The peace treaties were seen by the defeated powers as an imposed order, lacking moral legitimacy. This helped create a climate that was unfavourable to cooperation and unity, among victors and losers alike. The pan-European movement, the brainchild of Count Coudenhove-Kalergi, as well as concrete political measures, such as Aristide Briand's proposals for cooperation, lost all momentum amid the economic crisis in the early 1930s and the political radicalization in its aftermath.[10]

With a resounding rejection of democracy and liberalism, Adolf Hitler and the German Nazis launched a new, violent project to forcibly unite Europe, based on the principles of racial biology and the alleged superiority of the Germans over all other ethnic groups. The initial objective was to extend the German empire but, emboldened by repeated military victories in the first phase of the Second World War, the Nazi leadership drew up far-reaching plans for a Europe where the German master race would dominate inferior peoples and slaves in a community based on force and coercion.[11] Hitler's 'millennial' Reich (see Figure 7.2) proved more short-lived than Napoleon's

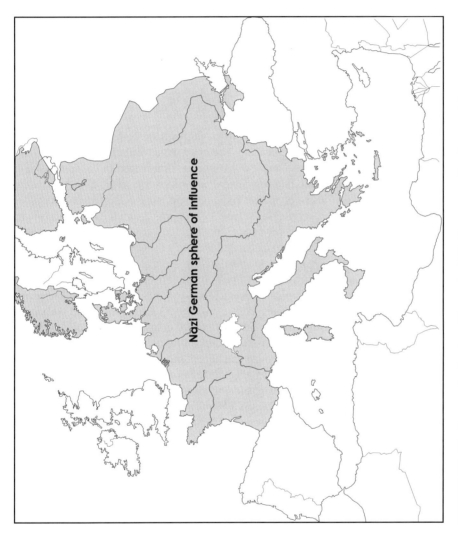

Nazi German sphere of influence

FIGURE 7.2 *The German domination of Europe in 1943 (Germany, militarily occupied states and territories, allied states)*

empire. A massive, concerted effort by Hitler's enemies was ultimately able to shatter the Nazi plans, but only at the cost of immeasurable human and material losses.

Hitler's and Napoleon's visions of a united Europe, though different in substance, had in common their roots in nationalistic power politics, where the interests of the state constituted the pillars of empire-building. Other states were forcibly to be joined to the new empire, without consideration of the wishes of the affected populations. The new regimes therefore lacked legitimacy in the eyes of their subjects and could survive only so long as they had sufficient military resources to subdue occupied territories.

European integration after the Second World War

If warfare and conquest failed to produce the uniting of Europe, could it be done through peaceful cooperation between rival European states? This question was addressed by a circle of influential statesmen in the wake of the Second World War. While lacking historical precedents, they could draw on a fairly rich set of literature propagating, and proposing plans for, cooperation between the European territorial states. Pervading themes in this literature were the overriding concern for peace, the wish to avoid hegemonic powers, and a preference for federation or confederation as the political expression of unity. These themes were elaborated in the seventeenth century by the influential English Quaker William Penn, in the eighteenth century by Abbé Saint-Pierre, François de Voltaire, Jean-Jacques Rousseau, Jeremy Bentham and Immanuel Kant, in the nineteenth century by Victor Hugo and Alexis de Tocqueville, and in the early twentieth century by Richard Coudenhove-Kalergi and Aristide Briand, to mention but a few.[12]

While the European movement gathered momentum after the Second World War, the Iron Curtain divided Europe into two political and ideological camps. The United States contributed to closer cooperation between West European states through the Marshall Plan of 1947 and the ensuing creation of OEEC as well as the establishment of NATO in 1949. Fear of communism and concern about too much dependence on the United States no doubt contributed to the renewed interest in European integration. But another immediate objective was to reconcile the archrivals Germany and France, which had been on opposite sides in so many devastating wars. This was the logic behind the creation of the European Coal and Steel Community (ECSC) in 1951, by which the production of coal and steel – the foundation of military power – was placed under supranational authority. The ECSC, in turn, was the precursor of the European Economic Community (EEC), which was established by the Treaty of Rome in 1957.

Even though Winston Churchill had made an eloquent albeit vague plea for a United States of Europe in his famous Zurich speech of 1946, the British balked at supranational solutions in subsequent negotiations. As a result, the ECSC and EEC included only 'the six', that is, France, Germany, Italy and the

Benelux countries. The early efforts at European integration thus largely coincided geographically with the Carolingian Empire, the cradle of the idea of Europe.[13] In 1959 'the outer seven' – Great Britain, Sweden, Norway, Denmark, Switzerland, Austria and Portugal – established the European Free Trade Association (EFTA), whose objectives were limited to the elimination of barriers to free trade among the member states.

The integration process

The evolution of European integration since then is reflected in changing designations and acronyms. In 1967 the political institutions of the ECSC, the EEC and Euratom were merged, and the term the European Community (EC) came into use. The Maastricht Treaty of 1992 brought into being the European Union (EU). Beyond altering labels, this development can be described in terms of widening geographical domain, expanding functional scope and enhanced institutional capacity.[14]

Geographical domain refers to the number of countries involved. Through four successive enlargements, the membership had grown from the original six to fifteen countries by the end of the twentieth century. In 1973 Great Britain, Denmark and Ireland joined. Greece became a member in 1981, followed by Spain and Portugal in 1986. Enlargement in 1995 added Austria, Finland and Sweden to the roster of member states. It was preceded by extensive negotiations between the EC and EFTA, which resulted in an agreement to create a joint European Economic Area (EEA). The agreement, which was originally designed as an alternative to enlargement, in fact came to serve as a stimulus to enlargement, as several of the EFTA countries drew the conclusion that the asymmetries of the EEA could only be overcome through full membership in the Union.[15] New applications for membership in the last half of the 1990s from Central and East European countries may eventually raise the number of member states from fifteen to twenty-seven.

Functional scope alludes to the issue-areas on the European agenda. To the original EEC scope of commercial, agricultural, competition and transport policies have been added several others, not foreseen in the Treaty of Rome, such as environmental issues. With the Single European Act (SEA) of 1986 everything that has to do with the realization of the internal market, such as regional policy and research and development, entered the European agenda. The Maastricht Treaty further expanded the scope to include monetary cooperation, education, culture, public health and a number of other issue-areas.

Institutional capacity has to do with the capacity to make, implement and enforce decisions. The development over time has been characterized by a growing role of the Commission, expanded applicability of majority voting in the Council of Ministers and extended legal authority of the European Court of Justice. Moreover, the EC/EU has acquired considerable external actor capacity, insofar as it participates in several international fora and negotiations, speaking on behalf of all member states.

The story of European integration – roughly but incompletely captured by the dimensions of domain, scope and institutional capacity – is not one of unidirectional evolution but rather one of twists and turns, of oscillations between 'Europhoria' and 'Eurosclerosis'. In the late 1970s and early 1980s, when Europe stagnated while the United States and Japan surged ahead in economic growth, the 'Eurosclerosis' rhetoric ran high. The end of the Cold War ushered in an era of intensified integration and pronounced 'Europhoria'. The new spirit was triggered by the Single European Act, signed in 1986, and came to be associated with the leadership of Jacques Delors, the dynamic President of the Commission. Today the European Union is the focus of attention of politicians, analysts and ordinary citizens alike to an unprecedented extent. There is a widespread perception that the European Union represents something new in world politics, at the same time as there is little consensus as to what kind of political creature it represents.

The opening phrase of the Treaty of Rome commits its signatories to 'an ever closer union among the peoples of Europe'. The phrasing points to two important aspects of the European integration project: first, that it involves a dynamic *process* with some kind of undefined union as the ultimate goal; secondly, the reference to 'peoples' indicates that *states* are not the only building blocs in this process. Thirty-five years into the process, the Treaty on European Union of 1992 (the so-called Maastricht Treaty) in its first paragraph refers to 'a new stage in the process of creating an ever closer union among the peoples of Europe'.

Of course, sceptics might argue that this continuity and sense of direction is primarily rhetorical and that European realities seldom live up to the proclaimed visions. There has always been an element of rhetorical or terminological inflation in the European project; the label 'European Community' came into official use before anything resembling a community existed, in the same way that a 'European Union' is prematurely proclaimed. Yet there is broad agreement among observers that the EU represents something new, something more than a temporary conglomerate of states pursuing their common interests.

What, then, is the nature of the phenomenon we are becoming used to calling the European Union? We tend to understand the unfamiliar with the help of familiar conceptual lenses. The two most common ones applied to the EU are to describe it either as an unusually ambitious *intergovernmental organization*, in principle limited to the pursuit of those tasks which are in the interest of the member states and which serve to protect and enhance their sovereign autonomy; or as a *supranational state* in the making, which is gradually taking over the functions traditionally performed by the member states.

At issue in the debate between proponents of the two simplified images of the EU is the role of the state. In the first perspective European states are still in command; they are the 'principals' which delegate varying degrees of authority to an 'agent', the EU, to use a vocabulary in current use.[16] In the second perspective the state is withering, to be replaced eventually by supranational structures. The end result will be a peacefully forged union of an unprecedented kind. Let us take a closer look at the two contradictory perspectives.

The EU as an international organization

To be sure, the EU has several traits in common with traditional inter-governmental organizations. For example, the ultimate decision-making authority of the Council of Ministers and the preparatory work done by diplomatic state representatives in Committee of Permanent Representatives (COREPER) are familiar stuff for students of international organization. Insofar as decision-making is characterized by negotiations between member states that search for their 'lowest common denominator', the EU does not differ significantly from other international organizations.

Some observers, like Alan Milward,[17] even argue that the creation of the European Community strengthened and consolidated the state rather than weakened it. Cooperation made it possible to carry out reforms jointly that the individual states would not have managed on their own. The term 'pooled sovereignty' is often used to indicate a gain rather than a loss of state capacity as a result of European integration. Similarly, 'liberal intergovernmentalists' maintain that all major or 'history-making' decisions in the EC/EU have in effect been bargains between the most powerful states.[18] Some even contend that the European Union fundamentally rests on a kind of German-French hegemony. While usually seeing Germany as the stronger partner, proponents of this view hold that without agreements between Germany and France nothing can be achieved. In this perspective, the smaller member states are reduced to supporting cast or mediators between the great powers.[19]

However, there are several aspects of the EU which do not square with our generalized understanding of *Realpolitik* as usual or intergovernmental organizations. The broad powers of the Commission to initiate policy and to monitor the implementation of Community law go far beyond the functions of other international secretariats. Moreover, the Commission is 'transnationally promiscuous', insofar as it considers itself free to establish relations with various non-governmental actors, in contrast to orthodox secretariats.[20] The European Court of Justice (ECJ), through the quiet accumulation of decisions, has established the supremacy of Community over national law and set precedents that can be used to resolve other disputes. This, too, is unprecedented in the history of intergovernmental organization. And the directly elected European Parliament is another repudiation of the intergovernmental logic.

These three bodies – the Commission, the ECJ and the European Parliament – are therefore commonly referred to as *supranational*. They enjoy a degree of autonomy from member-state governments, insofar as they have the capacity to define and pursue a politically relevant agenda. Furthermore, they are capable of constraining the behaviour of member states in specific policy domains. In short, they are more than 'passive structures', merely reflecting the interests of the member states, which sets the EU apart from other intergovernmental organizations.[21]

The EU as an emerging state

The tendency to emphasize the supranational aspects and thus see the EU as more or less 'state-like' is equally widespread. The EU is then usually seen as a state – or even a superpower[22] – in the making, and the disagreements concern what kind of state is emerging.

The most common conceptualization is in terms of a *federation*. Federalism was indeed an important source of inspiration for the 'founding fathers' of the Community project. And the EU shares some general characteristics with large federal systems, such as the United States and Germany, including a distribution of competencies across multiple levels of government and the inclusion of heterogeneous sub-units in a common institutional framework.[23] Both the American and European founding fathers 'were forced to confront the problem of bringing together on equal terms states that were manifestly unequal in size, population, economic prospects, religious commitments, and social dispositions'.[24] Both were divided between northern and southern traditions. However, Europe's differences in language and ancient sense of distinct national identification make integration far more difficult than in America. Nor do European leaders have a vision of a comprehensive national union comparable to that of Madison and Hamilton.[25]

It has been suggested that the European Union has followed the German rather than the American federal model. Common traits include dominance of the executive over legislative institutions, broad areas of joint competencies of various levels of government, incorporation of non-governmental actors into decision-making processes, and policy-making through negotiations between politically autonomous units in a political culture of compromise and consensus.[26]

On the whole, however, it is difficult to envision the EU as an embryonic federation. Whereas the actual distribution of powers and competencies between central and outlying units may vary across different federal systems, a federal order presupposes an explicit *Kompetenzkatalog*. This is missing in the European Union, where the relationship between the states and the EU is not legally fixed and static, but dynamic and intensely political.[27] Moreover, one common feature of most federal states is that foreign policy and defence are the prerogatives of the central, federal level rather than the sub-units. In the EU the member states retain these functions and are reluctant to delegate them to supranational bodies.

If not a federation, what kind of 'state' might the EU be or become? The academic literature proffers various answers. Paul Taylor, drawing on Arend Lijphart's work on 'consociational democracy', suggests that *consociationalism* may be a conceptual lens through which to view the EU.[28] Consociation implies four aspects: first, the existence of segmented, inwardly oriented groups; second, a cartel of elites of the various segments who are continuously involved in decision-making; third, political elites have veto rights over decisions of which they disapprove; fourth, the various segments have proportionate representation among the major institutions. Consociationalism is a way to maintain stability in a situation of actual or potential mutual tension.

The consociational model highlights crucial aspects of the EU. The political cultures of the member states are very heterogeneous; and the EU remains an elite project, insofar as only political elites participate in day-to-day politics and thus are the agents who have the ability to transcend cleavages and to accommodate the divergent interests and demands of the subcultures. Central institutions are compelled 'to adopt more frequently, and at an earlier stage of the decision-making process, the role of umpire'.[29]

Another conceptualization views the EU as a *regulatory state*, that is, a state that 'does not engage substantially in the redistributive, stabilization, and symbolic functions of government' and that 'relies on the administrative structures of states already in place to carry out its own policies rather than on independent ones created at the supranational level'. The regulatory state lacks a neat pyramidal structure of power or constitutional statement of the relations between citizen and state. By concentrating on 'the control and management of international externalities', it can manage with a very small revenue base. The extractive capacity of EU institutions is very modest: the EU spends only about 1.3 per cent of the combined GDP (Gross Domestic Product) of its member states.[30] The regulatory state, in short, is not the Westphalian state, the extractive state or the social democratic state, nor is it a federal state in the traditional sense. It is a construction that relies on a political division of labour between member states, focusing on social and redistributive policy, and the EU, focusing on regulatory policy.

The elusive nature of the EU

While conceptualizations in terms of federal, consociational or regulatory statehood may capture important aspects of the EU, they fail to give a comprehensive picture of the union. Most theoretical characterizations of the EU, laments one observer, 'have assumed caricatured shapes and have overly simplified very complex processes'.[31] One is reminded of the old story about the Indian prince who let learned but blind men describe an elephant and obtained totally different accounts depending on what part of the elephant they happened to touch. Similarly, prominent parts or aspects of the EU are magnified to represent the whole in simplified theoretical conceptualizations.

Today, students of the EU tend to agree that their object of study represents a political order based neither on intergovernmental organization nor on a supranational state; it is neither a *Staatenbund* nor a *Bundesstaat*.[32] Yet, as we have seen, the EU contains elements of both. While the EU rests on intergovernmental bargaining and decision-making, this is 'embedded in processes that are provoked and sustained by the expansion of transnational society, the pro-integrative activities of supranational organizations, and the growing density of supranational rules'.[33] Traditional models of polities do not seem to fit this new, unprecedented phenomenon.

Thus, the EU has given rise to inventive labels, such as 'neo-medieval', 'postmodern', or 'post-sovereign'.[34] It has been considered the first 'multi-perspectival polity' to emerge in the modern era.[35] While not necessarily adding to clarity, such labels reflect the realization that the emerging political structure does not correspond to the traditional format of territorial sovereignty and exclusivity but contains elements of diffuse and overlapping authority. They also raise the question whether the EU is better understood in functional rather than territorial terms. The distinction between 'three pillars' with different authority claims and decision rules is central to the self-understanding of the European Union.[36] Different policy fields have taken on different characteristics, which means that the EU may look different from different vantage points. In our terms, the EU is difficult to place squarely in the territorial field of tension.

There are several reasons why the EU is so difficult to catch in available theoretical nets. Most observers point to the *fluidity* and *complexity* of the union. The EC/EU is in constant transformation. There has been no time when the EC/EU has not been contemplating or undertaking some kind of extension of the existing order, with successive projects of 'deepening' and 'widening' the union.[37] The EU therefore should be understood as a *process* rather than a frozen institution. It is an 'experimental' process, moreover, that is not uni-directional.[38] Periods of 'Eurosclerosis' alternate with periods of 'Europhoria' in unpredictable patterns. This process of change affects not only EU institutions but also member states and their relationships with the EU. At different times, the EU may seem to be moving alternately toward the state, union, region and network mode of organizing territory, to refer back to our territorial field of tension.

The other factor that renders simple conceptualizations extraordinarily difficult is the complexity of the political apparatus and processes in the EU. The complexity pertains not only to the multitude of levels (local, regional, state, community) and participating actors (public as well as private, national as well as transnational, political as well as economic), but also to the fact that the EU is a political construction that strives to balance territorial and non-territorial claims.[39]

Does the EU, because of its fluidity and complexity, defy theoretical fixation? Was Jacques Delors right when he once characterized the EU as 'un objet politique non-identifié'?[40] No historian, political scientist or geographer would admit that, but there is greater humility, combined with avoidance of facile analogies with pre-existing political orders, in contemporary scholarship. One noticeable tendency is to use the term *governance* in characterizing the EU, in order to avoid associations with statehood. 'Government without statehood' is precisely the title of the concluding chapter of a recent textbook.[41]

Governance, it will be recalled, is about 'coordinating multiple players in a complex setting of mutual dependence' and refers to 'the patterns that emerge from governing activities' among these actors.[42] It is 'independent of the existence of a central authority and beyond the territorial congruence of those who govern with those who are subject to governance'.[43] James March and Johan P. Olsen's observation that 'governance becomes less a matter of engineering than of gardening' is quoted by students of the EU.[44]

Terms like *multi-level* or *multi-tiered* are frequently used to characterize governance in the EU. Scholars speak of a 'multi-level polity',[45] 'governance in a dynamic multi-level system',[46] 'a multi-tiered system of government',[47] and several variants of the same theme. Of course, these are mere labels. Yet they point to some significant features of the EU as a political system. Beyond indicating that the EU policy process takes place at several different levels, from the local to the supranational, notions of multi-level governance draw our attention to *negotiations* as key processes and *networks* as key structures. Negotiation processes at various levels are central to governance in the complex and dynamic EU, where the actors are not ordered hierarchically in a system of superordination and subordination. And the diffuse formal political structure of the EU gives rise to more informal structures; thus, the EU can be seen as a complex of policy networks, to use the term introduced in the previous chapter.

Negotiations in the European Union

The EU has been characterized as a 'negotiated order',[48] as an 'integrated system of multi-level bargaining',[49] as a 'permanent negotiation institute',[50] and as a 'multilateral inter-bureaucratic negotiation marathon'.[51] These and other characterizations bespeak the centrality of negotiations in the complex and fluid EU policy process. In Helen Wallace's words,

> The European policy process has been peculiarly dependent on negotiation as a predominant mode of reaching agreements on policy and of implementing policies once agreed. Much of the literature is misleading in suggesting that the model is either a negotiation model or something else. The analytical question is what characterizes the negotiation process, not whether it exists.[52]

One bone of contention among students of the EU concerns the role of states in the negotiation processes. One school of thought claims that the governments of member countries are the key negotiators. In that sense EU negotiations do not differ in kind from other international negotiations. In this view, the national interests and relative power of member states determine negotiation outcomes which typically have the character of 'the lowest common denominator', that is, they rarely go beyond what the least cooperative bargaining partner wishes to concede.[53] Another school points to the informality and accessibility of EU negotiations and emphasizes the multitude of actors rather than the predominance of states. Government representatives get involved in coalition building with lobbyists, experts and NGOs. Moreover, there is room for supranational leadership by the Commission and the European Parliament. Negotiation outcomes thus do not merely reflect the lowest common denominator among the most powerful member states, but may involve an 'upgrading of the common interest'.[54]

Which perspective describes the EU realities best? The best answer is probably that they depict different aspects of the same reality. In other words, it is a question of 'both–and' rather than 'either–or'. The formal interstate framework is a prerequisite for informal negotiations in networks, at the same time as these informal negotiations represent an important and necessary complement to intergovernmental deliberations. Another, complementary answer is 'it depends'. The character of negotiations depends on the circumstances. For instance, major, 'history-making' decisions, such as the Maastricht Treaty, are preceded by intergovernmental negotiations, whereas the many specific decisions in specialized issue areas, which are made continuously in Brussels, involve informal negotiations to a much larger extent. It is the combination of grand bargains and day-to-day negotiations that constitutes governance in the EU.

What, then, are some of the characteristics of negotiation processes in the EU, given their scope and variety? Obviously, EU negotiations are examples of multilateral negotiations, which are becoming increasingly common in contemporary diplomacy, but which have not been conceptualized and theorized to the same extent as bilateral negotiations in the academic literature.[55] At the same time, EU negotiations differ from traditional international negotiations in several respects. First, EU negotiations tend to be *informal*, only rarely taking place within formal institutions.[56] Secondly, 'no single individual is involved in the decision-making process from beginning to end'.[57] In contrast to other international negotiations, where the same sets of negotiators normally take part in a given negotiation process from beginning to end, the various stages of EU negotiations involve different sets of actors and move between different levels and fora.

Another important trait of EU negotiations is that they are *continuous*. It is difficult to pinpoint the beginning and end of bargaining processes in the EU. The outcome of one round of negotiations creates a new bargaining situation, and the parties are continually in contact with each other. One celebrated theory holds that the prospects for cooperation increase the longer the 'shadow of the future' is.[58] If the negotiating parties know that their relationship is not temporary but lasting, they are less tempted to seize opportunities to make one-sided gains at the expense of the others than if the negotiations concern a well-defined issue during a limited time span. The infinity of EU negotiations, accentuated by the lack of any exit clause in the Treaty of Rome, would make for a more cooperative climate than in other international negotiations, according to this theory.

Students of the EU tend to agree that the realization that the parties will be in continuous negotiations, with no endgame and no exit option in sight, does indeed facilitate cooperative solutions. Knowing that their relationship is not merely a temporary but a durable one, negotiators 'think twice before ruthlessly seeking to maximize their individual interests'.[59] While this does not imply consensus on values or on outcomes, it does imply a consensus that collaboration will produce mutual efficiency gains. Thus, despite considerable and bitter conflicts, the game continues to be played in order to secure mutual gains or avoid individual losses.[60]

A related aspect concerns the *institutionalized* nature of EU negotiations. This means that there are norms and rules impinging on the negotiations and persistent negotiation patterns over time. For example, protection of the minority is an EU *norm* which is reflected, *inter alia*, in the voting rules of the Council of Ministers. The principle of *juste retour* governs EU negotiations to a considerable extent.[61] To the extent that this norm permeates negotiations, we may hypothesize that small states have more influence than their size would indicate.

Formal EU decision *rules* may affect negotiations as well. For one thing, many issues can ultimately be decided by voting rather than by consensus, in contrast to most other multilateral international settings. A qualified majority may then decide an issue in the final analysis. Negotiation theorists have coined the acronym BATNA (Best Alternative to Negotiated Agreement). The idea is that negotiators use the consequences of no agreement as the yardstick against which possible negotiation outcomes are evaluated; only if a negotiated solution is better than their BATNA will they agree.[62] Applied to the EU, the expected outcome of an ultimate vote represents an obvious alternative to a negotiated agreement. For states and coalitions with great voting strength, majority decisions are always an alternative to a negotiated agreement. This can be used as a tactical instrument, and anticipation of ultimate voting may influence negotiations. For states and coalitions with less voting strength it means an imperative to negotiate seriously to modify the majority proposal, as it is better to agree to a less unacceptable proposal than to be outvoted. Merely obstructing the majority proposal makes sense only if the ultimate decision rule is unanimity. Thus, 'majority rule lowers the costs of cooperation which stem from the danger of non-decision'.[63] It is assumed to speed up negotiations by enhancing anticipation among the majority of possible opposing coalitions, while at the same time functioning as a 'shadow of hierarchy' for the minority.[64]

Persistent patterns in the institutionalized EU negotiations have to do with so-called 'path dependence'. Once certain choices are made, they constrain future possibilities and determine the range of options available to policy-makers, in terms of both policy substance and political process. Thus, any round of negotiations is constrained by the outcome of previous negotiations, at the same time as it may contribute to the institutionalization process by framing future negotiations.[65]

In sum, the multitude of issues along with different ultimate decision rules engenders great variability among negotiation processes in the EU. Even if there is no one typical EU negotiation pattern, certain characteristic tendencies can be discerned. First, the continuous and institutionalized nature of EU negotiations makes for a considerably greater probability of cooperative solutions than in other international negotiations. Secondly, the informality of EU negotiations and the variety of participants, in combination with prevailing norms of *juste retour*, imply that relative state power is a determinant of outcomes to a lesser degree than in other international negotiations. Thirdly, 'path dependence' is a significant aspect of continuous and institutionalized EU negotiations, insofar as each negotiation episode is conditioned by previous negotiations and agreements.

Networks in the European Union

In the wake of formal organizations – especially complex ones like the EU – informal networks typically emerge. International cooperation often requires more than state-to-state interaction, and informal networks provide access points for a variety of non-state actors. In the European case, moreover, the Treaty of Rome created a social and political space that intentionally emphasized and encouraged transnational economic interests and exchange across state boundaries.[66] The EU thus represents a new mode of governance which rests on continuous interaction, where 'instead of being objects of governance, actors in European networks, be they interest groups, enterprises, regions or research institutes, become partners of joint problem-solving'.[67] EU decisions are 'preceded and accompanied by intensive processes of consultation, information exchange, interest accommodation and alliance formation in the framework of policy networks'.[68] The EU has even been described as a 'hothouse' for different types of networks.[69] The proliferation of networks in the EU can be seen as a condition as well as a consequence of the fluidity and complexity of the formal European framework. As the dispersion of power renders hierarchical governance impossible, networks provide an alternative mode of policy coordination.[70]

> Bargaining through networks in a densely structured game reduces frictions and produces results for which the formal system may be ill attuned, even on ostensibly formal matters such as easier implementation and enforcement of laws. It allows for wide, flexible participation; it reduces inconsistencies; it gives rise to conventions, rather than formal rules, which can be adapted more easily over time.[71]

Throughout the different negotiation stages, issues are dealt with – at times simultaneously – at national, subnational and supranational levels. Rather than being neatly separated, these different levels or arenas are linked by transnational networks.[72] An EU composed of 'an elaborate set of networks', in the words of former Belgian Foreign Minister Willy Claes, helps Europe 'to reconcile its undeniable diversity with its equally undeniable common interests and aspirations'.[73] The EU has become the centre of a vast system of expert-based networks. To understand this new polity, we need to get rid of notions of hierarchy inherent in the Westphalian state model.

The diffusion of networks obviously contributes to the informality of EU negotiations, noted above. According to one observer, 'subterfuge' – the creative use of informal strategies to avoid deadlock in formal policy-making – has become second nature to the European Community.[74] One senior Brussels official has argued that 'if you were to stick to the formal procedures, it would take ten years every time' and that 'the more there is disagreement, the more the informal is necessary'.[75]

Interpersonal links are considered important in the continuous, institutionalized EU negotiations. In the words of a Commission cabinet official:

> The European Community is a very strange animal. One would expect it to be run on a very businesslike basis, like a major multinational company. Instead of that, it is run like a small, local theatrical society in that it is relationships between people at different levels that allow it to work.[76]

EU networks tend to transcend organizational boundaries, involving governmental as well as non-governmental organizations (NGOs), national as well as regional and subnational organizations. A 1992 inventory identified some 3,000 special interest groups of various kinds in Brussels, employing up to 10,000 persons – approximately the same number as Commission officials, excluding translators and secretarial staff.[77] These groups represent business interests (cross-sectoral organizations such as the European Round-table of Industrialists, sectoral organizations and individual firms), labour interests, public interests (for example, environmental and consumer groups) as well as territorial interests (regions and localities).[78] The EU, in short, provides an unusual abundance of access points to the policy-making process for interested actors. And several types of actors have accumulated significant political resources. There is, in other words, great potential for networks spanning a variety of organizations and individuals.

Furthermore, EU networks are relatively non-hierarchical. The element of hierarchy that is often noted is the Commission's 'linking-pin' role. While there are multiple points of access, the Commission enjoys a privileged position by being the only participant that is constituted as a community body and by serving as 'process manager' – setting the timing, prescribing consultation procedures and deciding which interest representation will be recognized.[79] Networks usually coalesce around the Commission, and Commission representatives are often the most permanent and central participants in negotiation processes. Moreover, the Commission is known to frequently pursue a deliberate networking strategy, actively encouraging informal sectoral links and empowering – or building coalitions with – transnational and subnational groups.[80] These groups thus may become vehicles of 'reverse lobbying', supporting the Commission's policies by putting pressure on governments, business associations and other actors at the national level.[81]

This points to important elements of resource dependency in EU networks. Several NGOs are financially dependent on funds from the Commission which, in turn, needs these NGOs as coalition partners in policy-making. In brief, the 'bureaucratic deficit' in terms of limited personnel places the various Directorates-General (DGs) of the Commission in mutual resource dependencies *vis-à-vis* other bureaucracies and organizations. In some of these symbiotic relationships, it is difficult to disentangle who controls whom.

In sum, multi-level governance in the European Union appears to rely on negotiations as the predominant mode of collective decision-making and takes place in an organizational setting that encourages continuous, informal contacts and networking. In terms of our territorial field of tension, the EU today emerges as neither a full-blown state nor a perfect union, but rather as a complex set of networks. Manuel Castells, for example, uses the term 'network state' to describe the European Union.[82] As it is in constant flux, it seems appropriate, in conclusion, to speculate about the EU's possible future development.

Conclusions

It is obviously extremely difficult to encapsulate the EU into any simple categorization. It has developed from an interstate treaty to a complex system of governance. In its present form, it represents a 'pioneering phenomenon', an 'attempt to provide a political form for a globalized world'.[83] If, as we have argued, the EU has developed in the direction of the network sphere in our territorial field of tension, then what about the future? Let us take a look at current and future developments in terms of the initial categories of geographical domain, functional scope and institutional capacity.

Enlargement of the geographical domain in Eastern Europe and the Mediterranean raises a number of thorny questions concerning the decision-making structures and redistributive policies of the EU. One pertinent question following from our analysis is whether a dramatic increase in the number of member states with different political and administrative traditions will undermine the network-like character of the EU. There is a limit to the number of nodes and links effective networks can encompass.

The steadily widening functional scope of the EU requires legitimacy in terms of popular support. Criticism of the 'democratic deficit' and the relative lack of accountability tends to increase with expanding EU responsibilities. The initial Danish 'no' and the French '*petit oui*' in the referendums on the Maastricht Treaty are harbingers of the limits to popular support of an essentially elite project. The implementation of the European Monetary Union (EMU) is an important touchstone, insofar as it appears to challenge the current division of labour between the EU and the member states. While a number of state functions have gradually been taken over by the EU, member states have retained their monopoly concerning control of the means of coercion, fiscal powers and locus of popular identity. To a certain extent, the EMU threatens the fiscal autonomy of the states. Perhaps even more importantly, national currencies are for many citizens closely associated with national identity. This means that the introduction of the Euro may have a symbolic and psychological significance beyond the economic effects foreseen by its architects.

The EMU also reanimates the perennial discussion of 'variable geometry', 'multi-speed Europe', 'flexible integration', 'Europe of concentric circles', 'Europe *à la carte*', or whatever the term in fashion may be. The discussion concerns the possibility that member states participate to differing extents in European integration projects, which has already become a reality with the EMU and the Schengen Agreements on the relaxation of border controls within the EU and the creation of common external border controls. In each area, the emerging political landscape is that of a core of enthusiastic integrationists and a periphery of reluctant ones. If we compare the EMU and Schengen, there is some, but not perfect, overlap between these categories of states. The Amsterdam Treaty of 1997 explicitly refers to flexible integration as a way toward the future, as it opens up the possibility for a majority of member states to establish closer cooperation between themselves without the participation of other member states. If this becomes a widespread phenomenon, it no doubt adds to the complexity of the EU and to the difficulty of defining it in unequivocal terms.

The institutional capacity of the EU, finally, may be weakened by future enlargements. The common wisdom is that a growing number of participants aggravates the capacity to make, implement and enforce decisions. Thorny issues of voting weights and the national distribution of commissioners need to be solved in connection with the envisaged Eastern and Mediterranean enlargement. From another angle, the expanding external actor capacity of the EU, epitomized by the Common Foreign and Security Policy (CFSP), may prove to be a mixed blessing. As its external position typically rests on complex multi-layered compromises among member states and other interested parties, which are next to impossible to renegotiate, the EU will often be a rather inflexible partner in international negotiations and deliberations.

The bottom line is that the European Union remains a constantly changing phenomenon. Moreover, the EU looks different, not only depending on when you look at it, but also depending on which issue and which national vantage point you select. The variability and institutional vagueness of the EU, we have argued, make for the proliferation of informal networks. In its present stage of development, the EU can thus be seen as an elaborate set of policy networks. Of course, our emphasis on the contingent and variable nature of the European Union does not imply that the range of possible future developments is unlimited. The EU is in a process of institutionalization, which means that its *acquis* – the accumulated obligations, commitments and conventions stipulated under the treaties and legislation over the years – creates a considerable degree of 'path dependence'. Yet within those limits, there is room for alternative futures.

NOTES

1 William H. McNeill, 'Introductory Historical Commentary', in *The Fall of Great Powers*, ed. Geir Lundestad (Oslo: Scandinavian University Press, 1994), 4–5.

2 Rune Johansson, 'Idéer om Europa – Europa som idé', in *Europa – Historiens återkomst*, 3rd edn, ed. Sven Tägil (Hedemora: Gidlunds, 1998), 54ff.

3 Louis Halphen, *Charlemagne et l'empire carolingien* (Paris: Albin Michel, 1947); Gerd Tellenbach, *The Church in Western Europe from the Tenth to the Early Twelfth Century* (Cambridge: Cambridge University Press, 1993).

4 Horst Fuhrmann (eds), *Das Constitutum Constantini* (Hannover: Hahnsche Buchhandlung, 1968).

5 Øyvind Østerud, *Nasjonenes selvbestemmelsesrett* (Oslo: Universitetsforlaget, 1984).

6 See, for example, Jean-Baptiste Duroselle, *L'Idée d'Europe dans l'histoire* (Paris: Denoël, 1965).

7 On the Holy Alliance, see, for instance, Francis Ley, *Alexandre 1er et sa Sainte Alliance (1811–1825)* (Paris: Fischbacher, 1975).

8 On the nineteenth-century balance-of-power philosophy, see, for instance, Carsten Holbraad, *The Concert of Europe: A Study in German and British International Theory, 1815–1914* (London: Longman, 1970).

9 On the dissolution of empires, see Max Engman (ed.), *När imperier faller: Studier kring riksupplösningar och nya stater* (Stockholm: Atlantis, 1994); Paul M. Kennedy, *The Rise and Fall of the Great Powers* (New York: Random House, 1987); Shmuel N. Eisenstadt (ed.), *The Decline of Empires* (Englewood Cliffs, NJ: Prentice Hall, 1967); Geir Lundestad (ed.), *The Fall of Great Powers*, (Oslo: Universitetsforlaget; Oxford: Oxford University Press, 1994).

10 Rolf H. Foerster, *Europa: Geschichte einer politischen Idee* (Munich: Nymphenburg, 1967).

11 See, for instance, Andreas Hillgruber, *Hitlers Strategie: Politik und Kriegführung 1940–1941* (Frankfurt am Main: Bernhard & Graefe, 1965).

12 Cf. Johansson, 'Idéer om Europa'.

13 Ibid., 83.

14 Cf. Finn Laursen, 'On Studying European Integration: Integration Theory and Political Economy', in *The Political Economy of European Integration*, ed. Finn Laursen (The Hague: Kluwer Law International, 1995), 7–9.

15 Cf. Thomas Pedersen, *European Union and the EFTA Countries: Enlargement and Integration* (London: Pinter, 1994).

16 See, for example, Mark A. Pollack, 'Delegation, Agency, and Agenda Setting in the European Community', *International Organization*, 51 (1997), 99–134; Mark A. Pollack, 'The Engines of Integration? Supranational Autonomy and Influence in the European Union', in *European Integration and Supranational Governance*, eds Wayne Sandholtz and Alec Stone Sweet (Oxford: Oxford University Press, 1998); Karen J. Alter, 'Who Are the "Masters of the Treaty"?: European Governments and the European Court of Justice', *International Organization*, 52 (1998), 121–47.

17 Alan S. Milward, *The European Rescue of the Nation-State* (Berkeley, CA: University of California Press, 1992).

18 Andrew Moravcsik, 'Negotiating the Single European Act: National Interests and Conventional Statecraft in the European Community', *International Organization*, 45 (1991), 19–56. Whereas Moravcsik, in this seminal article, used the term 'inter-governmental institutionalism' to characterize his approach, 'liberal intergovern-mentalism' has later become the prevalent label. See, for example, Andrew Moravcsik,

'Preferences and Power in the European Community: A Liberal Intergovernmentalist Approach', *Journal of Common Market Studies*, 31 (1993), 473–524.

19 See Thomas Pedersen, *Germany, France and the Integration of Europe: A Realist Interpretation* (London and New York: Pinter, 1998).

20 Jeremy Richardson, 'Policy-Making in the EU: Interests, Ideas and Garbage Cans of Primeval Soup', in *European Union: Power and Policy-Making*, ed. Jeremy Richardson (London/New York: Routledge, 1996), 10.

21 For a thorough discussion of the meaning of the term 'supranational', see Alec Stone Sweet and Wayne Sandholtz, 'Integration, Supranational Governance, and the Institutionalization of the European Polity', in Stone Sweet and Sandholtz (eds), *European Integration and Supranational Governance*, especially pp. 8–11.

22 For an early formulation of the superpower thesis, see Johan Galtung, *EF: en supermagt i verdenssamfundet* (Copenhagen: Ejler; Oslo: Universitetsforlaget, 1972).

23 Craig Parsons, 'European Integration and American Federalism: A Comparative Perspective', in *European Integration and American Federalism: A Comparative Perspective*, eds Richard Herr and Steven Weber (Berkeley, CA: IAS [International and Area Studies] Publication, 1996), 1.

24 Richard M. Abrams, 'The Relevance of American Federalism to the European Union: From Confederation to Federal Union to Nation-State', in Herr and Weber (eds), ibid., 15.

25 Ibid., 15–16.

26 Cf., e.g., Fritz W. Scharpf, 'The Joint-Decision Trap: Lessons from German Federalism and European Integration', *Public Administration*, 66 (1988), 239–78; Parsons, 'European Integration and American Federalism', 4.

27 Janne Haaland Matlary, 'Internal Market Regime or New Polity Model: Whither the European Union?', Working paper no. 26, ARENA (Advanced Research on the Europeanisation of the Nation-state, Oslo, 1996), 7.

28 Paul Taylor, 'Consociationalism and Federalism as Approaches to International Integration', in *Frameworks for International Co-operation*, eds A.J.R. Groom and Paul Taylor (London: Pinter, 1990). The notion of consociationalism was originally developed in Arend Lijphart, *The Politics of Accommodation: Pluralism and Democracy in the Netherlands* (Berkeley/Los Angeles, CA: University of California Press, 1968).

29 Taylor, 'Consociationalism', 179.

30 James A. Caporaso, 'The European Union and Forms of State: Westphalian, Regulatory or Post-Modern?', *Journal of Common Market Studies*, 34 (1996), 39. The characterization of the EU as a regulatory state was first expressed in Giandomenico Majone, 'Regulatory Federalism in the European Community', *Environment and Planning C: Government and Policy*, 10 (1992), 299–316.

31 James A. Caporaso, 'The European Union between Federalism and Regulation', in Herr and Weber (eds), *European Integration and American Federalism*, 34.

32 Cf. Philippe C. Schmitter, 'Imagining the Future of the Euro-Polity with the Help of New Concepts', in Gary Marks, Fritz W. Scharpf, Philippe C. Schmitter and Wolfgang Streeck, *Governance in the European Union* (London: Sage, 1996), 131; Haaland Matlary, 'Whither the European Union?', 6.

33 Stone Sweet and Sandholtz, 'Integration, Supranational Governance', 5.

34 See, e.g., Ole Waever, 'Identity, Integration and Security: Solving the Sovereignty Puzzle in E.U. Studies', *Journal of International Affairs*, 48 (1995), 389–431.

35 John Gerard Ruggie, 'Territoriality and Beyond: Problematizing Modernity in International Relations', *International Organization*, 47 (1993), 172.

36 The first pillar encompasses the treaties establishing the EEC, ECSC and Euratom;

questions related to the single market and the Common Agricultural Policy (CAP) are prominent contemporary policy areas. First-pillar issues are generally decided by qualified majority in the Council of Ministers. The Common Foreign and Security Policy (CFSP) constitutes the second pillar, and the third pillar comprises justice and home affairs. Unanimity is the prevalent decision rule on second- and third-pillar issues.

37 Michael Smith, 'The European Union and Concepts of Negotiated Order in Europe' (paper presented at the annual conference of the British International Studies Association, Durham, December 1996).

38 Helen Wallace, 'Politics and Policy in the EU: The Challenge of Governance', in *Policy-Making in the European Union*, eds Helen and William Wallace (Oxford: Oxford University Press, 1996), 3.

39 Caporaso, 'The European Union between Federalism and Regulation', 36.

40 Quoted in Philippe C. Schmitter, 'Examining the Present Euro-Polity with the Help of Past Theories', in Marks et al., *Governance in the European Union*, 1.

41 William Wallace, 'Government without Statehood: The Unstable Equilibrium', in *Policy-Making in the European Union*, eds Helen and William Wallace (Oxford: Oxford University Press, 1996).

42 Beate Kohler-Koch, 'The Strength of Weakness: The Transformation of Governance in the EU', in *The Future of the Nation State*, eds Sverker Gustavsson and Leif Lewin (Stockholm: Nerenius & Santérus, 1995), 188.

43 Markus Jachtenfuchs and Beate Kohler-Koch, 'The Transformation of Governance in the European Union' (paper presented at the Fourth Biennial Conference of the European Community Studies Association, Charleston, SC, May 1995), 5.

44 James G. March and Johan P. Olsen, 'Organizing Political Life: What Administrative Reorganization Tells Us about Government', *American Political Science Review*, 77 (1983), 292; quoted in Kohler-Koch, 'Strength of Weakness', 190; and Jachtenfuchs and Kohler-Koch, 'Transformation of Governance', 9.

45 Marks et al., *Governance in the European Union*, vii.

46 Jachtenfuchs and Kohler-Koch, 'Transformation of Governance', 1.

47 Kohler-Koch, 'Strength of Weakness', 169.

48 Smith, 'Negotiated Order in Europe'.

49 Edgar Grande, 'The State and Interest Groups in a Framework of Multi-Level Decision-Making: The Case of the European Union', *Journal of European Public Policy*, 3 (1996), 325.

50 Leendert Jan Bal, 'Decision-Making and Negotiations in the European Union', discussion paper no. 7, Centre for the Study of Diplomacy, University of Leicester, 1995, 1.

51 Kohler-Koch, 'Strength of Weakness', 181; Beate Kohler-Koch, 'Catching Up with Change: The Transformation of Governance in the European Union', *Journal of European Public Policy*, 3 (1996), 367.

52 H. Wallace, 'Challenge of Governance', 32.

53 For an influential and representative work in this tradition, see Moravcsik, 'Negotiating the Single European Act'.

54 Cf. Christer Jönsson, Bo Bjurulf, Ole Elgström, Anders Sannerstedt and Maria Strömvik, 'Negotiations in Networks in the European Union', *International Negotiation*, 3 (1998), 319–44.

55 I. William Zartman, 'Two's Company and More's a Crowd: The Complexities of Multilateral Negotiation', in *International Multilateral Negotiation*, ed. I. William Zartman (San Francisco: Jossey–Bass, 1994).

56 John Peterson, 'Decision-Making in the European Union: Towards a Framework for Analysis', *Journal of European Public Policy*, 2 (1995), 75.

57 Bal, 'Decision-Making and Negotiations', 15.

58 See Robert Axelrod, *The Evolution of Cooperation* (New York: Basic Books, 1984).

59 Adrienne Héritier, 'The Accommodation of Diversity in European Policy-Making and Its Outcomes: Regulatory Policy as a Patchwork', *Journal of European Public Policy*, 3 (1996), 157.

60 Richardson, 'Policy-Making in the EU', 13.

61 Cf. John Peterson, 'Technology Policy in Europe: Explaining the Framework Programme and Eureka in Theory and Practice', *Journal of Common Market Studies*, 29 (1991), 283.

62 Roger Fisher and William Ury, *Getting to Yes: Negotiating Agreement Without Giving In* (New York: Penguin, 1983); cf. Howard Raiffa, *The Art and Science of Negotiation* (Cambridge, MA: Harvard University Press, 1982).

63 Kohler-Koch, 'Strength of Weakness', 176.

64 Héritier, 'Accommodation of Diversity', 157.

65 Two papers presented at a workshop on 'The European Union as a Negotiated Order' at the Third Pan-European Conference on International Relations and Joint Meeting with the International Studies Association, Vienna, September 1998, elaborate this theme: Brigid Laffan, 'The European Union Budget: From Negotiation to Authority'; and Morten Kelstrup, 'Institutionalisation and Negotiation in the Process of European Integration'.

66 Cf. Stone Sweet and Sandholtz, 'Integration, Supranational Governance', 2.

67 Jachtenfuchs and Kohler-Koch, 'Transformation of Governance', 9.

68 Volker Schneider, Godefroy Dang-Nguyen and Raymund Werle, 'Corporate Actor Networks in European Policy-Making: Harmonizing Telecommunications Policy', *Journal of Common Market Studies*, 32 (1994), 477.

69 Peterson, 'Decision-Making in the European Union', 69.

70 Cf. Jachtenfuchs and Kohler-Koch, 'Transformation of Governance', 8; Schneider et al., 'Corporate Actor Networks', 495.

71 Keith Middlemas, *Orchestrating Europe: The Informal Politics of European Union 1973–1995* (London: Fontana Press, 1995), xvi.

72 Kohler-Koch, 'Catching Up with Change', 368.

73 Quoted in Peterson, 'Decision-Making in the European Union', 88.

74 Adrienne Héritier, 'Policy-Making by Subterfuge: Interest Accommodation, Innovation and Substitute Democratic Legitimation in Europe – Perspectives from Distinctive Policy Areas', *Journal of European Public Policy*, 4 (1997), 171–89.

75 Quoted in Middlemas, *Orchestrating Europe*, xxii.

76 Quoted in Peterson, 'Decision-Making in the European Union', 78.

77 Grande, 'State and Interest Groups', 320; Justin Greenwood, *Representing Interests in the European Union* (London: Macmillan, 1997), 3.

78 For a comprehensive assessment of the operation and significance of organized interests in the EU, see Greenwood, *Representing Interests*.

79 Kohler-Koch, 'Catching Up with Change', 368.

80 Cf. Gerhard Fuchs, 'Policy-Making in a System of Multi-Level Governance – The Commission of the European Community and the Restructuring of the Telecommunications Sector', *Journal of European Public Policy*, 1 (1994), 191; Grande, 'State and Interest Groups', 323; Héritier, 'Policy-Making by Subterfuge', 178.

81 Schneider et al., 'Corporate Actor Networks', 480, 490.

82 Manuel Castells, *End of Millennium* (Oxford: Blackwell, 1998), 332.

83 Interview with Anthony Giddens, 'Third Way's the Charm', *Newsweek*, 28 September 1998, 50.

8

Spatial Fragmentation

Europe's regions can be seen as the geographic building blocks of history. Descriptions of everyday life, residential settlement and commerce in Europe, from the Middle Ages through to the nineteenth century, reflect a *regional mosaic*. This was the framework within which the consciousness, experiences and therefore the *identity* of individuals evolved. Strong vertical relations linked *nature* and *culture*. Material sustenance as well as ideational structures were shaped by the physical environment and accessible resources. Research in regional geography, beginning with a number of classic studies in the early twentieth century, confirms the fundamental importance of regions. Production of goods, services and foodstuffs were organized primarily in geographically closed, self-sufficient entities – a kind of 'atomistic' production system. Outside this system was a rudimentary market economy with scattered markets and growing cities. Long-distance trade was limited, and a traveling elite was casting a thin net across the regional mosaic. Political fragmentation and diversity mirrored the ethnic, cultural and economic circumstances of the time.[1]

One major cause of this regional fragmentation and isolation was the prevailing distance-related friction. Waterways remained the principal means for transporting goods and people. Roads were scarce and primitive. Messages had to be delivered in person. Information could take weeks or months before it reached the recipient. Social communication, essential for developing a sense of solidarity and community, required that people lived within sight of each other and were able to talk to each other. This is what life in Europe looked like until quite recently.[2]

The concept of region today

Before looking into the significance of regions today, it may be worthwhile to pause and examine the theoretical implications of the term. The problem is that 'region' has come to be used in a variety of meanings and contexts. Even if we exclude the concept of *macro-regions* and concentrate on smaller territorial units, the term remains multifaceted. Table 8.1 attempts a rough classification.

TABLE 8.1 *Types of regions and classification principles*

Basis of division	Principle of division	Example
Nature	Transportation facilities	Islands, peninsulas, plains, valleys
Culture	Linguistic and ethnic similarity. Shared history and religion	Basque, Catalonia, Wales, Scotland, Wallonie, Sicily, Lombardy
Function	Intensity of flows (goods, people, ideas)	City-regions, urban regions, daily urban regions
Administration	Territorial range of decisions and regulations	*Länder*, *départements*, cantons, counties

As mentioned, physical geography determined the regional boundaries of earlier periods. Waterways and primitive roads united areas, mountains and forests separated areas. Transportation facilities left their mark on early settlements and created a pattern that has remained largely unchanged over the centuries. The regions of Italy and Spain, like the cantons of Switzerland, are examples of *physical-geographic regions*. The Norwegian fjord valleys, the Danish islands and the Finnish isthmuses also count as physical-geographic regions.

Ethnic and *cultural regions* often originated within the physical confines discussed above. Yet their remarkable endurance has less to do with transportation problems than with phenomena associated with *identity*. Identity is a dual concept. It connotes remoteness and delimitation as well as commonality and community – external remoteness and internal community. Identity rests on linguistic, cultural and ethnic similarity, and often includes a shared history and religion. Identity-bearing regions are the principal pillars of diversity of Europe.

The *functional region* is demarcated from the outside world in terms of travel, transportation, contacts and other dependency relations that connect people and structures. This type of region is usually described as *centred*, since it typically has an obvious core in the form of an urban centre. According to the so-called central-place theory, the influence of such centres diminishes with distance. Every centre has a field of influence, which grows thinner in the periphery. The regional borders thus become the interfaces between such fields of influence. This theory was developed as early as the 1930s by the German economist and geographer Walter Christaller.[3] Since the Second World War, Christaller's perspectives have been employed in community planning. The boundaries of functional regions can be altered in response to social change, especially developments in transportation and communications.

The modern form of functional region is often labelled an *urban* or *city region*, within which people move daily between their residence, their place of work and different service establishments. Contacts within the region are far more frequent and intensive than contacts across its boundaries (the term 'daily urban region' can be found in the literature). Increasingly, cities in close proximity to each other are creating regions with multiple cores, the largest of which are known as *conurbations*.

The *administrative region* is in essence a type of functional region, where a system of administrative regulations forms the basis for the division. Administrative regions serve as decision-making territories. They are used throughout Europe as territorial units for the collection and publication of public statistics. The French *départements*, the Swedish counties, the Swiss cantons, the Italian regions and the German *Länder* are examples of administrative regions. In terms of geographic size and decision-making authority, these regions lie in between the state (national) and the municipal (local) levels.

The types of regions described above together form a motley patchwork. In Europe there are abundant examples of both congruity and discrepancy between different principles of division. Historically, ethnic and cultural particularities usually evolved over the centuries within the shelter of physical barriers. Successive generations then created social, administrative, economic and political institutions to strengthen this cohesion. Yet there are also cases where administrative divisions fractured physical regions, territorial identities and functional areas. It is often in areas where administrative divisions, identity, contacts and patterns of daily movements coincide that we find the best examples of homogeneous, strong and robust regions.

The Finnish geographer Anssi Paasi employs the term 'institutionalization' to describe the emergence of regions. Paasi distinguishes four phases of the process that results in internal cohesion and external delimitation. Roughly speaking, the first phase involves *demarcation*, establishing the physical configuration of the territory. In the second stage, the region is anchored in the consciousness of its inhabitants. This is achieved with the help of *common symbols*. The third step entails the development of *common institutions*. The fourth phase involves the crystallization of a *regional identity*. Paasi views the region as a 'collective' category. 'Individual' categories include the concept of *place*, which connotes the individual's awareness of, and connection to, his/her immediate environment. A *sense of place* develops gradually as a result of daily activities and life experience.[4]

The various types of regional units differ in the extent to which they jointly cover a given area. Every country includes administrative divisions that border with each other and together span the entire territory. According to geography's central-place theory and several empirical studies, functional regions tend to be jointly comprehensive as well. Ethnic and cultural distinctiveness, however, is not equally tangible everywhere. History has given rise to a panorama of ethnic and cultural concentrations, yielding a map with an archipelago of distinctive identity spots among areas with weaker identity.

Regional democracies

While the significance of regions in history has seemed quite natural to posterity, their role in current societal development is more bewildering. There is no doubt that, in recent years, regions have attracted growing attention from scholars in the social sciences and humanities. As implied in Chapter 2, there is today a widespread view that increased internationalization, or globalization, goes hand in hand with various forms of regionalization. The two trends appear to reinforce, rather than counteract, each other. Let us take a brief look at a couple of studies of the political and economic prerequisites of regionalization, which tend to support this claim.

History and regional development

In the early 1970s, the political system of Italy underwent a thoroughgoing process of regionalization. Political power and public services were transferred from the central government in Rome to administrations and councils in twenty regions. The reforms provided scholars with an opportunity to study an unprecedented social experiment. American political scientist Robert Putnam and a group of researchers took the opportunity to follow developments in the Italian regions over a period of twenty years. They noted significant differences between the northern and southern parts of the country. In the north, the effectiveness of public institutions seemed to increase, as did the involvement of citizens in the political arena. By contrast, the reforms seemed not to bring any notable changes to the south.

By referring back to the turn of the century and analysing developments in the economy and civil society in Italy's regions, the scholars demonstrated that civic involvement was the most important factor behind institutional effectiveness. To be sure, economic prosperity was found to co-vary with effectiveness; but the scholars concluded that economic progress was the result of a well-developed civil society. In other words, the economy does not predict civic traditions; rather, 'civic-ness' predicts the economy. Dense social networks are the most important pillars of regional development in northern Italy. It is within a social fabric that various forms of public involvement evolve. In northern Italy civil society has deep roots in history. It has taken several decades to construct institutions, and generations to engender communities. In southern Italy, on the other hand, public life is organized vertically rather than horizontally. For centuries, power has rested on clientism and a 'protection mentality'. The concept of 'citizen' never took root. From the perspective of the individual citizen, societal issues are the responsibility of others. Few citizens attempt to participate in the public debate. Political involvement, to the extent that it occurs, is driven by a desire for personal gain, not for any collective purpose. Civic activity is dwindling, and personal piety becomes a substitute for civil involvement.[5]

Of course, examples of 'path-dependent' differences are found outside Italy as well. There are cases where the formal institutions, resources, relative prices and individual preferences of two societies are similar, but where striking differences in effectiveness none the less exist. Economic historian Douglass North, for instance, has traced the divergent economic development of North and South America to their different colonial legacies. The Anglo-American population inherited civic traditions, Latin Americans a tradition of vertical dependence and exploitation.[6]

It has also been argued that similar measures to promote economic development can have totally different results in different countries. The colonial experience is significant in this context as well. For instance, a glance at Palermo in Sicily may provide us with clues to the future of Moscow. Many of the former communist states had only weak civic traditions prior to the communist takeover. The totalitarian government exhausted what little social capital was available. Without networks and traditional communities, there is the risk of amoral nepotism, clientism, lawlessness, ineffective institutions and economic stagnation.[7]

Regional economies

In recent years, there has been much research on the growing economic importance of regions. The proposition that globalization and regionalization proceed apace and reinforce each other has been tested and verified in a number of countries within the OECD area.[8] How can this interrelation be explained?

Home bases

Home base is a concept that has gained currency among economists in recent years, with Michael Porter as the best-known proponent. According to Porter, firms, rather than states, are the main competitors in global markets, and their international competitiveness is rooted and sustained in their home base. It is from these home bases that rival firms operate. Home bases can be states, as in Porter's treatment, but may also be regions. Successful corporations employ global strategies and draw on points of support in many different parts of the world. Why, then, is a home base important?

One fundamental assumption is that several factors *conjointly* yield a competitive edge. Each home base has attributes that Porter classifies into four broad categories. First, *factor conditions* refer to a broad range of assets. Physical resources include land and energy. Human resources can be understood in terms of the availability, quality and cost of labour. Skills and knowledge are linked to individuals, but are generally administered by institutions such as universities, research institutes, firms, libraries, databases and registers. To this can be added capital resources and a well-developed infrastructure.

As for the relative importance of different factor conditions, Porter considers physical resources and less skilled labour as fundamental, generic and omni-present. They are inherited and are available in different combinations in most places. Their relevance has diminished, while resources that have to do with knowledge and technology are becoming more significant. These cannot be inherited in the same manner. They must consistently be 'upgraded' or recreated. This requires repeated investments in human capital and equipment.

Second, *demand conditions* refer to demand in the firm's immediate environment, which Porter considers important for the firm's international competitiveness. Yet he does not build his argument on conventional ideas about the significance of transportation costs. Instead, he emphasizes closeness in terms of cultural similarity. If there is a high degree of cultural similarity in its home base, the firm can more readily adapt its production to the needs of the consumer. The home base market can then serve as a 'nursery' for the producer, preparing it for later entry into international markets.

Concerning the third attribute, *related and supporting industries*, cluster is a key concept. Clusters include sub-contractors, services and other interacting entities. Together, they create resources that can be shared by many – for example, skilled labour, shared technology and 'know-how'. Clusters are characterized by cultural similarity and are held together by organizational and social networks.

The last attribute has to do with the firm's *strategy, structure and rivalry*. The conditions under which the firm works and the manner in which it adapts to changing conditions vary between different countries and cultures. The variation may concern financing and ownership, the objectives of owners and executives, marketing strategies and the organization of work. Porter argues that not only clusters of *supporting* entities but also *rivalry* between different firms in the same home base may be an advantage. Firms that have become successful internationally often began to develop in areas marked by strong competition. This is true not only of small, specialized businesses, but also of large industrial complexes such as the Swiss pharmaceuticals industry, the Swedish car industry, the German chemical industry and, for that matter, the American computer industry. Local competition incites firms to improve and innovate, puts pressure on prices and enhances service. Competition is particularly effective when the rivals are in close proximity to each other. It is therefore not surprising that geographic concentration of rival corporations is a common occurrence in the industrialized world. The production of knives and other tools in Solingen, Sheffield and Eskilstuna are examples from different periods and countries. Shoes in Bologna and leather in Florence are other illustrations.[9]

The core question in our context is whether regions, of the type discussed in this chapter, are sufficiently large to function as home bases. Michael Porter is vague on this point, and, as noted earlier, has tended to focus on states. He does provide a few examples, however, that imply that regional and local environments constitute home bases. States, on the other hand, tend to be so large that they obscure important aspects of the economic landscape. In the next chapter, we shall take a further step away from a top-down perspective and see how scholars in economics and geography have looked at the role of local units, *places*, within regions.

A Europe of regions

Regional self-reliance has increased in much of Europe. At the same time, the strength and independence of the regions differ widely. Moreover, administrative, ethno-cultural and functional regions frequently overlap, complicating the picture. It is therefore impossible to paint a uniform picture of a Europe of regions (cf. Table 8.2).

France has approximately 36,000 municipalities (*communes*) and is, since the French Revolution, a centralized, unitary state. Under Napoleon the country was partitioned by central directives into hundreds of administrative entities known as *départements*. In 1982 these were grouped into twenty-two regions, a division with historical roots. Each region is formally governed by a directly elected council and an administration headed by a president. The authority of the regional councils, however, remains quite limited.

Switzerland has over 3,000 municipalities distributed among twenty-six cantons with a high degree of autonomy. The cantons are, as a rule, governed by a parliament and an executive council that are both elected. Each canton has full sovereignty in all matters that are not explicitly designated as the concern of the confederation in the Swiss constitution. Cantons have taxation rights and legislative powers. Most cantons are age-old configurations originating in physical geographic conditions.

While officially a unitary state, Spain is composed of seventeen regions that enjoy far-reaching political independence, with some variation from region to region. Catalonia, Andalusia, Galizia, the Basque provinces and Navarre have greater autonomy than the other regions. A strong sense of regional identity remains in these historic regions.

Germany is a federation of sixteen *Bundesländer*, each of which has its own constitution and legislative powers. Each is governed by a directly elected parliament, which in turn appoints a government headed by a *Minister-präsident*. Since 1993, Belgium is also a federal state composed of three territories: Flanders, Wallonia and greater Brussels. Tensions between French-speaking and Flemish-speaking Belgians are today so severe that they threaten to fracture the state.

TABLE 8.2   *Regional divisions in some European countries*

Country	Name	Number of units	Average population (millions)
France	regions	22	2.3
Switzerland	cantons	26	0.25
Austria	*Länder*	9	0.8
Spain	regions	17	2.3
Italy	regions	20	2.9
Germany	*Länder*	16	4.9
Portugal	regions	7	1.5
Belgium	regions	3	3.3

Other states have comparatively weak regions. Sweden is a case in point. The country has been a centralized, unitary state since the sixteenth century. Feudalist structures never prevailed in Sweden. During its great power era in the seventeenth century, a powerful central administration was created. On the other hand, local self-government was developed throughout this sparsely populated, large country. Grass-roots democracy flourished within villages, parishes and municipalities, rather than in provinces or regions. Over the centuries, Sweden developed a comparatively homogeneous culture.

Whatever regional tradition did exist in Sweden was tied mainly to the *landskap*, or provinces, which were vehicles of identity and regional uniqueness. Provincial assemblies survived in many places into the nineteenth century, although they had been stripped of most of their functions. When Sweden was divided into *län*, or counties, in 1634, new borders were drawn for these administrative units. Territoriality, which had evolved from below, was destroyed by centralist forces from above. The counties became the monarchy's and the government's administrative areas at the regional level. County governments were the extended arms of the monarchy, and county governors were representatives of the king. When the county councils were introduced in 1862, to allow citizens greater influence in the regional arena, they were almost without exception tied to the centrally determined division into *län*. However, even in Sweden regions have experienced a renaissance in the 1990s. Efforts to revive the old *landskap* as an administrative unit and to expand the decision-making authority of county councils have been initiated.

Both within the Council of Europe and the European Union, there are today organs whose task is to promote regional interests. The Council of Europe's *Congress of Local and Regional Authorities* (CLRAE) was created in 1994, to allow counties and regions to participate in the Council's decision-making. The European Union's *Committee of the Regions*, established in 1993, has 200 members representing local and regional organs. Member-state governments nominate members, who are formally appointed for a four-year term by the Council of Ministers. The members are to be independent of their national parliaments and governments and to act in the interest of the European community. Thus far, the Committee of the Regions has consultative rather than decision-making functions. It advises the Council of Ministers and the Commission on matters of concern to counties and regions.

Besides these regional organs, there are the *Council of European Municipalities and Regions* (CEMR), and the *Assembly of European Regions* (AER). These bodies have brought together a large number of regions and counties from all over Europe, for the purpose of strengthening their influence and representation within the different supranational institutions and cooperative organs in today's Europe.

In collaboration with different directorates of the Commission, the EU bureau of statistics has divided the Union into territorial units, so-called NUTS (Nomenclature of Territorial Units for Statistics). There are three levels in this division, ranging from larger to smaller areas. As far as possible, the statistical division is based on existing administrative divisions in the fifteen EU member states. The resulting map clearly demonstrates the heterogeneity of the 'Europe of regions'. Some member states, such as Denmark, Luxembourg, Ireland, Finland and Sweden, have such small populations that they qualify as regions at the first level (NUTS I). Eleven of Germany's *Länder* also belong to this category; thirty-one *Regierungsbezirke* are defined as regions at the second level (NUTS II), while 328 *Kreise* are third-level regions (NUTS III). In Italy, eleven *Gruppi di regioni*, twenty *Regioni* and ninety-five *Provincie* are considered NUTS I, II and III. In Sweden, eight groups of provinces are regions at the second level, and twenty-three are third-level regions.

On the basis of this brief survey, it is difficult to draw any firm, generalized conclusions concerning the political significance of European regions. Two additional pieces should be added to the jigsaw puzzle. First, a growing number of regions have opened offices in Brussels, engaging in interest representation and lobbying *vis-à-vis* EU organs. Whereas before the mid-1980s there were almost no regional offices in Brussels, in the mid-1990s there were well over 120, according to some estimates.[10] Second, the subsidiarity principle, one of the products of the Maastricht Treaty, stipulates that decisions in issue-areas, where the EU organs do not have exclusive competence, should be made at the lowest possible effective level – that is, at the national, regional or local level. Only if the objectives are better served that way, are decisions to be made at the Union level. This principle has been the subject of much debate, in part because of its lack of precision. Some observers argue that the subsidiarity principle primarily strengthens the regional level in Europe. At any rate, the European Union has brought regions to the foreground to an unprecedented extent.

Different forms of regionalization

One may distinguish three different forms of regionalization. *Decentralization* means that functions that were previously state prerogatives are transferred to the regions. This trend is today visible in most of Europe. The EU subsidiarity principle can also be viewed as supranational support of decentralization to the benefit of regions. A second form of regionalization is associated with cultural expressions and identities with deep roots in history. This kind of regionalism stands in evident opposition to the state government, and in some instances develops into *separatism*. A third form, *region-building*, applies to cases where local and regional forces deliberately strive to create a new region, or to strengthen a weak one. Decentralizing, separatist and region-building processes may proceed in parallel and can mobilize mutually supporting forces. This is especially likely in border areas where today cross-border regions are emerging throughout Europe.[11]

As mentioned, region is a multifaceted concept. In addition, not even regions of the same type – identity regions, functional regions and administrative regions – are necessarily comparable but may vary significantly with respect to area, population, income, investments and several other variables. The largest functional city-regions in Europe have a population of over 10 million, while in the Nordic countries some barely count one million inhabitants. In Italy, regions such as Piedmont, Veneto, Emilia Romagna, Tuscany, Lazio, Campania and Sicily have between 4 and 5 million inhabitants, while Lombardy has 9 million. Several French and a few of Spain's most successful regions have similar numbers. Among the German *Länder*, Nordrhein–Westfalen has 17 million, Bavaria 11 million and Baden–Württemberg 10 million residents. In an EU context, the Nordic countries can be seen as regions in terms of population; but measured by surface area, only France is larger than Sweden.

Cross-border regions

Regions in state peripheries appear most likely to undergo profound changes in the foreseeable future. As the central governments gradually relinquish their traditional hegemony and as the European Union grows, border areas, which are located far from the national centres, will most likely be quick to take advantage of the new circumstances. While Nice and Strasbourg are peripheral cities from the national French perspective, they occupy central positions in a Europe of permeable boundaries. Malmoe is a peripheral city in relation to Stockholm, but is the most central area in Sweden from a Brussels viewpoint.

   Many of Europe's old conflict areas and risk zones have today been transformed into areas of cooperation and development. Both within and outside the European Union, cross-border collaboration is burgeoning, along peaceful frontiers as well. Cross-border regions are regional configurations that span one or more state boundaries. In other words, this is a form of regionalization that neutralizes international borders and nibbles at the sovereign state. This new form of regionalization has increased dramatically in recent years. A 1996 study identifies sixty-five such regional formations between 1947 and 1991, and refers to a database with 116 European cross-border regions in 1996. The swift rise in cooperative agreements in border regions can be related to three processes of change: deepening integration within the European Union, the political collapse of the Soviet system in Eastern Europe, and the general wave of regionalization discussed above.[12]

   Cross-border regions form clusters along virtually all of the state boundaries in Europe. At the same time, certain regions have begun to cooperate without sharing a common boundary. A long band of cross-border regional formations stretches from the Benelux states southward into the Rhineland, the historical conflict zone between France and Germany and since Antiquity a borderland between the Roman and Germanic worlds. One of the most publicized regions in this zone is EUREGIO, at the border between the Netherlands and Germany. Along the same border, there are four other cross-border regions with far-reaching cooperation. EUREGIO was created as early as 1958 and is one of the oldest transnational formations in Europe. It comprises areas between the rivers Rhine, Ems and Ijssel. Regio Baseliensis spans the remaining Rhine valley and includes parts of France, Switzerland and Germany. Many others are scattered between these two major regions.

In Central Europe, or *Mitteleuropa*, a large number of agreements have been reached between regions on different sides of state borders, and on both sides of the former Iron Curtain. German, Czech and Polish regions have agreed to mutual cooperation in various fields. Along the rivers Oder and Neisse, Pomerania has been created as a result of cooperation treaties between Poland and Germany. Hungary has quickly developed contacts in the border zones to neighbouring countries. In 1989, Hungary proposed collaboration between the border areas in Austria, Italy and Yugoslavia, under the regional label Danube–Adria. When Czechoslovakia came into the picture, the project was renamed the Pentagonal, which was transformed into the Hexagonal when Poland joined.

When it comes to the number of cross-border regions and their economic significance, only the Alpine area can compete with Rhineland and Benelux. Austria's entry into the European Union has strengthened cross-border cooperation in the eastern parts of the Alpine belt, and Austria has become a link between this area and Central Europe. Interestingly, a geopolitical pattern from the Habsburg dual monarchy appears to re-emerge. The northern parts of Italy are firmly linked to their neighbours to the north. In the western sections of the Alps lies another zone of overlapping interests that dates far back in history. Savoy, a disputed area coveted by the German emperor and the French king alike, was once part of this zone. Savoy was a realm with elastic boundaries and a shifting centre. Roughly speaking, its rulers exercised control over much of the Alpine valleys from Lake Geneva in the north to the Mediterranean in the south, from Nice in the west to Turin in the east. In the thirteenth and fourteenth centuries, more than 200 cities were founded in the area. In 1860 Savoy was divided between France and Italy. Today, there is far-reaching cross-border regional cooperation around cities such as Geneva, Basle, Lugano and Nice.

Given the turmoil in the Balkans in recent years, it is hardly surprising that cross-border projects are scarce in the southeastern parts of Europe. In the Pyrenees, however, the borders between Spain and France and between Spain and Portugal have been virtually neutralized. Boundaries in the northern peripheries of Europe also appear to be diminishing in importance. Following a proposal by the Nordic Council, an agreement for cross-border cooperation between counties was signed as early as 1977 between Denmark, Finland, Sweden and Norway in the areas of culture, environmental policy, health care, communications and tourism. There is currently an ambitious effort to strengthen cross-border ties between areas along Øresund, the sound between Denmark and Sweden with Copenhagen on the Danish side and Malmoe on the Swedish side as centres. In the far north, cooperation is taking root within the large Barents area – *Barents Euro-Arctic Region* (BEAR) – following an agreement between Norway, Sweden, Finland and Russia.

The Barents project can be seen as an example of a general trend toward cross-border agreements comprising larger territories, so-called macro-regions. These are significantly larger than the regional units that are the focus of this chapter. The cooperation that was launched in 1992 within the framework of the Council of the Baltic Sea States, with the Nordic countries, the Baltic states, Russia, Poland and Germany as participants, is another example of the rise of what may prove to be important European macro-regions.

Driving forces, motives and forms of cooperation

The patchwork of cross-border regions no doubt contains formations of varying character and stability. Yet they all constitute examples of a region-alization that does not take place within national perimeters. The traditional form of regionalization can be described as *vertical*. Functions are transferred from the state to the region, resulting in some kind of decentralization. Cross-border regionalization, by contrast, is *horizontal*. It takes place along the external boundaries of the state and requires foreign contacts and a partnership between public authorities and other organizations at the regional level. The traditional adjective 'international' seems inadequate to capture the true nature of cross-border regionalization and the emergence of autonomous networks. The term *transnational* better describes these dynamics.

Proposals for developing cross-border regions often emanate from both public and private local and regional actors. The formation of the region thus takes place in a sort of grey zone between civil law and public law. Important actors include firms, universities, chambers of commerce, trade unions, political parties and cultural organizations. Cooperation is facilitated by the emergence of political and administrative networks, in which local and regional authorities participate. It is also common at some stage to create an 'umbrella organization' or network with a wider geographic reach, sometimes with state governments as members.

The support of various international organizations has frequently facilitated regionalization efforts. Thus, both the Council of Europe and the European Union have actively worked to increase cross-border regional cooperation. The Assembly of European Regions (AER), with its secretariat in Strasbourg, has a close relationship with the Council of Europe. The Association for European Border Regions (AEBR) was formed in 1971 at the initiative of several border regions in the Rhineland, and in 1995 included fifty full members and an even higher number of associated regions. AEBR represents the interests of the border regions *vis-à-vis* national and international organs, and enjoys a certain degree of influence within the Council of Europe and the European Union. Since 1988, the Union has lent its support to cross-border cooperation through the programme known as Interreg I. With the advent of Interreg II, the Union extended its support to include cooperation between non-bordering regions in different countries.

In different parts of Europe there are similar motives behind the development of cross-border cooperation. Originally, security concerns predominated. The creation of regions between Germany, on the one hand, and Benelux and France, on the other, was considered to have a stabilizing and peace-keeping effect. Today, the evolution of regions is seen as a natural component of the European integration process, as reflected in the active EU support of the trend. In addition, regionalization appears to facilitate community planning in many border areas. Economic motives are prominent. Cooperation across state borders creates opportunities for economic growth, by enlarging the local markets and by merging physical and human resources. Since border areas have tended to lag behind economically compared with national core areas, cross-border cooperation is often intended to mobilize the peripheries of Europe.

Finally, a number of transnational issues, including transportation, communications, cultural affairs and environmental problems, have fostered growing interest in cooperation between regions. Cultural barriers have long impeded innovation in border areas. Environmental concerns can be dealt with more effectively in a wider forum. The chief spheres of cross-border cooperation today include infrastructure, environmental protection and cultural exchange. Research and development, tourism, education and industrial development follow at a lower rung in the ladder of priorities.

In summary, this chapter has demonstrated how regions have become the nexus of local, state and international attention and influence attempts. The next chapter will focus on the cities and places that constitute the core of different regions. As we shall see, it is here that important nodes in different networks are found, and it is here that global, national and regional interests converge and diverge.

NOTES

1 Classic works in the field of regional geography include Paul Vidal de la Blache, *Tableau de la géographie de la France* (Paris: Armand Colin, 1911); Paul Vidal de la Blache, *La France de l'Est* (Paris: Armand Colin, 1917). The largest economic history overview, describing the issues touched upon here, is Fernand Braudel, *Civilization and Capitalism*, 3 vols (London: Collins, 1981–1984).

2 For examples on travel and transportation times in earlier periods, see ibid. and Norbert Ohler, *The Medieval Traveller* (Woodbridge: Boydell Press, 1989). An overview appears in Gunnar Törnqvist, *Sverige i nätverkens Europa: Gränsöverskridandets former och villkor* (Malmoe: Liber-Hermods, 1996).

3   Walter Christaller, *Die zentralen Orte in Süddeutschland* (Jena, 1933). See also Walter Christaller, *Das Grundgerüst der räumlichen Ordnung in Europa: Frankfurter Geographische Hefte* (Frankfurt am Main: Verlag Dr. Waldemar Kramer, 1950).

4 Anssi Paasi, 'The Institutionalization of Regions: A Theoretical Framework for Understanding the Emergence of Regions and the Constitution of Identity', *Fennia*, 164 (1986): 1, 105–46; Anssi Paasi, 'Deconstructing Regions: Notes on the Scales of Spatial Life', *Environment and Planning A: International Journal of Urban and Regional Research*, 23 (1991), 239–56.

5 Robert D. Putnam, *Making Democracy Work: Civic Traditions in Modern Italy* (Princeton, NJ: Princeton University Press, 1993).

6 Douglass North, *Institutions, Institutional Change and Economic Performance* (New York: Cambridge University Press, 1990).

7 See these and other examples in Putnam, *Making Democracy Work*. See also Stefan Hedlund and Niclas Sundström, 'Does Palermo Represent the Future for Moscow?', *Journal of Public Policy*, 16 (1996), 113–56.

8 See, for example, Christopher Harvie, *The Rise of Regional Europe* (London: Routledge, 1994); Jan de Vet, 'Globalisation and Local and Regional Competitiveness', *STI Review*, 13 (1993), 89–121; Philip Cooke, 'Co-operative Advantages of Regions', unpublished paper, Centre of Advanced Studies, University of Wales, 1994.

9 Michael Porter, *The Competitive Advantage of Nations* (London: Macmillan, 1990); Örjan Sölvell, Ivor Zander and Michael Porter, *Advantage Sweden* (Stockholm: Norstedts, 1991).

10 Magnus Jerneck, 'Subnational Mobilization, Territoriality and Political Power in the European Union: A Challenge from Below?', in *The European Union and the Nation-State*, ed. Philippe Nemo (Paris: Groupe ESCP, 1997), 111.

11 Bjarne Lindström, *Regional Policy and Territorial Supremacy*, NordREFO 1996: 2 (Copenhagen/Stockholm: Nordiska institutet för regionalpolitisk forskning, 1996).

12 Anders Östhol, *Politisk integration och gränsöverskridande regionbildning i Europa* (Umeå: Department of Political Science, University of Umeå, 1996); Noralv Veggeland, *Regionbygging over grenser i det nye Europa: aktører, arenaer og regimer*, NordREFO 1994: 6 (Copenhagen/Stockholm: Nordiska institutet för regionalpolitisk forskning, 1994).

9

Places in Networks

The interrelationship between the two spheres *network* and *region* in Figure 2.1 can be used as a basis for describing a world that is not held together in the manner it used to be. The image that emerges is one of a fragmented territory, an archipelago of self-reliant regions linked together through different types of networks. Several trends discussed in this book have contributed to this configuration.

The process of globalization is reflected in steadily expanding international trade flows, foreign direct investment, global sourcing of components and transnational inter-firm cooperation. Even if these trends would seem to favour greater economic integration, there is still little evidence to suggest that *cross-border economic activity* has eliminated deep-seated differences between the advanced industrial economies. These concern not only technological and industrial specialization, but also such institutional conditions as the organization of scientific and industrial research, industrial training and the structure of labour and financial markets.

Because of globalization and the resulting international homogenization of formerly critical factors of production, firms have become progressively stimulated by, and dependent on, unevenly distributed *localized capabilities* that enhance learning and innovation. Through their buildings, firms and organizations within research and cultural life are tied to places and integrated into regional and local environments where people live and operate. 'Regions and localities do not disappear, but become integrated in international networks that link up their most dynamic sectors', argues Manuel Castells in his book on the emergence of the network society in our time.[1]

A global sense of place

In contemporary society, there are clear links between worldwide networks and local environments, through which information is exchanged between different geographical levels. A glance at different forms of culture and sports indicates, for example, how both worldwide relations and local isolation characterize our modern way of life. The British geographer Doreen Massey has used the expression 'a global sense of place' and offers as an example inhabitants of the favelas of Rio de Janeiro:

who know global football like the back of their hand, and have produced some of its players; who have contributed massively to global music, who gave us the samba and produced the lambada that everyone was dancing to last year in the clubs of Paris and London; and who have never, or hardly ever, been to downtown Rio. At one level they have been tremendous contributors to what we call time–space compression; and at another level they are imprisoned in it.[2]

Similarly, small-scale production that is developed under both competitive and cooperative conditions in dense regional environments would not be competitive or successful without close contacts with the outside world. These firms often sell their products in worldwide markets. They keep in touch with, and benefit from, the international flow of knowledge, capital and ideas.

The region of Veneto in northern Italy, which is the home base of the global corporation Benetton, may serve as one of many examples of the way global networks and narrow territoriality can complement one another. In 1955, Giuliana Benetton bought a knitting-machine and began making shirts for friends and relatives. Three brothers helped purchase yarn and sell textiles directly to shops that agreed to sell only Benetton products. Gradually the business expanded. Small firms in Benetton's home district became involved in the operation. Both the number of suppliers in the neighbourhood and the number of Benetton shops around the world grew. Today, the production chain employs some 30,000 people in 650 firms within a 50 kilometre radius of the small village Pozano Veneto. The Benetton family's own company has 6,000 employees and an annual turnover of US$1.65 billion. Approximately 7,000 shops have signed contracts that bind them to a network spanning 121 countries.[3]

Universities, in particular, act as strategic links between worldwide networks and local environments. The link runs in two directions. On the one hand, the university links up a place and region with centres of knowledge and excellence around the world. On the other hand, the university mobilizes local and regional competence and creativity.

Nodal economies

'Neo-Marshallian nodes'

The British economist Alfred Marshall was among the first to emphasize the importance of neighbourhood to industrial development. In the early twentieth century, Marshall argued that in the industrialized countries there existed areas characterized by an 'industrial atmosphere'; 'industry is in the air', in his expression. Related and similar industries were concentrated in such places. Agglomerations formed an archipelago of scattered islands. Marshall cited three main reasons why industries tended to concentrate and engender an industrial atmosphere in certain places or regions.[4] They are in many respects reminiscent of Michael Porter's classification, discussed in Chapter 8.

First, the agglomeration of related firms has an external effect, insofar as it creates a constant labour market for individuals with specific skills in a geographically limited space. The area thus becomes attractive to both employers and a specialized labour force. Secondly, access to specialized services grows. The third reason is that agglomeration generates competence, or, in Marshall's own words:

> The mysteries of the trade become no mystery; but are as it were in the air. . . . Good work is rightly appreciated, inventions and improvements in machinery, in processes and the general organization of the business have their merits promptly discussed: if one man starts a new idea, it is taken up by others and combined with suggestions of their own; and thus it becomes the source of further new ideas.[5]

In her noted book *Cities and the Wealth of Nations*, Canadian economist Jane Jacobs argues that states are not the appropriate territorial units for understanding how economies function. Each state is composed of a blend of regional economies. Rich and poor regions exist alongside each other. Without national policies of compensation, regional discrepancies would become unacceptably wide. Yet in spite of the regional policies that are pursued in many countries, economic differences remain far greater between regions than between national averages. Therefore, to gain deeper insights into the actual functioning of economies, Jacobs argues, the city and its immediate environment is the most adequate territorial unit of analysis. The functional *city-regions* are the constituent units of a larger economic landscape. In urban regions, a remarkable amount of economic activity takes place within a comparatively small area. In between cities, the economic landscape is surprisingly barren.[6]

Paul Krugman, another prominent economist, draws on Marshall's thinking. According to Krugman, states occupy a role in the international economy only because they are the seats of governments whose policies affect the geographic mobility of goods and production factors. Through political decisions, national boundaries can serve as obstacles to trade and mobility. However, there is no inherent economic sense in drawing a line in the terrain and construing the areas on either side as two separate countries. To understand how the international economy functions, we must observe what takes place *within* the boundaries of individual states. To understand why the economic growth rate differs from country to country, we must begin by analysing the differences in regional development.

When we speak of external effects and agglomerative advantages as factors influencing the localization of economic activity and the emergence of centre–periphery relations, there is no reason to assume that political boundaries define the relevant unit associated with these external effects. If we ask ourselves what is the most striking feature of the geography of economic enterprise, the obvious answer is concentration. According to both Marshall and Krugman, the concentration of firms in all the industrialized countries is the result of an economic trinity: a common labour market, access to specialized inputs and services, and the transfer of knowledge. Each of these factors originates in a city or a small cluster of cities, an area so small that people can easily switch jobs without leaving their habitat, an area where fewer mobile goods and services can be supplied and where regular face-to-face contacts can take place.[7]

Recent literature in economic geography offers a terminology that underlines the continued relevance of Marshall's early work. Successful regions and areas are described as having 'Marshallian benefits'. In the most monotonous spaces, 'intelligent regions' may break existing patterns. In the sea of traditional industrialism lie scattered 'neo-Marshallian islands'. To mix metaphors, these islands resemble raisins in a cake. As described in a cumulating literature, the successful regions and local units may be of varying size and are in some respects quite different in character. Cities, city districts, science parks, centres for development, so-called technopoles, local production complexes and industrial districts exist alongside counties, Italian regions, American states and German *Länder*. What these have in common is that they are all fractions of national territories.[8]

Where, then, are these neo-Marshallian islands, or nodes, as they are sometimes called? According to Krugman, for instance, the phenomenon of Silicon Valley is not unique either in space or time, but is simply a glossy version of a traditional phenomenon. In reality, there are other major industries in the United States that are narrowly concentrated to specific regions or areas: the motor industry in Detroit, the rubber factories of Acron, the aircraft industry in Seattle, textiles in the Piedmont area, photographic equipment in Rochester near New York, and the film industry in Hollywood. Today, the celebrated high-technology and electronic sectors are concentrated not only in Silicon Valley, but also along Route 128 in Boston and the Research Triangle in North Carolina.

Similarly, every European country has examples of areas with Marshallian attributes in its industrial history. Oft-cited examples include the axis Cambridge–Reading–Bristol, the southern part of the Paris area, Grenoble, Toulouse, Montpellier, Sophie–Antipolis, Baden–Württemberg and Santa Croce Sull'Arno in Tuscany. Arnaldo Bagnasco was allegedly the first to note that there existed a 'third Italy' besides the 'first Italy', the industrial triangle in the northwest, and the 'second Italy', the stagnant Mezzogiorno area in the south. The 'third Italy' is home to small-scale production, characterized by advanced technology and high capacity. The area comprises most of the region Emilia Romagna and parts of Veneto, and includes the cities of Bologna, Carpi, Sassuolo and Arezzo.[9]

The embryo of such successful agglomerations can surprisingly often be traced back to seemingly trivial historical coincidences. Behind the success stories, we often find individuals whose early initiatives launched a lengthy process, a spark that triggered a chain reaction. Only on rare occasions, however, are prosperous regions the result of deliberate, systematic planning.

One of the characteristics of integrated industrial districts is a seemingly contradictory combination of competition and cooperation. Firms act as rivals in regard to research and development, innovation and efficacy, but frequently collaborate when it comes to administrative services, financing, and utilizing physical resources. Technical innovations also spread rapidly between firms, and mutual support is common. Various 'external effects' ensue in the neighbourhood, which appear to compensate smaller companies for their lack of economy of scale.

Against the background of our discussion of functioning regional democracies in Chapter 8, it is not surprising that highly productive, small-scale industrial districts are concentrated in regions and places in northern and central Italy, which are characterized by a tradition of civic engagement and institutional effectiveness. These areas prosper from rich networks of private economic unions and political organizations that create healthy markets and allow small firms access to an infrastructure they could not afford on their own. The networks channel information about technological innovations, creditworthiness and reliability. The networks are upheld, expanded and upgraded through continuous informal contacts in cafés, bars and in the street.

A Europe of cities

Jane Jacobs's thesis that city-regions are key economic units is echoed by the French geographer Jean Labasse in his book *L'Europe des régions*. Economically successful regions are in essence nothing else than expansive cities and their vicinity. Moreover, Labasse maintains that large cities give regions their identity. As an example, he cites the dynamic development along the northern coast of the Mediterranean. According to Labasse, economic growth in the regions along this coast is concentrated to a few major cities: Lyons in the Rhône–Alps region, Turin in Piedmont, Milan in Lombardy and Barcelona in Catalonia. Even in Baden–Württemberg, which is considered one of Europe's most expansive regions, cities such as Stuttgart, Mannheim, Karlsruhe, Freiburg, Heidelberg and Ulm, along with some smaller cities, are the engines of growth.[10]

The city has two attributes, which make it strategic in the territorial field of tension outlined in Chapter 2. In a long historical perspective, settlement patterns seem to constitute the most stable spatial order underlying European social life. It is to this pattern that population, production and all forms of transportation are tied. In a broad panorama, cities appear as the principal carriers of Europe's diversity and variation. In a European history characterized by territorial tensions and change, cities represent geographic continuity. The second attribute of the city is that it provides an interface for the interaction between different geographic levels and spheres of interest, from the global to the local.

As will be recalled from the brief historical outline of urban development in Chapter 2, the *marketplace* was originally the core of the city, as epitomized by the *agora* in Athens and the *forum* in Rome. During the era of industrialization, the *factory* typified cities. Many of the older industrial centres of Europe have in recent decades experienced crises. This is apparent in Strathclyde, Merseyside, Teeside and Tyneside in Great Britain, the Ruhr and the Saar in Germany, the Nord-Pas de Calais and Lorraine in France, and Wallonia in Belgium, to cite a few prominent examples. In some places, skyrocketing unemployment and a decaying physical infrastructure suggest that the problems are not easily solved. On the other hand, there are cases where the forces of renovation have been mobilized in dense industrial environments.

The successful cities of our time are products of a combination of technology, a way of organizing labour, the integration of the financial world, and, not least, the dynamics of social communications. These interrelations can alternatively be described as an interplay between networks – physical, institutional, social and cultural. In cities, or rather city-regions, the nodes of these different networks are situated close to each other, which means that networks can easily be integrated. Thus, opportunities are created for synergies.

One of the city's most evident geographic advantages is that it offers two types of proximity. One is *territorial proximity*, in terms of density and social neighbourhood. But the city also offers *proximity in networks* in relation to other cities. Thanks to advanced means of transportation and communication, people, buildings and institutions are within reach and easy access despite physical distances. The nodes in institutional networks attract each other. The management of industry, finance, research, interest groups and public administration is concentrated in cities, as are clusters of specialized services. The media broadcast news, culture and entertainment from large cities. Cities represent the dense environments that throughout history have provided *meeting-places*, crucial to renewal and artistic creativity.

The city is not only a place where goods and services are exchanged, and where people meet and collaborate. It is also a breakpoint, the place in which different currents of ideas, lifestyles and belief systems intersect. Cities have been the springboards for almost all revolutions. They are the birthplace of new fashions, styles and technologies. They are the centres from which most news spreads, even news originating elsewhere.[11]

Saskia Sassen has coined the term *global city* to denote the new strategic role for major cities in a spatially dispersed, yet globally integrated organization of economic activity. Major cities, she argues, have become the sites for the *practice* of global control – the activities involved in producing and reproducing the organization and management of a global production system and a global marketplace for finance. These include (a) the production of specialized services needed by complex organizations for maintaining centralized control and management over spatially dispersed networks of factories, offices and service outlets, and (b) the production of financial innovations and the creation of new financial markets. Thus, international legal and accounting services, management consulting and financial services are heavily concentrated in major cities. The fundamental dynamic analysed by Sassen is that the more globalized the economy becomes, the higher the agglomeration of central functions in relatively few 'global cities'.

Moreover, the three principal 'global cities' of today – New York, London and Tokyo – constitute a sort of transnational urban system, according to Sassen. These three cities do not simply compete with each other for the same business, but function as one trans-territorial marketplace. What contributes to growth in the network of 'global cities' does not necessarily contribute to growth in states. The relaxed restrictions on direct foreign investment and the deregulation of financial markets have created a whole array of economic activities, concentrated to these cities, where governments participate only minimally. The triad of New York, London and Tokyo may thus serve as a harbinger of more widespread archipelagic structures of places in networks in the future. At the same time, such a development raises fundamental questions about the future relationship between cities and states.[12]

Sassen draws on Manuel Castells, who describes the modern city as an *informational city*, a centre of information processing and exchange. Further-more, both authors depict the modern city as *dual*, insofar as it is dominated by two contrasting social groups: an educated, affluent upper class with a wide network of contacts, on the one hand, and a low-paid class of service personnel, including many immigrants, on the other.[13]

As we have seen in Chapter 4, the birth of the modern state coincided with the emergence of a new social group in the cities with new sources of revenue and power, the burghers. Similarly, a new cosmopolitan social group with new lifestyles and consumption patterns is appearing in the 'informational' or 'global' cities. It consists of high-income earners who represent a cosmopolitan work culture. Their work conditions are world oriented, and their visions of the good life and lifestyles often clash with traditional middle-class values.[14] In the same way that the burghers did not fit the old feudal order in the late Middle Ages, today's cosmopolitan 'networkers' are not adjusted to a state-centric order. And just as the state can be seen as an institutional outcome of the burghers' search for political allies, so the future alignment of the emerging cosmopolitan groups may herald new patterns of political organization.

The European archipelago

Figure 9.1 shows 103 of the most important urban regions in Europe. These include all capitals, even small ones, and cities with more than 500,000 inhabitants. Numbers of the regions and names of the cities are found in Table 9.1. Figure 9.2 indicates the proximity to these cities of the total population in Europe: how many can reach Stockholm (number 1 in Figure 9.1 and Table 9.1) for a one-day visit; how many can go to London (number 28), how many to Moscow (number 92), and so on.[15]

The areas of the circles measure the proportion of the population that in principle can reach the centre of the respective cities for a one-day visit (round trip between 6 a.m. and midnight with a stay of at least four hours). Travellers are assumed to use the most rapid form of transportation available, or the optimal combination (car, train, airplane or boat). Two factors, in particular,

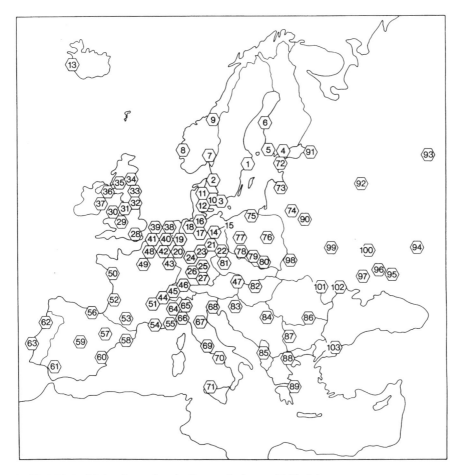

FIGURE 9.1   *Major city regions in Europe: for key see Table 9.1*

affect the size of the circles. The number of inhabitants in the regional neighbourhoods, the home region, carries great weight. In addition, swift and direct air or train connections add to the number of people for whom the city is accessible, regardless of distance. Thus, Figure 9.2 is no ordinary map of population density or distribution, but a map of accessibility in the all-European city system.[16]

Let us assume that the transportation system in Europe has been constructed according to market principles. This implies that transportation capacity can be expected to increase primarily along routes with the highest need and demand for transportation services. We might then glean from the map which are the most attractive centres in Europe. The map represents a rough yet uniform method for comparing different cities. Our approach is not dissimilar from that of economists who compare different economies only on the basis of the Gross National Product (GNP). The values that determine the size of the

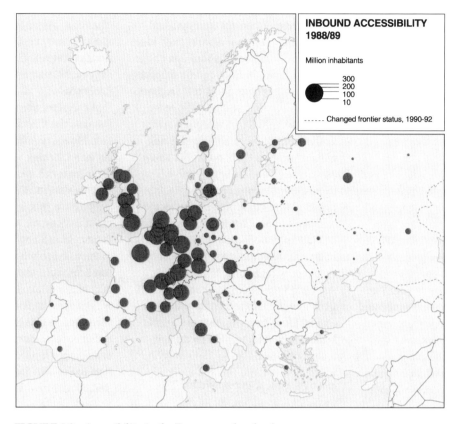

FIGURE 9.2 *Accessibility in the European urban landscape*

circles in Figure 9.2 co-vary well with data about the locations of the
administration and management of firms and other organizations. The circles
thus portray the most important meeting-places within business. They also
indicate where cultural manifestations take place, where important research
is conducted, and where capital investments and media are concentrated.

Paris and London appear to be the most central sites in Europe. They can be
considered the most international cities of the continent. If we consult the
map, we find that the economic strength of Europe is concentrated in an arch
of city-regions from London to Milan. The arch has been labelled the 'Blue
Banana', the 'Boomerang' and the 'Baroque Arch'. It covers an area where not
only important parts of economic activity, but also Europe's largest war
cemeteries and war monuments are concentrated. East of a line between Oslo,
Copenhagen, Berlin and Rome, the map is remarkably empty – not because
this part of Europe is sparsely populated, but because transportation is far less
developed than in the western areas. Network accessibility is low. This map
of the European urban landscape may serve as a background for a brief
discussion of future possibilities and risks.

TABLE 9.1 *Centres in city regions in Figure 9.1*

1	Stockholm	28	London	53	Toulouse	81	Prague
2	Gothenburg	29	Birmingham	54	Marseilles		
3	Malmoe	30	Liverpool	55	Nice	82	Budapest
		31	Manchester				
4	Helsinki	32	Leeds	56	Bilbao	83	Zagreb
5	Turku	33	Newcastle	57	Zaragoza	84	Belgrade
6	Vasa	34	Edinburgh	58	Barcelona		
		35	Glasgow	59	Madrid	85	Tirana
7	Oslo	36	Belfast	60	Valencia		
8	Bergen			61	Seville	86	Bucharest
9	Trondheim	37	Dublin				
				62	Oporto	87	Sofia
10	Copenhagen	38	Amsterdam	63	Lisbon		
11	Aarhus	39	Rotterdam			88	Thessalonica
12	Odense			64	Turin	89	Athens
		40	Antwerp	65	Milan		
13	Reykjavik	41	Ghent	66	Genoa	90	Minsk
		42	Brussels	67	Bologna		
14	West Berlin			68	Venice	91	St Petersburg
15	East Berlin	43	Luxemburg	69	Rome	92	Moscow
16	Hamburg			70	Naples	93	Kazan
17	Hannover	44	Geneva	71	Palermo	94	Volgograd
18	Bremen	45	Berne			95	Rostov
19	Düsseldorf	46	Zürich	72	Tallinn		
20	Cologne			73	Riga	96	Donetsk
21	Leipzig	47	Vienna	74	Vilnius	97	Zaporoshche
22	Dresden					98	Lvov
23	Erfurt	48	Lille	75	Gdansk	99	Kiev
24	Frankfurt am	49	Paris	76	Warsaw	100	Kharkov
	Main	50	Nantes	77	Poznan	101	Kishinov
25	Nuremberg	51	Lyons	78	Wroclaw	102	Odessa
26	Stuttgart	52	Bordeaux	79	Katowice		
27	Munich			80	Cracow	103	Istanbul

Centre–Periphery

In light of continuing economic and political integration in Europe, the need for a national centre within each state will probably decrease. The capitals are likely to lose some of their governing functions, both within public administration and private industry. Cities that are today in border zones in the periphery of the territorial states may become more important as a result. Cities such as Aachen, Strasbourg, Nice, Lille, Arnhem and Malmoe, peripheral from a national vantage point, may in the future emerge as central within a wider European framework.

Sparsely populated areas

One problem that affects several countries, including the Nordic states, concerns sparseness. The accessibility of the major continental city-regions is well established. Distances to secondary centres of significance are small. Express trains and airplanes complement each other, when the range of cars is insufficient. In other words, accessibility rests on alternative means of communication. The situation is quite different for the Nordic city-regions and other peripheral areas in Europe. According to the map in Figure 9.2, the accessibility of Nordic capitals is reasonably good, but it is vulnerable. Their 'reachability' depends entirely on air traffic; in the absence of air connections, the Nordic area would be quite isolated. From Helsinki, Stockholm and Oslo it would be impossible to take a one-day trip to any continental city; a business trip, for instance, would require several days. Thanks to the development of high-velocity trains, Copenhagen is in a somewhat better position.

Without air connections, it is questionable whether Oslo, Stockholm and Helsinki would be considered integrated parts of a European city-system. In terms of accessibility, these cities would probably once again become provincial capitals, as they were during the railroad era. In the future, railway traffic most likely will be significantly developed in the densely populated parts of western Europe. But travel by air will remain the principal means of transportation for the peripheries. To sustain their passenger traffic, large cities will be able to rely on subways and other mass transportation. The prospects for sparsely populated areas look different. Their future is dependent on the car.

Traffic infarct

The European cities are sites of progress. The constructions, installations and transportation channels testify to the advance in human efforts to improve the standard of living. Yet there is a downside to growing prosperity. Heightened standards of living and better material circumstances have taken a heavy toll. Natural resources are being depleted, the environment is damaged and the congestion in certain areas is intolerable. One fundamental problem is the constant growth and concentration of the population. Approximately 100 million persons lived in Europe in the seventeenth century. In the early nineteenth century, the continent was home to 180 million; by the end of that century, to 420 million people. Today, Europe has some 720 million inhabitants. Figure 9.2 gives us an idea of how unevenly this population is distributed, but primarily it illustrates the highly unequal distribution of purchasing power and consumption.

From another angle, the map shows how the problems associated with today's high degree of mobility are distributed in Europe. The environmental problem differs somewhat in character between the eastern and western parts of Europe. In the east, the predominant problems are linked to *immobile production sectors*. These are largely lingering problems from the heydays of industrialism. Old, pre-Second World War plants remain – obsolete, dilapidated, energy-devouring and fuelled by sulphurous coal. In the west, such conditions are far less common. A transition from large-scale, energy-demanding industries to flexible, small-scale production is in progress. New means of production are more fuel-efficient than older methods, and there are better methods of purifying industrial emissions. Many of the new, research-intensive, high-technology plants affect the environment no more than do schools, hospitals and office buildings.

There are other environmental problems in western Europe, however, some of which are becoming urgent. The constant increase in the number of people, and thus in consumption, is one such concern. The growing amount of garbage, resulting from high levels of consumption and turnover as well as 'packaging hysteria', is but one manifestation. Other problems, which refer back to Figure 9.2, have to do with the *mobile production sectors*. Modern society is characterized by increasing mobility and expanding needs for transportation. Since the 1960s, transportation within Europe of both people and goods has grown exponentially. In the economic centres and arteries, traffic is becoming increasingly congested. Many European cities today seem to be victims of *traffic infarct*.

The symptoms are evident in Europe's major cities during rush hour: streets are blocked, and traffic moves slowly. Car traffic is problematic in the central parts of many cities, which were originally built for pedestrians. Various efforts have been made to solve this dilemma; mass transportation, pedestrian streets and tunnels are examples. Despite these measures, however, many feel that some of Europe's large cities are not as accessible and as attractive for settlement as they once were.

Similar symptoms can be discerned in the links connecting cities. Traffic is congested even on major highways. It is becoming increasingly difficult to satisfy rising demand by building new roads and highways. Long-distance trucks, which in recent years have become an increasingly common means of transporting goods, travel the same roads as passenger cars and periodically block traffic in western Germany, Austria and Switzerland.

Overcrowding is becoming a problem in the air as well. In major airports, planes land and take off at ever-shorter intervals. The risk of accidents increases. As traffic is restricted to specific air corridors, a delay of a few minutes in take-off may lead to an hour-long wait for a new corridor. Such delays cost the airlines in Europe billions of dollars each year.

An EU expert group in 1992 concluded that Europe is heading toward a transportation crisis; that the transportation system will soon be paralysed, and the result will be a dramatic slowdown in economic growth, serious social tensions and further damage to the environment. A radical change in transportation policies is thus required. The objective must be to increase traffic by train, at the expense of other forms of transportation, the experts argued. The EU group recommended that railroads should once again become the principal means for transporting goods, while maritime traffic along coasts and via canals might also make a comeback. The group's report futher recommended that passenger traffic ought to be transferred from cars and airplanes to high-velocity trains and that new railroad lines should become the principal links connecting the patchwork of European cities.[17]

The infarct symptoms thus raise questions about the durability of archipelagic structures centring around major cities. There is a trade-off between the benefits and costs of the agglomeration of functions in 'global cities'. In the same way that traffic congestion today threatens the viability and attractiveness of major cities, the profits generated by global management, servicing and financial activities may be exhausted in the longer run as well.

Political implications

While the archipelago metaphor primarily reflects emerging economic configurations in Europe, it may well have political implications. Archipelagic structures entail three types of inequalities and tensions that might assume political significance. First, as we have seen, archipelagoes are located predominantly in the western parts of Europe, thus underscoring the inequalities between east and west on the continent. Secondly, the archipelago metaphor points to potential differences and tensions between 'global cities' and their home states. In many respects these cities have more extensive connections with each other than with the more distant parts of their home countries. With the emergence of 'functional spaces . . . that bear little resemblance to the political map',[18] the effective authority of states is reduced.

Thirdly, as mentioned above, archipelagoes give rise to new class structures and inequalities. The main tension appears to be between the new cosmopolitan class of network actors and locally bound low-paid workers. It is noteworthy that the pro-European vote in various referenda on EU matters has been most emphatic in the major cities, whereas nationalist sentiments are more firmly rooted in the peripheries. In sum, regional inequalities, tensions between cities and states as well as emerging class differences may create new political cleavages in the future.

NOTES

1 Manuel Castells, *The Rise of the Network Society* (Oxford: Blackwell, 1996), 381.

2 Doreen Massey, 'A Global Sense of Place', *Marxism Today*, June 1991, 26.

3 Christian Zaar, 'Syskonen Benetton driftiga som få', *Dagens Nyheter*, 18 December 1994.

4 Alfred Marshall, *Industry and Trade* (London: Macmillan, 1919).

5 Alfred Marshall, as quoted in Paul Krugman, *Geography and Trade* (Cambridge, MA: MIT Press, 1991), 37–8.

6 Jane Jacobs, *Cities and the Wealth of Nations* (Harmondsworth: Penguin, 1984).

7 Krugman, *Geography and Trade*.

8 See, for example, *Globalisation, Institutions, and Regional Development in Europe*, eds Ash Amin and Nigel Thrift (Oxford: Oxford University Press, 1994); Annelie Saxenian, *Regional Advantage: Culture and Competition in Silicon Valley and Route 128* (Cambridge, MA: Harvard University Press, 1994); Karl-Johan Lundquist, *Företag, regioner och*

internationell konkurrenskraft: om regionala resursers betydelse (Lund: Studentlitteratur, 1996).

9 Armand Bagnasco, *Tre Italie: La problematica territoriale dello sviluppo italiano* (Bologna: Il Mulino, 1977).

10 Jean Labasse, *L'Europe des régions* (Paris: Gallimard, 1991).

11 Manuel Castells, *The Informational City* (Oxford: Blackwell, 1992).

12 Saskia Sassen, *The Global City: New York, London, Tokyo* (Princeton, NJ: Princeton University Press, 1991).

13 Cf. Castells, *The Informational City*; Sassen, *The Global City*.

14 Sassen, *The Global City*, 335–7.

15 The map is from the National Atlas of Sweden, *Sweden in the World* (Stockholm: Almqvist & Wiksell, 1993). The calculations were made by Ulf Erlandsson at the Department of Social and Economic Geography, Lund University.

16 For a more detailed discussion, including empirical examples, see Gunnar Törnqvist, *Sverige i nätverkens Europa: Gränsöverskridandets former och villkor* (Malmoe: Liber-Hermods, 1996); Paul Knox, 'World Cities and the Organization of Global Space', in *Geographies of Global Change*, eds Robert J. Johnston, Peter J. Taylor and Michael J. Watts (Oxford: Blackwell, 1995).

17 Commission of the European Communities, *Green Paper on the Impact on the Environment* COM (92) (Brussels, 20 February 1992).

18 Alexander B. Murphy, 'The Sovereign State System as Political-Territorial Ideal: Historical and Contemporary Considerations', in *State Sovereignty as Social Construct*, eds Thomas J. Bierstecker and Cynthia Weber (Cambridge: Cambridge University Press, 1996), 107.

10

Towards a New State of Mind

The prominence of the state in our three disciplinary knowledge structures provided the point of departure for our trialogue. Moreover, in Chapter 1 we noted the symbolic and metaphorical underpinning of the central position of the state in scholarly as well as everyday discourses. In the course of our trialogue we have brought insights from history, geography and political science to our common purpose of putting the state into perspective and exploring alternative modes of organizing European space. We have also suggested alternative metaphors that might improve our understanding of complex realities. Hopefully, our transdisciplinary approach has provided new perspectives, insights and understandings beyond those offered by the individual disciplines. We would like to see our chief contribution as suggesting novel linkages and raising new research questions rather than revealing hitherto unknown facts or furnishing definitive answers.

While we have been struck by the degree of consensus and compatibility across disciplinary boundaries that our trialogue has revealed, our emphases may nevertheless differ somewhat. Therefore, we have decided to let the individual voices of the co-authors be heard in the final chapter. What kind of conclusions does our joint enquiry suggest to the historian, political scientist and geographer, respectively? Having related European historical experiences to current trends in the previous chapters, we now speculate about possible future developments and the mind-sets needed to understand them.

Territorial identity and historic legacy

The crossroads of history

To understand the present and evaluate alternative futures, we need knowledge about historical crossroads: which alternatives have existed in different periods, and why did Europe end up on the path it did? The historical perspective is also essential to a better understanding of the way humans have organized their existence in time and space, how and where their loyalties have been established, and how they have built their communities. The answer to these questions depends on the observer's vantage point and choice of approach.

In this book, we have focused on the interrelationship between the three basic concepts in its title, *Organizing European Space*. As for 'space', the fundament of this triad, we have primarily been interested in territory related to human beings, or 'human territory', rather than in physical-geographic or other aspects of the concept. Our study has also been limited to conditions and cultures within the boundaries of Europe, although certain conclusions may be applicable at the global level, particularly since European culture has had – and continues to have – worldwide influence.

The third defining – and at the same time confining – notion in our title concerns 'organization', a concept we use to analyse forms of control over the European territory. This control refers mainly to political controls and societal organization, although these cannot be treated as separate from other fundamental aspects, such as economy, religion and networks of communication. The terms 'organizing' and 'organization', as used in this book, imply a process perspective. The frequent use of 'organization' as a static concept – a 'frozen' process – is unsatisfactory for our purposes. In fact, our approach can be described as extremely process-oriented, insofar as it attempts to link a long-term historical perspective with present-day phenomena and to raise questions about the future.

The historical experiences that are highlighted have not been derived from any overarching theory, but have been selected to help bring concrete meaning to the four structural elements of our model of the 'territorial field of tension': state, region, union and network. Just as these vary in form and can be compared in a contemporary spatial context, a diachronic perspective provides a basis for comparisons in yet another dimension. This underlines our desire to juxtapose the two dimensions that are essential to all social science: time and space.

The point of departure for our analysis of territorial organization in Europe is the present, that is, the way Europe is organized today. As has become evident from the foregoing chapters, it is not easy to give an unequivocal description of complex realities. The fact that all the categories of the model exist in parallel – some reconcilable and perhaps even mutually reinforcing, others competing or perhaps even mutually exclusive – complicates the analysis. If the tendencies simultaneously point in different directions and appear with varying intensity, how are we to evaluate which path we are on?

To simplify, Europe today is characterized by overarching integration, as reflected in the European Union and its supranational organs and functions, on the one hand, and by fragmentation, as manifested in enduring national barriers and regional demands, on the other. These conflicting tendencies can be traced back to divergent views as to the optimal mode of organizing territory. The picture is complicated further by another development, which has called in question, or reduced the value of, territorial control at whatever level: the rapid growth in recent years of non-territorial networks.

The question of integration/fragmentation can be understood either from a top-down perspective or from a bottom-up perspective. Organization reflects power relations and resources among central actors, whether princes, estates, city oligarchies, parliaments or some other governing entity, depending on space and time. Territorial organization has not been determined only by economic, technical or military forces concentrated in the hands of specific elites or rulers, but has been shaped as well by the interests and loyalties of different groups. Successful exercise of power requires that rulers have secured a sufficient degree of legitimacy among the subjects, the citizens, or 'the people'.

In the rear-view mirror of history we can observe both the efforts of different actors and interest groups to design the most effective territorial organization, and the eternal interplay of individuals acting within or against existing structures. As discussed earlier, dramatic shifts in technical range often run up against the limits of the human mind, a factor that can be regarded as a constant in the short time perspective – a few millennia at the most – applied in this study. Thus, an enquiry into territorial identity inevitably draws attention to the values and mental frameworks of individuals and groups. To allude to a dichotomy that will be discussed later in this chapter, *human reach* then becomes more important than *technical range*, even if both dimensions are relevant in accounting for the genesis of identities.

Territoriality is a function of the emotional intensity and geographical scope of people's anchorage in space, on the one hand, and of the institutionalization of territorially based patterns, on the other. Moreover, the formation of identities is such a slow and protracted process that the individual is unlikely to experience any clear changes during his or her lifetime. Only in retrospect do transformations become discernible in this pattern of inertia.

Naturally, attachment to one's place of residence and work has been important to all generations of Europeans throughout the two thousand years dealt with in this study. This is not to say that territory has played the same role in every place and at all times, nor that territorial control has always been equally significant. In looking for prominent patterns, we should note, first, that different patterns might emerge simultaneously in different places within the European cultural sphere. Moreover, development has not been unidirectional. Already in Europe's earliest history, we can discern varying degrees of loyalty to, and different extensions of, the territorial objects of identification.

The city-state

A few examples may illustrate the point. In classical Greece, the city-states, which were small in terms of population and territory, played a major political role as independent entities. While important, citizenship was granted only to free men – not to women, slaves or immigrants. At the same time, the Greek city-states were part of a pan-Hellenic cultural community unified by language. This meant that an Athenian could, in turn, participate in a military raid against Sparta and participate in pan-Hellenic Olympic games. He could also belong to a Greek commercial network through contacts with compatriots around the Mediterranean and the Black Sea. The identity of an Athenian – the strength and depth of which we cannot know today – appears to have been stratified hierarchically, with compatible and overlapping levels.

A similar pattern can be observed in the medieval city-states. A Venetian merchant, for example, was based in the city of Venice but had access to a far-reaching commercial network around the Mediterranean. The merchant felt no affinity to the coexistent principalities in the Mediterranean region, beyond purely commercial relations. This applied to commercial cities else-where in Europe as well. A Hanseatic merchant from Lübeck was based in his hometown, but had access to business offices in, for instance, London, an extraterritorial base. At the same time, he took part in a non-territorial network of like-minded colleagues in the Hanseatic League. For the average Athenian, Venetian or Lübeckian, territorial identity was in all likelihood unconscious or only weakly developed. An individual's loyalty was more likely to be to his family, his kin or the guild to which he belonged, and was thereby indirectly linked to the immediate territorial environment, the city within its walls.

The city wall can be seen as a concrete expression of a conscious demarcation from surrounding territorial states and principalities. Entrance and exit took place through guarded gates and, for cities located by the sea, through the harbour or 'port', the linguistic origin of which is the Latin word for 'gate'.

The principality

Alongside the medieval city-states, there were social formations that rested on non-territorial ties and loyalties. The most common form of political organ-ization and control was exercised by rulers of various ranks: feudal lords, kings, dukes, counts, tyrants, bishops and a number of other potentates, frequently in conflict with each other and with the city-states.

Principality is a collective label for the most common form of territorial control during most of the Middle Ages, up until the emergence of the modern state in the late Middle Ages and the Renaissance. People's loyalties were tied to their ruler and ruling family, rather than to defined territories, the configuration of which was liable to shift in connection with wars or dynastic activities. This is most evident in the case of the migration states in the middle of the first millennium, when popular loyalty was linked to a military leader rather than to any definite territory.

Over time, as the migration states gained permanence, both the ruler and the territory became part of the identification of peoples, a process that of course was encouraged by the rulers themselves. The medieval monarchies are the political entities that most successfully strengthened their position and eventually evolved into territorial states in the modern sense. Such territorial formations could vary greatly in scope, ranging from quite small units in terms of geographic size and population – historical regions, dynastic configurations and different types of functional entities – to large integration projects, such as France, Spain or Sweden, embryos of later nation-states.

The nation-state

The nation-state – or national state – proved to be the most influential model for state-building in Europe, particularly after the principle of nationality gained currency and nationalism was promoted as an ideology in the nineteenth century. As is often noted, there was great discrepancy between ideal and reality, and true nation-states with perfect congruence between state and nation have been exceptions in the history of Europe. The principle of nationality thus has often played a destabilizing role in multinational states and in so-called part-nation states, which comprise nationalities residing in more than one state.

The principle of nationality had particularly important consequences for the multinational empires, which were unable to survive the convulsions of the First World War. The Wilhelmian empire was reduced to an ethnic German territory after the war, and the Habsburg domain was replaced by a number of small states based on the principle of nation-statehood, albeit imperfectly applied. Similarly, the Romanov and Ottoman empires were fractured into smaller units, often with new waves of instability as a result.

The European experience of large integration projects after the fall of the Roman Empire has hardly been felicitous. To be sure, the Holy Roman Empire of the German Nation lasted over 800 years, but most of this time it existed in name only. And subsequent pan-European empires had far shorter life spans – Napoleon's survived for a decade and a half, Hitler's for only a few years.

Historically, the European nation-state has proven to be the most viable form for the political organization of territory. The fact that states for two hundred years have occupied this unique position by no means implies that the system has been static, however. State-building, on the contrary, is a highly dynamic process. New states emerge, change, are fragmented, merge with others and decline. Multiple processes affect the life of any given state, not least in Europe.

In light of the development of the European Union, the question arises, whether the ethno-territorial states of Europe have played out their traditional role. Many claim that the strength and independence of the state is being eroded both from above, under the pressure of supranational governance, and from within or below, by various particularist forces. As its traditional power withers, the state will disappear altogether, the argument goes. Those lacking legitimacy and the confidence of their people will vanish first, and the others will follow as a consequence of the integrative momentum.

It seems premature, however, to declare the territorial state dead. All previous attempts to integrate Europe have foundered on the opposition of powerful structures in Europe, on the diversity of the continent in regard to peoples, languages, cultures and political experiences. To be sure, states are today in the process of transferring decision-making authority in certain important issue-areas to the European Union (areas they in practice no longer control unilaterally: defence/security, economy, international regulation, etc.). But new tasks surface continuously, and in many of these the state retains control over policy and implementation. Just as the princes in the Holy Roman Empire of the Middle Ages retained the key control apparatus and tax collection within their domain, while the emperor lacked the resources to exercise overarching power; so it will be difficult for EU organs to take over and maintain the powers that historically have been exercised within the framework of the territorial states.

Territorial control has thus played a central role throughout European history, although it has taken varying forms. Modes of organization have been time- and culture-specific. Continued integration within the European Union and the emergence of supranational organs for economic and political control raise the question whether or not we are experiencing something qualitatively different and are entering an entirely new era of European history.

Networks

While territory has been a central part of societal organization, other patterns have always existed in parallel. In these non-territorial networks have played an equally essential role. The feudal system of enfeoffment rested on loyalty between lord and vassal, which in principle was not linked to any specific territory. A successful feudal ruler could build a net of fortified places, which were controlled by the lord in a hierarchical network where horizontal contacts between vassals were suppressed.

Other early historical networks were represented by the Catholic Church with its overarching ideology and its control over the channels of communication, primarily through the Latin language, which for several centuries was the *lingua franca* of European elites. The church controlled people's souls rather than their territories. However, this did not prevent the church from exercising power over people's material possessions, including land.

A clearer alternative to both the feudal system and the territory-based social structure of the principalities was the medieval network of commercial cities that spread through most of Europe. A network of cities had existed already during Roman Antiquity; but only through the expansion of the Italian cities, resulting from the growth of long-distance trade in the tenth century, did such networks gain importance. The Italian city-republics could be viewed as islands surrounded by a sea of feudally organized society, and they were thus subjected to constant pressure. The city-republics were seldom stable. Indeed, their republican foundations often could be abolished by warlords and replaced with dictatorial rule under so-called tyrants.

The cities north of the former Roman Empire suffered similar pressures. Some were from the outset under the protection and control of princes, such as Hedeby and Birka, two major centres in the realm of Baltic commerce in the ninth century. In general, the princes could use their military resources to strengthen their influence, by offering 'protection' in exchange for taxes and tariffs, or 'extraction'. To some extent, the fortified walls of the city could protect its dwellers from such intrusions, but the lines of communication between the cities, particularly by land, were too vulnerable for the network system to survive in the long run.

Regions and places

In present-day Europe, cities once again occupy a position that challenges established decision-making structures, essentially the traditional territorial states. Now more than ever before, resources – people, knowledge, capital and infrastructures – are concentrated to cities. Technological advances have reduced distances and improved accessibility to an unprecedented degree. The nodes of the IT society are linked quite regardless of geographic dimensions, such as distance and territories in between. Actors in modern networks no longer confront highwaymen, confiscatory customs duties, or insurmountable physical barriers. Rather, they are restrained primarily by human limitations; not even the most talented and well-educated individuals can reach beyond their given, comparatively limited abilities. If history teaches us anything, it is the paramountcy of people interacting with their environment, the human need for a palpable community, which encompasses families, friends, a residence and a workplace – a space in which the individual feels at home. This has remained true throughout the period dealt with in this study.

Despite inherent limitations to human capacity, Europeans throughout their history have exhibited a remarkable ability to organize and to adapt structures and organizations to constantly changing needs and conditions. European culture has been dynamic and expansive, both in terms of ideas, politics and economic power. Many of the original elements of European culture eventually became cornerstones of a wider phenomenon, generally called Western civilization. Although the forms of political dominance in the international system have changed in more recent times, much of the fundamental influence and advantage that Europe obtained through its global political and economic reach still remains. Thus, the impact of European culture and organization is not confined to the continent, but continues to be a global concern.

Power and accountability: the future of the democratic state

To a political scientist, two central themes suggest themselves in summarizing the evolution described and analysed in the preceding chapters, and in attempting to extrapolate into the future: (1) the dispersion of power, and (2) the multiplying problems of accountability. The first theme concerns competing authority claims and the future role of the state; the second alludes to the prospects for democratic governance under multi-layered complexity and globalization.

The power of the sovereign state, as we have seen, rested on extensive authority claims. The institution of sovereignty endowed states with 'meta-political' authority, insofar as states claimed the authority to relegate issues to the political realm where they were recognized to have ultimate authority. This kind of exclusive authority is no longer for the state to claim. The evolution from the traditional sovereign state to the contemporary state, it has been suggested, represents a qualitative change similar to that of a lobster in the sea ending up on a plate: 'Their borders remain largely intact and their constitutions are in place, but the shells of these sovereign crustaceans have often proved too porous to prevent their contents from being cooked to someone else's taste.'[1]

As is particularly graphic in Europe, the state is losing power 'upwards', to supranational entities, as well as 'downwards', to regional entities and transnational networks. It has been argued that the state has become too big for the little things and too small for the big things.[2] This reflects a widespread impression that the sovereign power of the state has been diluted and dispersed among other types of actors in recent times.

From state to market

Technological and economic factors are usually pointed to as the main determinants of this development, and 'globalization' is the buzzword used – and frequently misused – to capture their combined effect. The favoured manner of describing the power shift is to portray the state as the victim of the globalized market economy. Robert Cox, drawing on Karl Polyani's work, describes a kind of cyclical movement in the relations between state and market.[3] The early European states, from the fifteenth through the eighteenth century, were mercantilist; the pursuit of state power was carried out through the accumulation of economic power and wealth. States strove to regulate production as well as export and import and to control shipping. During the industrial revolution, the state gradually withdrew from substantive economic activity, leaving it to the presumedly self-regulating market, while assuming the role of enforcer of the rules of the market.

Eventually states reacted to unanticipated socially destructive consequences of the self-regulating market by resuming its regulatory authority and guaranteeing a modicum of social equity, and in the twentieth century the welfare state was born. By the early 1970s this renewed pattern of state regulation seemed to have reached its limits. Stagflation and fiscal crises led to a deregulation movement around the world. The state abdicated from the economic realm in the same way it had done during the industrial revolution. The crucial difference is that now the economy is global, and the autonomous capacity of states to control their national economies and regulate their relationship to the external world economy has been reduced.

To some observers, this kind of historical sketch suggests an irrevocable change in the balance of power between states and markets: 'the impersonal forces of world markets, integrated over the postwar period more by private enterprise than by the cooperative decisions of governments, are now more powerful than the states to whom ultimate political authority over society and economy is supposed to belong'.[4] In this perspective, the vertical boundaries separating states are being replaced by horizontal boundaries separating economic and technical elites from other citizens, and sovereign states are being replaced by sovereign markets.[5]

In the proliferating globalization literature there is no doubt a tendency to exaggerate the extent to which power has slipped away from states to markets. First of all, states may be portrayed as midwives rather than victims of globalization. A number of states are promoting and encouraging rather than constraining the globalization of corporate activity. The opening up of capital markets occurred as a direct result of decisions by a series of governments to deregulate. They may have done so willingly or unwillingly, ceding to pressures from financial interests or trying to prevent international crises, but deregulation was none the less the outcome of political decisions. The changing balance of power between states and markets is thus largely the result of the diffusion of national deregulation policies, the widespread susceptibility of governments to the 'fashion' in economic policy or the 'mood of the time', rather than impersonal forces of globalization above and beyond states. Moreover, the globalization literature has tended to draw an exaggerated picture of state powers in the past in order to claim powerlessness in this day and age.[6]

If anything, the long sweep of history teaches us that the state has proved to be an extraordinarily adaptive type of organization. As we have seen, the modern state emerged from the challenges of military competition and increased trade in the late Middle Ages. European states have since had to respond to new challenges of industrialization, nation-building and democratization. In the process, they have redefined their purposes and added new functions and institutions while retaining the old ones.[7] Will they be able to adapt to the challenges of today and tomorrow as well? A negative answer to this question is by no means given, as the 'transformationalists' contend. As a matter of fact, the states of Europe may once again serve as a model for the rest of the world and provide a key to the future.

As alluded to in Chapter 7, the European Union, in its present form, can be seen as a kind of adaptation to globalization. The EU is often taken to be *sui generis*, a unique phenomenon with no historical precedent or counterpart in the contemporary world. Yet it is possible to regard the EU as a harbinger of the future role of the state. Let us pursue that perspective and look for components of such a role, as suggested by the EU experience.

From dominance to negotiations

The changing role of the state, we concluded in Chapter 5, entails negotiation instead of domination. Rather than claiming absolute authority domestically and exclusive agency externally, the 'negotiating state' mediates between domestic and international and between political and economic interests. As demonstrated graphically by the EU, the shift from domination to negotiation does not only involve increased cooperation among states but interaction with other types of actors as well. In the wake of globalizing markets, traditional notions of diplomacy as state–state activity need to be broadened to include state–firm as well as firm–firm diplomacy.[8] In addition, the state becomes increasingly engaged in negotiations with the expanding and variegated community of transnational actors and movements, 'activists beyond borders',[9] which are often lumped together under the label of non-governmental organizations (NGOs). By virtue of their commitment to, and expertise in, a focused set of concerns, NGOs may gain considerable leverage on selected policy issues *vis-à-vis* states, which have to attend to a wide array of demands.[10]

As we have seen, the EU has become an arena for interaction between the 'negotiating state' and these other types of actors. The EU experience also illustrates that they enter into a bargaining relationship, characterized by interdependence and the coincidence of common and conflicting interests.[11] States need firms to create the economic foundation of their existence, and firms need the predictable environment of a stable state to prosper. States are often dependent on NGOs to reach out 'where the action is' on such issues as protecting the environment, providing development aid or halting the spread of epidemics, whereas NGOs are dependent on states or interstate organizations for the provision of channels of action and, sometimes, funding. Along with the common or complementary interests in the creation of wealth and the solution of certain issues, important conflicting interests obviously enter into the bargaining relationship among states, firms and NGOs. For example, states want to extract as much in taxes as possible, firms prefer to pay as little tax as possible. As the identity of NGOs is often based on opposition to governments, too close collaboration with governments may threaten their autonomy. In short, firms and NGOs sometimes challenge, sometimes supplement the state; but they nearly always act in counterpoint with governmental actors.

While such incipient bargaining relationships are not limited to European states, the peculiarity of the EU is that these various actors tend to interact conjointly in informal networks. It could be argued that throughout history formal organizations have been created in order to discipline and control informal networks exercising unchecked influence, be they families, clans or churches. The modern state is no exception in that regard, and outside the European Union states remain more concerned with controlling networks than with participating in them. The EU member states, by contrast, seem to be following the motto 'if you can't beat them, join them'. This represents an innovation in international relations, which can be taken to illustrate the adaptive capacity, and foreshadow the future role, of the state.

If we situate the state in the context of negotiations in networks, as the EU experience suggests, we may identify its relative bargaining strengths and weaknesses. A tentative, but by no means exhaustive, list of bargaining assets of the contemporary state might focus on network position, sovereignty and information. First, as demonstrated by the EU, states tend to occupy *central positions in policy networks*. In graphic representations of policy networks, with points symbolizing organizational nodes and arrows symbolizing connections, states usually constitute central nodes in terms of being reachable from, and able to reach, most other organizations in the network. This 'linking-pin' position makes it difficult for other actors to neglect or bypass the state when negotiating an issue. Secondly, *sovereignty* remains a bargaining asset in transnational networks. As we concluded in Chapter 5, sovereignty still confers on states legal authority which can be exercised to the detriment of other actors' interests or be bargained away in return for influence over others' policies. The EU is a primary example of this. Thirdly, the state still has a certain advantage in the collection and assemblage of *information*, even if it has lost some of its previous preponderance to multinational media conglomerates. The preparation of statistics is typically a state function. In addition, states have diplomatic and intelligence branches which system-atically gather information about the international environment. Being well informed is essential in negotiations in networks, and information can be used as a bargaining resource in exchange relations.

By the same token, one can draw up a list of relative weaknesses of the state in network and bargaining terms. For the sake of symmetry, let us highlight three disadvantages under the rubrics of territoriality, decision time and intersocietal penetration. First, states are *territorially bound*, whereas their business and NGO counterparts are transnational in character. By virtue of their presence in many countries, multinational corporations and NGOs are not dependent on any one state. For instance, a firm can exit if it dislikes the policies of a host country; a state cannot run away from its geopolitical situation. Secondly, states – especially the kind of democratic states that predominate in Europe – have *lengthy decision processes*, whereas their counterparts – in particular the actors in globalized financial markets – can make speedy decisions, unrestrained by public opinion or constitutional checks and balances. The contrast between the extreme speed of decisions in the financial markets and the inertia of government decision-making becomes palpable in times of currency crises. Thirdly, in comparison with multinational firms and NGOs, states lack the capacity for what we, for lack of better words, may call *intersocietal penetration*. The institution of sovereignty, it will be recalled, allows the state to make extensive claims of authority within its own society while excluding it from any influence over the societies of other states. To be sure, states have by no means adhered strictly to the principle of non-intervention, but the asymmetry remains that multinational firms and NGOs are vastly more embedded in – and have considerably greater potential to influence – a number of societies.

In sum, a perspective that puts emphasis on states as negotiating entities, participating in transnational networks, yields a more multifaceted and fine-grained picture of the adaptability and changing role of states than the simplistic alternatives of demise or survival dominating the debate between 'transformationalists' and 'sceptics'. In that respect, the EU may be a key to the future of the state more generally.[12]

Problems of accountability

At the same time, the notion of the negotiating state in networks raises thorny questions about democratic values in general, and accountability in particular. Accountability is the touchstone of representative democracy. The government is accountable for its actions before the people in elections at regular intervals. For citizens to be able to make informed judgements of accountability two fundamental requirements must be fulfilled: *transparency*, in the sense that the voter should be fully informed as to what the government has in fact done during its term, and *responsibility*, in the sense that it should be clear to the voter who is responsible for what action. The picture of the changing role of the state, drawn above on the basis of the EU experience, is problematic on both accounts.

Negotiations in networks rarely take place in the open. The accepted wisdom is that effective negotiations require confidentiality and a measure of secrecy, and one of the advantages of informal network structures is precisely their limited visibility. The lack of transparency, associated with negotiations in networks, is therefore a major problem in terms of government accountability before the voters; the heated debate about transparency in the EU testifies to that. Added to the general problem of transparency is the difficulty of ascribing unequivocal responsibility to specific actors for decisions reached through negotiations in networks. Negotiated outcomes imply shared responsibility among a number of actors who have all had to modify their initial positions. Unpopular aspects of the outcome can always be blamed on other actors.

In short, as agency and power become more anonymous, the difficulty of pinning responsibility to individual actors is magnified. Again, the EU provides ample illustrations as to how the traditional image of individual governments being held responsible for discrete policy measures, affecting only citizens of its own state, is eroded by multi-level governance through negotiations in networks. 'If the efficacy of the system of representative democracy is being strained and eroded in the face of regional and global interconnectedness, what mechanisms could ensure accountability in the new international order?'[13] That question remains unanswered.

Another principal democratic problem concerns the delimitation of a *demos*, the people entitled to suffrage and other democratic rights and responsibilities. Nationalism laid a foundation for modern democracy, in this regard, by defining the *demos* in terms of the nation which, in turn, was to coincide with the state. The *demos* of modern democratic practice thus became territorially bound. If we envisage the future of Europe as negotiation and power sharing between territorial states and non-territorial entities, this seemingly firm foundation begins to crumble. One problem derives from the increased demographic mobility. Voting rights have traditionally been based on birth and citizenship. With a growing number of persons residing and working in other countries than those of their citizenship, this principle raises questions. Why should, say, a Swede, who has worked for many years in the EU bureaucracy in Brussels, or in a multinational firm in Spain, be entitled to vote in elections in remote Sweden but not in his or her country of residence and work, where political decisions directly affect his or her daily life?

This touches on a perhaps even more fundamental problem, which is accentuated by the EU experience: democracy presupposes perfect coincidence between the *demos* with voting rights and the people affected by the resulting policy measures. This forges the link between voting and accountability judgements. In our era of globalization, however, 'territorial systems of accountability no longer necessarily coincide with the spatial reach of sites of power'.[14] Increasingly voters are affected by decisions made in other states or by other types of actors, on the one hand, and outcomes of negotiations between their own state and other states and actors, on the other. 'National communities by no means exclusively make and determine decisions and policies for themselves, and governments by no means determine what is appropriate exclusively for their own citizens'.[15] The European Union epitomizes new 'possibilities of governance independent of the existence of a central authority and beyond the territorial congruence of those who govern with those who are subject to governance'.[16] The new realities seem to call for a move away from reliance on a single source of democratic legitimation and accountability. Yet, the unresolved question in the contemporary trans-formation of European space will be how to define *demos* and retain the fundamentals of democratic governance.

To summarize, the dispersion of power we can note in Europe and the rest of the world does not necessarily entail the withering of the state, as much of the current literature on globalization contends. However, we are witnessing a profound transformation of the state's role, and the state's adaptability to new circumstances, proven by the historical record, is again being tested. The EU experience points to one possible mode of adaptation: the state as a negotiating entity, participating in transnational networks. This invites a discussion of interdependencies, common and conflicting interests, and the relative strengths and weaknesses of states *vis-à-vis* other prominent types of actors, such as multinational corporations and NGOs. A scenario of negotiating states in networks calls traditional democratic practices into question. Unresolved problems include how to ensure accountability and how to define the *demos* that might be the foundation of future democratic governance.

The changing geography: does territory matter?

Transportation and communications technology is, in essence, a question of finding technical solutions to the problem of moving goods, people and information. This fundamental problem has been a continuous challenge to human ingenuity, and history abounds with examples of technical innovations that have dramatically altered our geographic scope for action. New oppor-tunities have been created for exploiting natural resources, for producing goods and services, for managing enterprises, and for improving human living conditions. The correlation between new technology and increased mobility is evident. Diminishing distance-related friction has entailed increased volumes of transportation as well as multiplying and more rapid flows of communication. It is more difficult to evaluate in which ways new technologies have affected, and will continue to affect, the location of industrial plants, settlement patterns and modes of organization. This has been the subject of divergent visions, hopes and apprehensions.

Napoleon did not travel faster than Caesar

At the root of the local self-subsistence and regional isolation of earlier societies lay considerable distance-related friction. Through vertical links, natural resources bound production to specific places. Transport by land was dependent on the physical capacity of animals and people to carry and pull. Information could be transmitted to remote places only through messengers. Navigable waters provided the best form of transportation. Roads were few and primitive.

Over the centuries, human ability to master geographic space changed quite slowly. That Napoleon Bonaparte did not travel faster than Julius Caesar was not merely a figure of speech, but a reality. In the eighteenth century, the ancient Roman roads remained the most trafficable paths south and west of the *limes*, the boundary along the Rhine and the Danube that separated the barbarians in the north and east from the civilized populations in the south and west.

It was only in the nineteenth and twentieth centuries that a qualitative change in technical range triggered a veritable social revolution. To be sure, even before then there were intermittent advances in the capacity to transport people and goods over long distances, but they were modest in comparison to those set in motion by the industrial revolution.

The Belgian historian Henri Pirenne has distinguished three 'logistic revolutions'. The first took place during the Middle Ages, when new transport links connected previously separated trade systems and cultures. With better vessels, such as Venetian crusader ships and Hanseatic cogues, trade evolved between ports along Europe's major navigable rivers. As political territories grew, it became easier to avert robbery and plundering along transportation routes, over land as well as water. The second logistic revolution connected continents. With the advent of caravels it became easier to carry goods across the seas. The pivot of long-distance trade shifted from the Mediterranean and the Baltic Sea to the coasts of the Atlantic and the North Sea. Not only advances in transportation technology account for the expansion of trade, however. The emergence of uniform means of payment, a credit market and banks contributed as well by facilitating commercial transactions. This, in turn, boosted the need for transmitting and processing information. The third logistic revolution began with industrialism in England by the end of the eighteenth century.[17]

Technology that transfigures time and space

With industrialism, the technical range began to expand at an accelerating pace. The advent of steamships facilitated rapid transportation of large quantities across the seas, regardless of weather conditions. Railroads linked large territories. This process started around the year 1800, when local railroad tracks and horse-drawn wagons were introduced in the coal district of Newcastle in the northeast of England. A century later, Europe was replete with railroad tracks. For the first time in history, an expansion of technical range came to affect the public at large. People were no longer dependent for their livelihood on local markets and resources. It became possible to move and sustain mass armies. Long-distance travel was no longer the privilege of a small elite.

The invention of the automobile launched another revolution in the transport of people and goods. Its principal advantages had little to do with increasing range or speed, and more to do with the automobile's adaptability to individual travel needs. Air transport can be said to represent the opposite: it has quickly developed into the outstanding means of rapid transportation, while having pronounced nodal network properties. This means that access is provided only through a few far-apart nodes. The radical impact of automobiles and aircraft became apparent in Europe only after the Second World War. Later, when motor traffic started causing congestion in narrow city streets and on overcrowded roads, railroads experienced a sort of renaissance. Overcrowding in the air has also contributed to new investment in express trains along major traffic routes.

The advent of railways in the early nineteenth century undermined earlier perceptions of time and space. As railroad traffic effectively shrunk the distances between areas, the incongruous local times throughout Europe were exposed. Before the railroad era, time was 'variegated', based on astronomical phenomena. This meant that places and regions at different latitudes had different local times, determined by the position of the sun. In the 1840s, the railroad companies of Great Britain introduced uniform railroad times, which until the end of the century pertained only to railroad traffic and schedules. As the railroad network grew denser, affecting more and more places and regions, the need to replace 'variegated' time with 'uniform' time became apparent. In 1880, railroad times became the standard throughout Great Britain, and in 1884 an international conference coordinated national standard times and divided the world into the time zones that are still in effect today.

While contributing to making time uniform, railroads punctuated space. A pattern of discrete points linked by more or less straight lines was superimposed on a continuous geographic space. 'The railroads know only departure, pause and arrival in places that are normally far apart. With the space in between, which they contemptuously crisscross and condescend only to glance at, they create no connection.' These words were written in 1840.[18] The transfiguration of time and space experienced by nineteenth-century travellers seems minor in comparison to present-day realities.

The cost of transporting goods has been reduced to a greater extent than other costs that businesses attempt to minimize, and transportation times have shrunk. One result of this development is that a significant part of the manufacturing industry has become 'footloose', with wide options of location and relocation. Another development is that the transportation sector has expanded dramatically. Goods are transported between producers, suppliers, wholesalers, retailers and consumers regardless of distance, and regardless of the fact that substitutes are available closer at hand. Congestion and 'traffic infarct' in large cities and along highways is the price paid for this enhanced mobility.

At the utmost limit of mobility

Even more dramatic is the history of the range of the media, the channels for conveying information. For thousands of years, information travelled only as fast as the horse or the ship. In the 1840s, when Samuel Morse had invented his alphabet and telegraph services were initiated, it took ten weeks to dispatch a message back and forth between London and Bombay. In the 1870s, by which time telegraph wires linked much of the world, it took only four minutes.

Before the turn of the century, the invention of the telephone made it possible to exchange spoken messages over long distances. Later refinements of telecommunications technology, such as mobile phones and facsimile machines, have increased the ease and speed of exchanging information. With computers in networks there are virtually no limits to the transfer and storage of information, whether as text, image or sound. Firms and other organizations today have built internal computer networks that connect their different sites. In principle, the physical distance between these sites is of no relevance. Such networks can also link up independent but collaborating companies, thus blurring traditional notions of firms.

Modern information technology promises limitless range. Today, the daily operations of complex transportation systems, multilateral corporations and financial markets rely on telecommunications and computers. Key actors in these spheres with global range may have the impression of sharing the same locality. Manuel Castells, for instance, speaks in paradoxical terms of 'timeless time' and a 'space of flows'.[19]

The development of mass communication has been no less dramatic. In earlier eras, information could reach a great number of people simultaneously only if these people assembled, for example in the amphitheatre, the agora, the forum, the piazza, or the marketplace. Only with the invention of the printing press in the fifteenth century could the written word start reaching larger audiences. Even if newspapers were being published in many parts of Europe by the seventeenth century, the major expansion of newspaper distribution took place in the nineteenth and the first half of the twentieth century. In early industrial society, daily newspapers became the most important medium for news, debates and political propaganda, with a circulation that affected nearly every household.

Radio transmissions were initiated in the 1910s. Early television broadcasts took place in London and Berlin in 1936. Today the broadcasting media occupy an exceptional position in mass communications, by virtue of the speed with which identical information can reach different audiences around the globe. Information spread via broadcasting media is public and unidirectional. It is not directed to any particular recipient, and it does not allow for immediate feedback. In the context of a society without any distance-related friction, it is important to recall that all forms of mass communications are 'asymmetrical'. The senders can reach out to multiple audiences, whereas the recipient can only tune in to one channel at the time. This asymmetry is illustrated most dramatically by television. Reporters, anchormen and artists appear before anonymous audiences who, for their part, may experience a sense of presence and community with the performers. Indeed, one-way communication and technical reach make for individual fame and stardom in our age.

The French urban planner Paul Virilio is one of many who have argued that accelerating speed is the governing principle of social change. In his book *Vitesse et politique*, Virilio portrays technology as our destiny, and technological progress as an inevitable incentive for change. The history of science and technology, he claims, is a history of acceleration. Technological development has led to, or soon will lead to, a world where physical distance is of no relevance. Before long, it will be possible to travel between Paris and Tokyo in less time than it takes many people to commute from home to work in a large urban region today. Democracy was born when citizens gathered in the centre of the city, in an agora or a forum. New technology has given rise to medial proximity with no sense of physical distance or space. The public sights and sounds of the broadcasting media, transmitted at the speed of magnetic waves, that is, 300,000 kilometres per second, have replaced the public marketplace. Paul Virilio regards the development as alarming, but inevitable. In a 1991 interview, he stated: 'Either we do away with technology or we accept acceleration until we have reached the utmost limits of mobility, that is, the speed of light. Beyond that there is nothing, unless Einstein was mistaken and the theory of relativity is incorrect and there do, in fact, exist superluminous speeds.'[20]

The lack of friction and restrictions does not entail only advantages, but also causes a new set of problems. For instance, financial markets in our electronic age are often blamed for reacting too hastily and unreflectingly. Opinion polls, registering temporary swings in the electorate, may influence long-term political decisions. Automation and remote control eliminate the 'social friction' that is an essential part of negotiations, discussions and conversations. Without such friction, it is more difficult to reach prudent and pragmatic decisions. Individual experience becomes a less important input. The possibility for individuals to control, discover errors and inform diminishes. Reduced friction entails more uncertainty, unexpected outcomes and risks.[21]

Liberated space and settlement patterns

Modern means of transportation and communication would seem to make production and settlement less bound to places and limited regional environments. And no doubt reduced distance-related friction has entailed a broader range of options concerning location. With more alternatives, mobility can be expected to increase. Yet this freedom of choice has not been widely used either by firms or individuals. Rather, it seems to have facilitated concentration.

Today choices of location are influenced by access to transportation routes and network nodes. Air routes and express trains connect cities in 'nodal landscapes', whereas today's 'remote areas' are those without railway stations, located along railroad tracks on which express trains pass, and those far from airports. It is well known that the advantages of large-scale production become more significant with increasing technical range. The theoretical literature refers to 'agglomerative advantages' and 'external local effects', which come to the fore in a society where the distance-related friction is insignificant.[22] Thus, we find that firms tend to cluster in strategic locations.

What about individual freedom of choice? Are there human, rather than technological, factors that tie individuals to specific geographic environments and make certain places and areas more attractive than others? In our attempt to address this question, 'social communication' and 'human reach' are key concepts.

Terms of social communication

The previously used term 'technical range' can be contrasted with 'human reach'. Range implies technical scope, the possibilities of, and limits to, moving goods, people and messages. Reach, on the other hand, is contingent on the biological and mental capacity of human beings, the ability to include the surrounding world in a mental sphere of interest. Human reach changes through personal experiences and incoming information.

Given the remarkable development of technical range, it is easy to forget that human reach has by no means been transformed correspondingly. The physical and mental capacities of human beings are not much different from a few generations ago. If anything, without technical aids, our physical aptitude would most likely be lower today. It is also questionable whether our ability to handle information has grown significantly. There is nothing to indicate that the present generation would have greater sensory and perceptual capacities – or different gifts for empathy, identity, involvement and trust – than previous ones.

The verb 'reach' means to extend, stretch out, grasp, and achieve communication. As a noun, it denotes scope and something attainable, including comprehension. As such, 'reach' is widely used in phenomenological research. The Swedish geographer Torsten Hägerstrand describes reach thus:

To say that something is within a person's reach refers not only to his/her being able to reach it in a purely physical sense. It includes economic, cognitive and emotional dimensions as well. Figuratively speaking, each person is during his/her lifetime embedded in a *reach space* that in various ways stretches sideways, backward to the past, and forward toward desired futures. What is contained in the space depends on the individual's own capacity and biography, but also on what is offered by the environment in terms of resources to draw from and recipients to give to.[23]

To understand human reach we need to draw on insights from information theory, physiology and psychology concerning the human ability to process and convey information. All information that reaches us is screened and classified. Every second, individuals sift out millions of information bits, thus creating organization and order out of the confusing mass of information and laying the foundation of human *consciousness*. It is this screening process that creates consciousness, not the information *per se*. Consciousness is filtered, organized and assimilated information. At any given moment we perceive but a fraction of the information that is bombarding our sensory organs. The 'bandwidth' of our consciousness is far narrower than that of our senses.

At the same time, consciousness is remarkably versatile. The bandwidth for 'internal' handling of information is a thousand times greater than that which our senses can utilize to receive 'external' impulses. An extensive thought process takes place in the nervous system of each human being, a process of association, sorting, organization and filtering, in which new information blends with memories, dreams and emotions. People's internal mental worlds contain a wealth of information. By contrast, the amount of information that can be exchanged between complex mental worlds is small. The channel that is available for this process has a very narrow bandwidth. Language is insufficient to convey the major share of our experiences. The effect of our efforts to transmit information depends, to a certain extent, on the clarity of the signals we send; but even more on the distance between mental worlds. Social communication is most effective between individuals whose mental worlds have been 'formatted' analogously over lengthy periods of time.[24]

Our need for boundaries

These observations concerning human consciousness have geographic implications. They draw attention to the fact that human thought requires boundaries. To draw boundaries can be viewed as a mental self-defence mechanism. At the same time, we need boundaries to share our views and experiences with others and to determine our identity, in terms of being able to distinguish 'us' from 'them'. As pointed out in Chapter 2, physical proximity, likeness and linkage are three fundamental principles underlying our drawing of boundaries.

In short, boundaries do not only refer to the physical terrain but are drawn in mental maps as well. *Realm of experience* and *epistemic community* are some of the concepts used to describe areas within which people are united by a common language, religious community, a collective history, shared memories and mutual trust. The French speak of *sémiosphère*, the Germans of *Lehrgemeinschaft*. These realms or communities can easily be conceptualized as territorial categories – places, regions and countries. Yet, as discussed in previous chapters, there is every indication that a sense of belonging and loyalty can be nurtured in networks as well. However, as indicated in Chapters 8 and 9, several factors suggest that place, neighbourhood and region will continue to play important roles as realms of experience and epistemic communities.

While technical range stands for rapid change, human reach, personal networks of contact and epistemic communities represent remarkably tenacious structures. These are passed on from generation to generation through upbringing and education. Inherited knowledge is preserved in texts and images in our archives, museums, libraries, statues and memorials. Resting on the experiences of overlapping generations, human reach fosters local anchorage and regional identity. Our daily patterns of movement and dense social networks reinforce the importance of our immediate environment. If an individual resides in a certain area for a relatively long time, the place and the neighbourhood become his/her realm of experience. This realm includes not only social and cultural ties, but also the physical environment. During childhood and adolescence, experiences of place are likely to have a particularly strong influence on the development of an individual's psyche. In recent years, questions related to the emergence and preservation of regional identity and sense of place have attracted renewed interest among scholars.[25]

Our need for conversation

Our discussion of social communication points to our need for conversation. No other form of communication offers the same advantages. Weak or ambiguous signals can be amplified and clarified through the back-and-forth flow of information. Only within sight can kinetic and paralinguistic signals be sent and interpreted. When more than two individuals need to communicate, the advantages of direct conversation become even more apparent. Participants are then able to observe and interpret not only the speaker but also the reactions of the listeners. Technical aids cannot convey the richness of impressions offered by direct contacts. All known media filter information, and mass media reduce communication to a one-way process.

Here we can trace one of the great paradoxes of our time. Modern, computer-backed information systems make it possible to process virtually boundless amounts of information. Via telecommunications and media, information can be transferred at the speed of light across any distance. Yet at the same time, the need for consultation and direct person-to-person contacts has increased. Today, more and more businessmen and civil servants devote more and more of their time to meetings and other contact activities. Travel to various types of meetings, even over great distances, has surged dramatically in recent years, despite undeniable costs in terms of money, time and effort. Modern society, characterized by far-reaching division of labour and specialization, is becoming ever more complex and less transparent. In a world of fragmented knowledge and expertise, conferences and meetings are means of overcoming uncertainty, of combining bits of information into a comprehensive basis for decision-making.

Well-structured, routine information can be transferred rapidly and effectively via telephone, facsimile and computers in networks. Such information transfers are today used in a wide variety of contexts, ranging from large-scale manufacturing to speedy check-in at airports. These flows of information are often unidirectional and follow established, formal channels. There is a low degree of uncertainty (Figure 10.1).

Technical aids are not as useful in dealing with questions involving *uncertainty*, *unpredictability* and *surprise*. Thus, negotiation, reconnaissance, renewal and other search processes require information exchange via face-to-face contacts and group conversation. Media, on the other hand, are most suitable for transferring information *within* established social networks, characterized by a low degree of uncertainty. They cannot replace direct contacts between strangers or *between* networks, which are typified by uncertainty.[26]

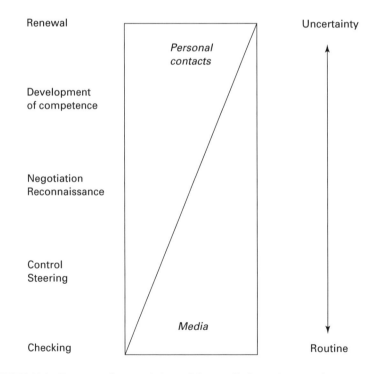

FIGURE 10.1 *Purposes, characteristics and forms of information transfer*

The archipelago: the metaphor of our times

Existing global networks would hardly be feasible without almost boundless technical range. On the other hand, the prevalence of local anchorage would be unintelligible without reference to the potency and limitations of human reach. The overall picture that emerges is one of fragmented space, of an *archipelago* of scattered urban regions, connected via networks of different kinds.

As discussed above, it is the interplay of several factors that creates this picture. Modern transportation systems contribute to the fragmentation of geographical space, whereas strong agglomerative forces favour concentration. Firms and institutes of research and culture erect buildings and are embedded in local and regional environments where people live and work, but without links with transnational flows of knowledge, capital and ideas they would face stagnation. Hence networks grow that transcend national and other geographic boundaries. The interplay of global forces of change and regional ambitions, which is essential to our material prosperity, is made possible through the links that connect a kaleidoscopic world of home bases and creative places.

Quo vadis, Europe?

Our trialogue has not yielded any hard and fast predictions as to which mode of organizing European space will prevail in the future. Nor was that our intention from the outset. Rather, we have tried to provide a set of conceptual tools, which hopefully will help the reader to better understand the multi-layered organizational complexity characterizing contemporary Europe. To refer back to the metaphors used in Chapter 1, we have offered a whole set of floodlights to avoid leaving parts of the stage in the shade or in the dark, or – to use a different metaphor – a variety of nets to catch different fish in different ponds.

Our main message, therefore, is to accept and welcome complexity and variability rather than relying on any *one* model or theory. Different lines of development coexist in today's Europe. In that sense the present is not that different from the past. In fact, it could be argued that the multiplicity and variability of organizational forms may have contributed to the dynamism that accounts for the relative success of the European continent throughout history. And, as we have seen, this complexity and variability can be captured in a 'territorial field of tension' which, though of a general nature, may look somewhat different at different times and in different parts of the world.

The state constituted the benchmark in our analysis of the contemporary 'territorial field of tension'. We have identified a number of challenges to the sovereign territorial state. One can be subsumed under the label of 'globalization'. Its determinants are chiefly technological and economic in nature. As a result of the revolution in transportation and information technology, ever larger shares of business, research and development can be conducted in transnational networks that are beyond the control of individual states. The EU, as we have argued, can be seen as an incipient effort to create a political form for globalized space.

Another tendency, proceeding in parallel, can be labelled 'regionalization'. Regional proximity and local anchorage have not lost their significance in a globalized world. In large measure, identification needs rather than material forces, human reach rather than technical range, underlie this tendency. As the bonds with the national centre are weakened, regional and local self-identities tend to be strengthened. This trajectory does not contradict the globalization trend. On the contrary, when mobility across national boundaries increases, the significance of local identities seems to grow as well. In a world of global flows of capital, people, ideas and technology specific local and regional features become competitive advantages. Regional and local organizations are emerging as international actors not only economically but in the political arena as well. The cross-border regions, regional representation and regional lobbying in the EU are prominent examples of this. In short, globalization and regionalization tendencies interact and shape each other, which has given rise to such synthesized labels as 'glocalization' and 'fragmegration'.[27]

Our conclusions as historian, political scientist and geographer have one thing in common: a caveat not to forget the limitations of human nature and the inertia of basic human values, as we live through an era of dramatic and unprecedented changes in technical range. Depending on disciplinary background, we may emphasize different aspects of human reach, be it identity, democratic values or a sense of place. But we do agree that mental structures can prove to be barriers to rapid technological and organizational change.

We are also in agreement that these complementary processes of spatial integration and fragmentation do not necessarily herald the end of the state. Our analysis has emphasized the adaptability of the state in the past and the changing *role* of the state today. As we have seen, the 'negotiating state' retains certain advantages in its interactions with other actors. And one should not forget that the same states that promoted globalization through a series of liberalization and deregulation measures may in the future act to restrain that process and close their borders. To be sure, most observers believe that states are no longer able to reverse the process – the globalization genie cannot be put back into the bottle. But the political arsenal of the state has not yet been exhausted.

We have suggested the network metaphor to capture the essence of the three simultaneous processes of globalization, regionalization and state adaptation. The European Union is the primary example of a multi-level political organization based on networks that include representatives of states as well as subnational and supranational entities. The network metaphor induces us to view territory, organization and interorganizational relations in a new light. Moreover, the archipelago metaphor sensitizes us to constellations that have yet to find their political expression.

Our principal argument, in short, is that theories and conceptions of Europe which privilege the state at the expense of other organizational forms are of limited value in trying to understand the dynamism and complexity of European realities today, in the past or in the future. By providing a multitude of conceptual tools and perspectives from different disciplines we hope to have contributed, however marginally, to a new state of mind. We also hope to have avoided the three most common mistakes people make when thinking about the future.[28] The first is to assume that the future will be entirely different from the past; the second is to believe that it will be just the same; and the third, and most serious, mistake is not to think about it at all.

NOTES

1 Frederick S. Tipson, as quoted in James N. Rosenau, *Along the Domestic–Foreign Frontier: Exploring Governance in a Turbulent World* (Cambridge: Cambridge University Press, 1997), 341.

2 Daniel Bell, as quoted in Mathew Horsman and Andrew Marshall, *After the Nation-State: Citizens, Tribalism and the New World Disorder* (London: HarperCollins, 1995), 187.

3 See Robert W. Cox, 'The Crisis in World Order and the Challenge to International Organization', *Cooperation and Conflict* 29 (1994), 99–113; Robert W. Cox with Timothy J. Sinclair, *Approaches to World Order* (Cambridge: Cambridge University Press, 1996), 527–9.

4 Susan Strange, *The Retreat of the State: The Diffusion of Power in the World Economy* (Cambridge: Cambridge University Press, 1996), 4.

5 Peter Dombrowski and Richard W. Mansbach, 'From Sovereign States to Sovereign Markets' (paper presented at the 38th Annual Convention of the International Studies Association, Toronto, March 1997).

6 See Linda Weiss, *The Myth of the Powerless State* (Ithaca, NY: Cornell University Press, 1998), 188–212.

7 Cf. Ibid., 9.

8 Susan Strange, 'Rethinking Structural Change in the International Political Economy: States, Firms, and Diplomacy', in *Political Economy and the Changing Global Order*, eds Richard Stubbs and Geoffrey R.D. Underhill (London: Macmillan, 1994).

9 This is the expression used by Margaret E. Keck and Kathryn Sikkink, *Activists beyond Borders: Advocacy Networks in International Politics* (Ithaca, NY: Cornell University Press, 1998).

10 Cf. Ann Marie Clark, 'Non-Governmental Organizations and their Influence on International Society', *Journal of International Affairs*, 48 (1995), 510.

11 These elements – the coincidence of cooperative and conflictual elements in combination with interdependent decisions – are commonly included in definitions of 'bargaining situations'. See, for example, Christer Jönsson, *Communication in International Bargaining* (London: Pinter, 1990), 2.

12 Of course, this does not imply that the EU in its entirety is likely to serve as a model for the world.

13 David Held, *Democracy and the Global Order* (Stanford, CA: Stanford University Press, 1995), 138.

14 Anthony McGrew, 'Globalization and Territorial Democracy: An Introduction', in *The Transformation of Democracy?*, ed. Anthony McGrew (Cambridge: Polity Press, 1997), 12–13.

15 Held, *Democracy and the Global Order*, 16–17.

16 Markus Jachtenfuchs and Beate Kohler-Koch, 'The Transformation of Governance in the European Union' (paper presented at the Fourth Biennial International Conference of the European Community Studies Association, Charleston, SC, May 1995), 5.

17 Henri Pirenne, *Economic and Social History of Medieval Europe* (London: Paul, Trench and Trubner, 1949); Henri Pirenne, *Medieval Cities: Their Origins and the Revival of Trade* (Princeton, NJ: Princeton University Press, 1952).

18 W. Schivelbusch, *Geschichte der Eisenbahnreise: Industrialisierung von Raum und Zeit im 19. Jahrhundert* (Munich: Carl Hanser Verlag, 1977).

19 Manuel Castells, *The Rise of the Network Society* (Oxford: Blackwell, 1996), Chapters 6 and 7.

20 Paul Virilio, *Vitesse et politique* (Paris: Hachette/Reclus, 1977); Paul Virilio, *L'espace critique* (Paris: Hachette/Reclus, 1984); 'Full fart mot evigheten', *Dagens Nyheter*, 8 December 1991.

21 For a multifaceted overview of different forms of friction and their significance, see Nordal Åkerman, *The Necessity of Friction: Nineteen Essays on a Vital Force* (Heidelberg: Physica-Verlag, 1993).

22 Gunnar Törnqvist, 'Studier i industrilokalisering', *Meddelanden från Geografiska institutionen vid Stockholms universitet No. 153* (Stockholm, Department of Geography, Stockholm University, 1963).

23 Torsten Hägerstrand, 'Att skapa sammanhang i människans värld – problemet', in *Att forma regional framtid* (Stockholm: Liber, 1978).

24 See, for example, Tor Nørretranders, *Märk världen: En bok om vetenskap och intuition* (Stockholm: Bonnier Alba, 1993). Cf. Gunnar Törnqvist, *Renässans för regioner: Om tekniken och den sociala kommunikationens villkor* (Stockholm: SNS Förlag, 1998).

25 Cf. Anssi Paasi, 'The Institutionalization of Regions: A Theoretical Framework for Understanding the Emergence of Regions and the Constitution of Identity', *Fennia*, 164 (1986): 1, 105–46; Kay Anderson and Fay Gale (eds), *Inventing Places: Studies in Cultural Geography* (London: Longman, 1992).

26 For empirical documentation, see Gunnar Törnqvist, *Contact Systems and Regional Development* (Lund: C.W.K. Gleerup, 1970).

27 See Rosenau, *Along the Domestic–Foreign Frontier*, 38.

28 Cf. Horsman and Marshall, *After the Nation-State*, 270.

Bibliography

Abrams, Richard M. (1996) 'The Relevance of American Federalism to the European Union: From Confederation to Federal Union to Nation-State', in Richard Herr and Steven Weber (eds), *European Integration and American Federalism: A Comparative Perspective*. Berkeley, CA: IAS (International and Area Studies) Publication.

Adler, Emanuel (1997) 'Seizing the Middle Ground: Constructivism in World Politics', *European Journal of International Relations*, 3 (3): 319–63.

Agnew, John (1994) 'The Territorial Trap: The Geographical Assumptions of International Relations Theory', *Review of International Political Economy*, 1 (1): 53–80.

Åkerman, Nordal (1993) *The Necessity of Friction: Nineteen Essays on a Vital Force*. Heidelberg: Physica-Verlag.

Allison, Graham T. (1971) *Essence of Decision: Explaining the Cuban Missile Crisis*. Boston, MA: Little, Brown.

Alter, Karen J. (1998) 'Who Are the "Masters of the Treaty"?: European Governments and the European Court of Justice', *International Organization*, 52 (1): 121–47.

Amin, Ash and Thrift, Nigel (eds) (1994) *Globalisation, Institutions, and Regional Development in Europe*. Oxford: Oxford University Press.

Anderson, Benedict (1991) *Imagined Communities: Reflections on the Origin and Spread of Nationalism*, rev. edn. London/New York: Verso.

Anderson, Kay and Gale, Fay (eds) (1992) *Inventing Places: Studies in Cultural Geography*. London: Longman.

Anderson, Malcolm (1996) *Frontiers: Territory and State Formation in the Modern World*. Cambridge: Polity Press.

Andersson, Lars (1989) 'Pirenne, Bolin och den nya arkeologin', *Scandia. Tidskrift för historisk forskning*, 55 (2): 163–83.

Arnold, Benjamin (1991) *Princes and Territories in Medieval Germany*. Cambridge: Cambridge University Press.

Arnold, W.T. (1974) *The Roman System of Provincial Administration to the Accession of Constantine the Great*. Chicago: Ares Publishers.

Avruch Kevin (1999) 'Reciprocity, Equality, and Status-Anxiety in the Amarna Letters', in Raymond Cohen and Raymond Westbrook, (eds), *The Beginnings of International Relations: Amarna Diplomacy*. Baltimore, MD: Johns Hopkins University Press.

Axelrod, Robert (1984) *The Evolution of Cooperation*. New York: Basic Books.

Axelsson, Björn and Easton, Geoffrey (eds) (1992) *Industrial Networks: A New View of Reality*. London/New York: Routledge.

Bachrach, Bernhard S. (1973) *A History of the Alans in the West*. Minneapolis: Berna.

Bagnasco, Armand (1977) *Tre Italie: La problematica territoriale dello sviluppo italiano*. Bologna: Il Mulino.

Bal, Leendert Jan (1995) 'Decision-Making and Negotiations in the European Union', discussion paper no. 7, Centre for the Study of Diplomacy, University of Leicester.

Barkin, Samuel J. and Cronin, Bruce (1994) 'The State and the Nation: Changing Norms and the Rules of Sovereignty in International Relations', *International Organization*, 48(1): 107–30.

Barrett, John C., Fitzpatrick, Andrew P. and Macinnes, Lesley (eds) (1989) *Barbarians and Romans in North-West Europe from the later Republic to late Antiquity*. Oxford: BAR.

Barrow, G.W.S. (1973) *The Kingdom of the Scots*. London: Arnold.

Bartelson, Jens (1995) *A Genealogy of Sovereignty*. Cambridge: Cambridge University Press.

Bartlett, Robert (1993) *The Making of Europe: Conquest, Colonization and Cultural Change 950–1350*. London: Penguin.

Bautier, Robert H. (1971) *The Economic Development of Medieval Europe*. London: Variorum.

Bautier, Robert H. (1991) *Sur l'histoire économique de la France médiévale: la route, le fleuve, la foire*. London: Variorum.

Beech, George T. (1995) 'Aquitaine', in William W. Kebler and A. Zinn Grover (eds), *Medieval France: An Encyclopedia*. New York: Garland.

Bérenger, Jean (1994) *A History of the Habsburg Empire, 1273–1700*. London: Longman.

Berridge, G.R. (1995) *Diplomacy: Theory and Practice*. London: Prentice Hall/Harvester Wheatsheaf.

Beumann, Helmut (1962) 'Das Kaisertum Ottos des Grossen', *Historische Zeitschrift* 195: 529–73.

Beumann, Helmut (1978) 'Die Bedeutung des Kaisertums für die Entstehung der deutschen Nation in Spiegel der Beziehungen von Reich und Herrscher', in Helmut Beumann and Werner Schröder (eds), *Aspekte der Nationenbildung im Mittelalter*. Sigmaringen: Thorbecke.

Beumann, Helmut (1981) 'Der deutsche König als "Romanorum Rex"', *Sitzungsberichte* XVIII:2 (Frankfurt am Main: Johann Wolfgang Goethe-Universität).

Beumann, Helmut and Schröder, Werner (eds) (1978) *Aspekte der Nationenbildung im Mittelalter*. Sigmaringen: Thorbecke.

Bierstecker, Thomas J. and Weber, Cynthia (1996) 'The Social Construction of State Sovereignty', in Thomas J. Bierstecker and Cynthia Weber (eds), *State Sovereignty as Social Construct*. Cambridge: Cambridge University Press.

Börzel, Tanja A. (1997) 'What's So Special about Policy Networks: An Exploration of the Concept and Its Usefulness in Studying European Governance', *European Integration Online Papers* 1, [http://eiop.or.at/eiop/texte/1997-016a.htm].

Bosl, Karl (1970) 'Staat, Gesellschaft, Wirtschaft im deutschen Mittelalter', in Herbert Grundmann (ed.), *Gebhardt: Handbuch der Deutschen Geschichte 1*, 9th edn. Stuttgart: Klett.

Braudel, Fernand (1981–1984) *Civilization and Capitalism*, 3 vols. London: Collins.

Braudel, Fernand (1995) *The Mediterranean and the Mediterranean World in the Age of Philip II*. Berkeley/Los Angeles, CA: University of California Press.

Bretherton, Charlotte (1996) 'Introduction: Global Politics in the 1990s', in Charlotte Bretherton and Geoffrey Ponton (eds), *Global Politics: An Introduction*. Oxford: Blackwell.

Brunner, Otto (1968) 'Feudalismus: Ein Beitrag zur Begriffsgeschichte', in *Neue Wege der Verfassungs- und Sozialgeschichte*. Göttingen: Vandenhoeck & Ruprecht.

Buttimer, Anne (1989) *The Wake of Erasmus*. Lund: Lund University Press.

Cameron, Averil (1993) *The Mediterranean World in Late Antiquity AD 395–600*. London: Fontana.

Camilleri, Joseph A. and Falk, Jim (1992) *The End of Sovereignty? The Politics of a Shrinking and Fragmenting World*. Aldershot: Edward Elgar.

Camilleri, Joseph A., Jarvis, Anthony P. and Paolini, Albert J. (eds) (1995) *The State in Transition: Reimagining Political Space*. Boulder, CO: Lynne Rienner.

Caporaso, James A. (1992) 'International Relations Theory and Multilateralism: The Search for Foundations', *International Organization*, 46 (3): 599–632.

Caporaso, James A. (1996) 'The European Union and Forms of State: Westphalian, Regulatory or Post-Modern?', *Journal of Common Market Studies*, 34 (1): 29–52.

Caporaso, James A. (1996) 'The European Union between Federalism and Regulation', in Richard Herr and Steven Weber (eds), *European Integration and American Federalism: A Comparative Perspective*. Berkeley, CA: IAS (International and Area Studies) Publication.

Carr, E.H. (1939) *The Twenty Years' Crisis 1919–1939: An Introduction to the Study of International Relations*. London: Macmillan. (Reprinted 1984.)

Castells, Manuel (1992) *The Informational City*. Oxford: Blackwell.

Castells, Manuel (1996) *The Rise of the Network Society*. Oxford: Blackwell.

Castells, Manuel (1998) *End of Millennium*. Oxford: Blackwell.

Cederlund, Kerstin (1995) 'Universitet i internationella nätverk', Rapporter och notiser 140. Lund: Department of Social and Economic Geography, Lund University.

Cerny, Philip (1990) *The Changing Architecture of Politics: Structure, Agency, and the Future of the State*. London: Sage.

Cerny, Philip (1995) 'Globalization and the Changing Logic of Collective Action', *International Organization*, 49 (4): 595–625.

Chekel, Jeffrey T. (1998) 'The Constructivist Turn in International Relations Theory', *World Politics*, 50 (2): 324–48.

Chevallier, Raymond (1972) *Les Voies romaines*. Paris: Colin.

Chilton, Paul A. (1996) *Security Metaphors: Cold War Discourse from Containment to Common House*. New York: Peter Lang.

Chisholm, Donald (1989) *Coordination Without Hierarchy: Informal Structures in Multi-organizational Systems*. Berkeley / Los Angeles, CA: University of California Press.

Christaller, Walter (1933) *Die zentralen Orte in Süddeutschland*. Jena: Gustav Fischer.

Christaller, Walter (1950) *Das Grundgerüst der räumlichen Ordnung in Europa: Frankfurter Geographische Hefte*. Frankfurt: Verlag Dr. Waldemar Kramer.

Christensen, Paul R., Eskelinen, Heikki, Forsström, Bo, Lindmark, Leif and Vatne, Eriik (1990) 'Firms in Networks: Concepts, Spatial Impacts and Policy Implications', in Sven Illeris and Leif Jacobsen (eds), *Networks and Regional Development*. NordREFO 1990: 1. Copenhagen / Stockholm: Nordiska institutet för regionalpolitisk forskning.

Clark, Ann Marie (1995) 'Non-Governmental Organizations and their Influence on International Society', *Journal of International Affairs*, 48 (2): 507–25.

Claude Jr, Inis L. (1964) *Swords into Plowshares: The Problems and Progress of International Organization*, 3rd edn. New York: Random House.

Claval, Paul (1987) 'The Region as a Geographical, Economic and Cultural Concept', *International Social Science Journal*, 112: 159–72.

Clover, Frank M. (1993) *The Late Roman West and the Vandals*. Aldershot: Variorum.

Commission of the European Communities (1992) *Green Paper on the Impact on the Environment*, COM (92). Brussels, 20 February.

Conze, Werner (1990) 'Staat und Souveränität', in Otto Brunner and Werner Conze (eds), *Geschichtliche Grundbegriffe 6*. Stuttgart: Klett–Cotta.

Cooke, Philip (1994) 'Co-operative Advantage of Regions'. Unpublished paper, Centre of Advanced Studies, University of Wales.

de Coulanges, Fustel (1994) *La Gaule romaine*, rev. edn. Paris: Editions de Fallois.

Cox, Robert W. (1994) 'The Crisis in World Order and the Challenge to International Organization', *Cooperation and Conflict*, 29 (2): 99–113.

Cox, Robert W. with Sinclair, Timothy J. (1996) *Approaches to World Order*. Cambridge: Cambridge University Press.

Cróinín, Dáibhí O. (1995) *Early Medieval Ireland: 400–1200*. London: Longman.

Davies, Norman (1996) *Europe: A History*. Oxford: Oxford University Press.

Der Grosse Ploetz: Auszug aus der Geschichte (1980). Freiburg: Verlag Ploetz.

Dictionary of the Middle Ages (1982–1989) Joseph R. Strayer editor-in-chief, 12 vols. New York: Charles Scribner's Sons.

Diesner, Hans-Joachim (1975) 'Zur Rolle der Religion unter besonderer Berücksichtigung des Christentums', in Rigobert Günther and Helga Köpstein (eds), *Die Römer an Rhein und Donau*. Vienna: Böhlau.

Dollinger, Phillippe (1981) *Die Hanse*, 3rd edn. Stuttgart: Kröner.

Dombrowski, Peter and Mansbach, Richard W. (1997) 'From Sovereign States to Sovereign Markets'. Paper presented at the 38th Annual Convention of the International Studies Association, Toronto, March 1997.

Doyle, Michael (1986) 'Liberalism and World Politics', *American Political Science Review*, 80 (4): 1151–69.

Duroselle, Jean-Baptiste (1965) *L'idée d'Europe dans l'histoire*. Paris: Denoël.

Duroselle, Jean-Baptiste (1990) *Europe: A History of its Peoples*. London: Viking.

Duval, Paul-Marie (1979) *Gallien: Leben und Kultur in römischer Zeit*. Stuttgart: Reclam.

Eisenstadt, Shmuel N. (ed.) (1967) *The Decline of Empires*. Englewood Cliffs, NJ: Prentice Hall.

Elton, Hugh (1996) *Frontiers of the Roman Empire*. London: Batsford.

Engman, Max (ed.) (1994) *När imperier faller. Studier kring riksupplösningar och nya stater*. Stockholm: Atlantis.

Ennen, Edith (1972) *Die europäische Stadt des Mittelalters*. Göttingen: Vandenhoeck & Ruprecht.

Ferguson, Yale H. and Mansbach, Richard W. (1996) 'Political Space and Westphalian States in a World of "Polities": Beyond Inside/Outside', *Global Governance*, 2 (2): 261–87.

Fisher, Roger and Ury, William (1983) *Getting to Yes: Negotiating Agreement Without Giving In*. New York: Penguin.

Foerster, Rolf H. (1967) *Europa: Geschichte einer politichen Idee*. Munich: Nymphenburg.

Foucault, Michel (1991) 'Governmentality', in L. Martin, H. Gutman and P. Hutton (eds), *The Foucault Effect: Studies in Governmentality*. Amherst, MA: University of Massachusetts Press.

Fourquin, Guy (1976) *Lordship and Feudalism in the Middle Ages*. London: Allen & Unwin.

Fox, E. Whiting (1971) *History in Geographic Perspective: The Other France*. New York: W.W. Norton.

Frame, Robin (1990) *The Political Development of the British Isles 1100–1400*. Oxford: Oxford University Press.

Frances, Jennifer, Mitchell, Jeremy, Levaçiç, Rosalind and Thompson, Grahame (1991) 'Introduction', in Grahame Thompson, Jennifer Frances, Rosalind Levaçiç Rosalind and Jeremy Mitchell (1991) (eds), *Markets, Hierarchies and Networks: The Coordination of Social Life*. London: Sage.

Fritze, Wolfgang H. (1982) *Frühzeit zwischen Ostsee und Donau*, Berlin: Duncker and Humbolt.

Fuchs, Gerhard (1994) 'Policy-Making in a System of Multi-Level Governance – The Commission of the European Community and the Restructuring of the Telecommunications Sector', *Journal of European Public Policy*, 1 (2): 177–94.

Fuhrmann, Horst (ed.) (1968) *Das Constitutum Constantini*. Hannover: Hahnsche Buchhandlung.

Fukuyama, Francis (1992) *The End of History and the Last Man*. New York: The Free Press.

Galtung, Johan (1972) *EF: en supermagt i verdenssamfundet*. Copenhagen: Ejler; Oslo: Universitetsforlaget.

Gamillschegg, Maria-Helene (1996) *Die Kontroverse um das Filioque*. Würzburg: Augustinus Verlag.

Ganshof, Francois L. (1971) *The Carolingians and the Frankish Monarchy: Studies in Carolingian History*. London: Longman.

Gellner, Ernest (1983) *Nations and Nationalism*. Oxford: Blackwell.

Giddens, Anthony (1985) *A Contemporary Critique of Historical Materialism*, vol. 2, *The Nation-State and Violence*. Berkeley/Los Angeles, CA: University of California Press.

Glick, Thomas F. (1979) *Islamic and Christian Spain in the Early Middle Ages*. Princeton, NJ: Princeton University Press.

Goffart, Walter (1974) *Caput and Colonate*. Toronto: Phoenix.

Goldblatt, David (1997) 'Liberal Democracy and the Globalization of Environmental Risks', in Anthony McGrew (ed.), *The Transformation of Democracy?* Cambridge: Polity Press.

Goldgeier, James G. and McFaul, Michael (1992) 'A Tale of Two Worlds: Core and Periphery in the Post-Cold War Era', *International Organization*, 46 (2): 467–91.

Gordenker, Leon, Coate, Roger A., Jönsson, Christer and Söderholm, Peter (1995) *International Cooperation in Response to AIDS*. London: Pinter.

Grande, Edgar (1996) 'The State and Interest Groups in a Framework of Multi-Level Decision-Making: The Case of the European Union', *Journal of European Public Policy*, 3 (3): 318–38.

Green, Miranda J. (1995) *The Celtic World*. London/New York: Routledge.

Greenfeld, Liah (1993) *Nationalism: Five Roads to Modernity*. Cambridge, MA: Harvard University Press.

Greenwood, Justin (1997) *Representing Interests in the European Union*. London: Macmillan.

Grigg, David (1972) 'The Logic of Regional Systems', in Wayne Davies (ed.), *The Conceptual Revolution in Geography*. London: University of London Press.

Grundmann, Herbert (ed.) (1970) *Gebhardt: Handbuch der Deutschen Geschichte 1*, 9th edn. Stuttgart: Klett.

Guéhenno, Jean-Marie (1995) *The End of the Nation-State*. Minneapolis, MN: University of Minnesota Press.

Günther, Rigobert and Köpstein, Helga (eds) (1975) *Die Römer an Rhein und Donau*. Vienna: Böhlau.

Gurevitj, Aron J. (1979) *Feodalismens uppkomst i Västeuropa*. Stockholm: Tiden.

Haaland Matlary, Janne (1996) 'Internal Market Regime or New Polity Model: Whither the European Union?', Working paper No. 26, ARENA (Advanced Research on the Europeanisation of the Nation-state), Oslo.

Haas, Peter M. (ed.) (1992) *Knowledge, Power, and International Policy Coordination*. Boston, MA: MIT Press.

Hägerstrand, Torsten (1978) 'Att skapa sammanhang i människans värld – problemet', in *Att forma regional framtid*. Stockholm: Liber.

Hägerstrand, Torsten (1995) 'Resandet och den sociala väven', in *Färdande och resande*. Stockholm: KBF.

Håkansson, Håkan (1989) *Corporate Technological Behaviour: Co-operation and Network*. London: Routledge.

Halecki, Oscar and Polonsky, A. (1992) *A History of Poland*, 3rd edn. London: Dent.

Hall, Patrik (1998) *The Social Construction of Nationalism*. Lund: Lund University Press.

Halphen, Louis (1947) *Charlemagne et l'empire carolingien*. Paris: Albin Michel.

Hanf, Kenneth and O'Toole Jr, Laurence J. (1992) 'Revisiting Old Friends: Networks, Implementation Structures and the Management of Inter-Organizational Relations', *European Journal of Political Research*, 21 (1): 163–80.

Hanson, William S. (1989) 'The Nature and Function of Roman Frontiers', in John C. Barrett, Andrew P. Fitzpatrick and Lesley Macinnes (eds), *Barbarians and Romans in North-West Europe from the Later Republic to Late Antiquity*. Oxford: BAR.

Harrison, Dick (1993) *The Early State and the Towns: Forms of Integration in Lombard Italy AD 568–774*. Lund: Lund University Press.

Harvie, Christopher (1994) *The Rise of Regional Europe*. London: Routledge.

Hastings, Adrian (1997) *The Construction of Nationhood: Ethnicity, Religion and Nationalism*. Cambridge: Cambridge University Press.

Hedlund, Stefan and Sundström, Niclas (1996) 'Does Palermo Represent the Future for Moscow?', *Journal of Public Policy*, 16 (2): 113–56.

Held, David (1995) *Democracy and the Global Order*. Stanford, CA: Stanford University Press.

Held, David (1997) 'Democracy and Globalization', *Global Governance*, 3 (3): 251–67.

Henneman, John B. (1971/1976) *Royal Taxation in Fourteenth Century France*, 2 vols. Philadelphia: American Philosophical Society.

Héritier, Adrienne (1996) 'The Accommodation of Diversity in European Policy-Making and Its Outcomes: Regulatory Policy as a Patchwork', *Journal of European Public Policy*, 3 (2): 149–67.

Héritier, Adrienne (1997) 'Policy-Making by Subterfuge: Interest Accommodation, Innovation and Substitute Democratic Legitimation in Europe – Perspectives from Distinctive Policy Areas', *Journal of European Public Policy*, 4 (2): 171–89.

Herr, Richard and Weber, Steven (eds) (1996) *European Integration and American Federalism: A Comparative Perspective*. Berkeley, CA: IAS (International Area Studies) Publication.

Herz, John H. (1962) *International Politics in the Atomic Age*. New York: Columbia University Press.

Herz, John H. (1976) *The Nation-State and the Crisis of World Politics*. New York: David McKay.

Hillgruber, Andreas (1965) *Hitlers Strategie: Politik und Kriegführung 1940–1941*. Frankfurt am Main: Bernhard & Graefe.

Hobsbawm, Eric J. (1990) *Nations and Nationalism since 1780: Programme, Myth, Reality*. Cambridge: Cambridge University Press.

Hobson, John (1997) *The Wealth of States: A Comparative Sociology of International Economic and Political Change*. Cambridge: Cambridge University Press.

Hodges, Richard and Whitehouse, David (1983) *Mohammed, Charlemagne and the Origins of Europe*. London: Duckworth.

Holbraad, Carsten (1970) *The Concert of Europe: A Study in German and British International Theory, 1815–1914*. London: Longman.

Horsman, Mathew and Marshall, Andrew (1995) *After the Nation-State: Citizens, Tribalism and the New World Disorder*. London: Harper Collins.

Huxley, J.S. and Haddon, A.C. (1935) *We Europeans*. New York: Harper and Row.

Ibrahim, Taufic and Sagadeev, Arthur (1990) *Classical Islamic Philosophy*. Moscow: Moscow Progress Publishers.

Jachtenfuchs, Markus and Kohler-Koch, Beate (1995) 'The Transformation of Governance in the European Union'. Paper presented at the Fourth Biennial International Conference of the European Community Studies Association, Charleston, SC, May 1995.

Jackson, Robert (1990) *Quasi-States: Sovereignty, International Relations and the Third World*. Cambridge: Cambridge University Press.

Jacobs, Jane (1984) *Cities and the Wealth of Nations*. Harmondsworth: Penguin Books.

Jerneck, Magnus (1997) 'Subnational Mobilization, Territoriality and Political Power in the European Union: A Challenge from Below?', in Philippe Nemo (ed.), *The European Union and the Nation-State*. Paris: Groupe ESCP.

Johansson, Rune (1998) 'Idéer om Europa – Europa som idé', in Sven Tägil (ed.), *Europa – Historiens återkomst*, 3rd edn. Hedemora: Gidlunds.

Johansson, Rune (1999) 'The Impact of Imagination', in Sven Tägil (ed.), *Regions in Central Europe: The Legacy of History*. London: Hurst & Co.

Johansson, Rune, Rönnquist, Ralf and Tägil, Sven (1998) 'Territorialstaten i kris? Integration och uppsplittring i Europa', in Sven Tägil (ed.), *Europa – Historiens återkomst*, 3rd edn. Hedemora: Gidlunds.

Jönsson, Christer (1986) 'Interorganization Theory and International Organization', *International Studies Quarterly*, 30 (1): 39–57.

Jönsson, Christer (1990) *Communication in International Bargaining*. London: Pinter.

Jönsson, Christer, Bjurulf, Bo, Elgström, Ole, Sannerstedt, Anders and Strömvik, Maria (1998) 'Negotiations in Networks in the European Union', *International Negotiation*, 3 (3): 319–44.

Jordan, Grant and Schubert, Klaus (1992) 'A Preliminary Ordering of Policy Network Labels', *European Journal of Political Research*, 21 (1): 7–27.

Jouanne, Jacques (1994) 'L'image de l'Europe chez Hérodote et Hippocrate: essai de comparison', in Michel Perrin (ed.), *L'Idée de l'Europe au fil de deux Millénaires*. Paris: Beauchesne.

Keck, Margaret E. and Sikkink, Kathryn (1998) *Activists beyond Borders: Advocacy Networks in International Politics*. Ithaca, NY: Cornell University Press.

Kedourie, Elie (1960) *Nationalism*. London: Hutchinson.

Kelstrup, Morten (1998) 'Institutionalisation and Negotiation in the Process of European Integration'. Paper presented at the Third Pan-European Conference on International Relations and Joint Meeting with the International Studies Association, Vienna.

Kennedy, Paul M. (1987) *The Rise and Fall of the Great Powers*. New York: Random House.

Keohane, Robert O. (1995) 'Hobbes's Dilemma and Institutional Change in World Politics: Sovereignty in International Society', in Hans-Henrik Holm and Georg Sørensen (eds), *Whose World Order?: Uneven Globalization and the End of the Cold War*. Boulder, CO: Westview Press.

Klineberg, Otto (1964) *The Human Dimension in International Relations*. New York: Holt, Rinehart and Winston.

Knox, Paul (1995) 'World Cities and the Organization of Global Space' in Robert J. Johnston, Peter J. Taylor and Michael J. Watts (eds), *Geographies of Global Change*. Oxford: Blackwell.

Kohler-Koch, Beate (1995) 'The Strength of Weakness: The Transformation of Governance in the EU', in Sverker Gustavsson and Leif Lewin (eds), *The Future of the Nation State*. Stockholm: Nerenius & Santérus.

Kohler-Koch, Beate (1996) 'Catching Up with Change: The Transformation of Governance in the European Union', *Journal of European Public Policy*, 3 (3): 359–80.

Kormoos, J.B.F. (1987) 'The Geographical Notion of Europe over the Centuries', in Hendrik Brugmans (ed.), *Europe, Dream – Adventure – Reality*. New York: Greenwood Press.

Krasner, Stephen D. (1988) 'Sovereignty: An Institutional Perspective', *Comparative Political Studies*, 21 (1): 66–94.

Krasner, Stephen D. (1993) 'Westphalia and All That', in Judith Goldstein and Robert O. Keohane (eds), *Ideas and Foreign Policy: Beliefs, Institutions, and Political Change*. Ithaca, NY: Cornell University Press.

Krasner, Stephen D. (1998) 'Problematic Sovereignty'. Paper presented at the Annual Convention of the American Political Science Association, Boston, MA, September 1998.

Kratochwil, Friedrich (1986) 'Of Systems, Boundaries, and Territoriality: An Inquiry into the Formation of the State System', *World Politics*, 39 (1): 21–52.

Kratochwil, Friedrich (1995) 'Sovereignty as *Dominium*: Is There a Right of Humanitarian Intervention?', in Gene M. Lyons and Michael Mastanduno (eds), *Beyond Westphalia? State Sovereignty and International Intervention*. Baltimore, MD: Johns Hopkins University Press.

Krugman, Paul (1991) *Geography and Trade*. Cambridge, MA: MIT Press.

Kuehls, Thom (1996) *Beyond Sovereign Territory*. Minneapolis: University of Minnesota Press.

Kuhn, Arthur K. (1910) 'The Beginnings of an Aerial Law', *American Journal of International Law*, 4: 109–32.

Kulischer, Alexander and Kulischer, Eugen (1932) *Kriegs- und Wanderzüge: Weltgeschichte als Völkerbewegung*. Berlin/Leipzig: Walter de Gruyter.

Kvistad, John M. (1995) *The Barents Spirit: A Bridge-building Project in the Wake of the Cold War*. Oslo: Institutt for forsvarsstudier.

Labasse, Jean (1991) *L'Europe des régions*. Paris: Gallimard.

Lademacher, Horst (1983) *Geschichte der Niederlande: Politik – Verfassung – Wirtschaft*. Darmstadt: Wissenschaftlishes Buchgesellschaft.

Laffan, Brigid (1998) 'The European Union Budget: From Negotiation to Authority'. Paper presented at the Third Pan-European Conference on International Relations and Joint Meeting with the International Studies Association, Vienna.

Lakoff, George and Johnson, Mark (1980) *Metaphors We Live By*. Chicago: University of Chicago Press.

Långtidsutredningen 1995 SOU 1995: 4. Stockholm: Fritzes.

Lapidus, Ira (1988) *A History of Islamic Societies*. Cambridge: Cambridge University Press.

Laursen, Finn (1995) 'On Studying European Integration: Integration Theory and Political Economy', in Finn Laursen (ed.), *The Political Economy of European Integration*. The Hague: Kluwer Law International.

Lawrence, Robert Z. (1995) 'Emerging Regional Arrangements: Building Blocks or Stumbling Blocks?', in Jeffrey A. Frieden and David Lake (eds), *International Political Economy: Perspectives on Global Power and Wealth*, 3rd edn. London/New York: Routledge.

Lawson, Stephanie (1995) 'The Authentic State: History and Tradition in the Ideology of Ethnonationalism', in Joseph A. Camilleri, Anthony P. Jarvis and Albert J. Paolini (eds), *The State in Transition: Reimagining Political Space*. Boulder, CO: Lynne Rienner.

Lexikon des Mittelalters (1977–1997) 8 vols. Munich: Artemis/Lexma.

Ley, Francis (1975) *Alexandre 1er et sa Sainte Alliance (1811–1825)*. Paris: Fischbacher.

Lijphart, Arend (1968) *The Politics of Accommodation: Pluralism and Democracy in the Netherlands*. Berkeley/Los Angeles, CA: University of California Press.

Lindström, Bjarne (1996) *Regional Policy and Territorial Supremacy*. NordREFO 1996: 2. Copenhagen/Stockholm: Nordiska institutet för regionalpolitisk forskning.

Linklater, Andrew (1996) 'Citizenship and Sovereignty in the Post-Westphalian State', *European Journal of International Relations*, 2 (1): 77–103.

Lintott, Andrew W. (1981) 'What was the Imperium Romanum?', *Greece and Rome*, 28 (XXVIII), 53–67.

Lopez, Robert S. (1971) *The Commercial Revolution of the Middle Ages*. Cambridge: Cambridge University Press.

Löwe, Heinz (1970) 'Deutschland im fränkischen Reich', in Herbert Grundmann, (ed.), *Gebhardt: Handbuch der Deutschen Geschichte 1*, 9th edn. Stuttgart: Klett.

Lundestad, Geir (ed.) (1994) *The Fall of Great Powers*. Oslo: Universitetsforlaget; Oxford: Oxford University Press.

Lundquist, Karl-Johan (1996) *Företag, regioner och internationell konkurrenskraft: om regionala resursers betydelse*. Lund: Studentlitteratur.

Lundquist, Lennart (1992) *Förvaltning, stat och samhälle*. Lund: Studentlitteratur.

Lycklama à Nijeholt, J.F. (1910) *Air Sovereignty*. The Hague: Martinus Nijhoff.

McDonald, Thomas R. (1995) 'Lorraine', in William W. Kebler and A. Zinn Grover (eds), *Medieval France. An Encyclopedia*. New York: Garland.

McGrew, Anthony (1997) 'Democracy Beyond Borders? Globalization and the Reconstruction of Democratic Theory and Practice', in Anthony McGrew (ed.), *The Transformation of Democracy?* Cambridge: Polity Press.

McGrew, Anthony (1997) 'Globalization and Territorial Democracy: An Introduction', in Anthony McGrew (ed.), *The Transformation of Democracy?* Cambridge: Polity Press.

McNeill, William H. (1982) *The Pursuit of Power*. Chicago: University of Chicago Press.

McNeill, William H. (1994) 'Introductory Historical Commentary', in Geir Lundestad (ed.), *The Fall of Great Powers*. Oslo: Scandinavian University Press.

Majone, Giandomenico (1992) 'Regulatory Federalism in the European Community', *Environment and Planning C: Government and Policy*, 10: 299–316.

Mallory, J.P. (1989) *In Search of the Indo-Europeans: Language, Archaeology and Myth*. London: Thames & Hudson.

Malmberg, Bo (1990) 'The Effects of External Ownership', Geografiska regionstudier No. 24. Uppsala: Department of Human Geography, Uppsala University.

Malmberg, Torsten (1980) *Human Territoriality*. The Hague: Mouton.

March, James G. and Olsen, Johan P. (1983) 'Organizing Political Life: What Administrative Reorganization Tells Us about Government', *American Political Science Review*, 77 (2): 281–96.

Marks, Gary, Scharpf, Fritz W., Schmitter, Philippe C. and Streeck, Wolfgang (1996) *Governance in the European Union*. London: Sage.

Marsh, David and Rhodes, R.A.W. (1992) 'Policy Communities and Issue Networks: Beyond Typology', in David Marsh and R.A.W. Rhodes (eds), *Policy Networks in British Government*. Oxford: Clarendon Press.

Marshall, Alfred (1919) *Industry and Trade*. London: Macmillan.

Martinez y Riqué, Martin (1998) 'Spanien: kastilianskt imperium eller nationalstat i vardande?', in Sven Tägil (ed.), *Europa – Historiens återkomst*, 3rd edn. Hedemora: Gidlunds.

Massey, Doreen (1991) 'A Global Sense of Place', *Marxism Today*, June, 24–29.

Middlemas, Keith (1995) *Orchestrating Europe: The Informal Politics of European Union 1973–1995*. London: Fontana Press.

Millar, Fergus G.B. (1981) *The Roman Empire and its Neighbours*, 2nd edn. London: Duckworth.

Miller, Eugene F. (1979) 'Metaphor and Political Knowledge', *American Political Science Review*, 73 (1): 155–70.

Milward, Alan S. (1992) *The European Rescue of the Nation-State*. Berkeley, CA: University of California Press.

Minc, Alain (1993) *Le Nouveau Moyen Age*. Paris: Gallimard.

Moravcsik, Andrew (1991) 'Negotiating the Single European Act: National Interests and Conventional Statecraft in the European Community', *International Organization*, 45 (1): 19–56.

Moravcsik, Andrew (1993) 'Preferences and Power in the European Community: A Liberal Intergovernmentalist Approach', *Journal of Common Market Studies*, 31 (4): 473–524.

Morgan, Gareth (1986) *Images of Organization*. Beverly Hills/London: Sage.

Morgenthau, Hans J. (1966) *Politics Among Nations: The Struggle for Power and Peace*, 3rd edn. New York: Alfred A. Knopf.

Mulhearn, Chris (1996) 'Change and Development in the Global Economy', in Charlotte Bretherton and Geoffrey Ponton (eds), *Global Politics: An Introduction*. Oxford: Blackwell.

Murphy, Alexander B. (1996) 'The Sovereign State System as Political-Territorial Ideal: Historical and Contemporary Considerations', in Thomas J. Bierstecker and Cynthia Weber (eds), *State Sovereignty as Social Construct*. Cambridge: Cambridge University Press.

Musset, Lucien (1975) *The Germanic Invasions: The Making of Europe AD 400–600*. University Park, PA: Pennsylvania State University Press.

Nairn, Tom (1977) *The Break-up of Britain: Crisis and Neo-Nationalism*. London: New Left Books.

Nicholas, David (1992) *Medieval Flanders*. London: Longman.

Nilsson, Jan-Evert (1991) 'Svensk massa- och pappersindustri i förändring', Industridepartementet Ds 1991: 35. Stockholm: Department of Industry.

Nisbett, Richard and Ross, Lee (1980) *Human Inference: Strategies and Shortcomings of Social Judgment*. Englewood Cliffs, NJ: Prentice Hall.

Nordström, Kjell (1991) *The Internationalization Process of the Firm: Searching for New Patterns and Explanations*. Stockholm: Institute of International Business.

Nørretranders, Tor (1993) *Märk världen. En bok om vetenskap och intuition*. Stockholm: Bonnier Alba.

Nørretranders, Tor and Haaland, Tor (1990) 'Dansk dynamit. Dansk forsknings internationale status vurderet ud fra bibliometriske indikatorer', Forskningspolitik 8. Copenhagen: Forskningspolitisk råd.

North, Douglass (1990) *Institutions, Institutional Change and Economic Performance*. New York: Cambridge University Press.

O'Brien, Richard (1992) *Global Financial Integration: The End of Geography*. London: Pinter.

Ohler, Norbert (1989) *The Medieval Traveller*. Woodbridge: Boydell Press.

Ohlin, Bertil, Hesselbom, Per-Ove and Wijkman, Per Magnus (eds) (1977) *The International Allocation of Economic Activity*. London: Macmillan.

Østerud, Øyvind (1984) *Nasjonenes selvbestemmelsesrett*. Oslo: Universitetsforlaget.

Östhol, Anders (1996) *Politisk integration och gränsöverskridande regionbildning i Europa*. Umeå: Department of Political Science, University of Umeå.

Our Global Neighbourhood: The Report of the Commission on Global Governance (1995). Oxford/New York: Oxford University Press.

Paasi, Anssi (1986) 'The Institutionalization of Regions: A Theoretical Framework for Understanding of the Emergence of Regions and the Constitution of Regional Identity', *Fennia*, 164 (1): 105–46.

Paasi, Anssi (1986) *The Institutionalization of Regions: Theory and Comparative Case Studies*. Joensuu: Joensuun Yliopisto.

Paasi, Anssi (1991) 'Deconstructing Regions: Notes on the Scales of Spatial Life', *Environment and Planning A: International Journal of Urban and Regional Research*, 23 (2): 239–56.

Parisse, Michel (ed.) (1978) *Histoire de la Lorraine*. Toulouse: Privat.

Parry, John Horace (1963) *The Age of Reconnaissance*. London: Weidenfeld & Nicolson.

Parsons, Craig (1996) 'European Integration and American Federalism: A Comparative Perspective', in Richard Herr and Steven Weber (eds), *European Integration and American Federalism: A Comparative Perspective*. Berkeley, CA: IAS (International and Area Studies) Publication.

Pedersen, Thomas (1994) *European Union and the EFTA Countries: Enlargement and Integration*. London: Pinter.

Pedersen, Thomas (1998) *Germany, France and the Integration of Europe: A Realist Interpretation*. London/New York: Pinter.

Persson, Olle (1980) 'Informell kommunikation bland forskare och tekniker', Reseach Report No. 56. Umeå: Department of Sociology, University of Umeå.

Persson, Olle (1983) 'Svensk kunskapsimport – några indikatorer', Inforsk Papers on Communication Studies No. 19. Umeå: Department of Sociology, University of Umeå.

Peterson, John (1991) 'Technology Policy in Europe: Explaining the Framework Programme and Eureka in Theory and Practice', *Journal of Common Market Studies*, 29 (3): 269–90.

Peterson, John (1995) 'Decision-Making in the European Union: Towards a Framework for Analysis', *Journal of European Public Policy*, 2 (1): 69–93.

Petit, Paul (1967) *La Paix romaine*. Paris: Nouvelle Clio.

Pirenne, Henri (1937) *Mahomet et Charlemagne*. Paris: Félix Alcan.

Pirenne, Henri (1949) *Economic and Social History of Medieval Europe*. London: Paul, Trench and Trubner.

Pirenne, Henri (1952) *Medieval Cities: Their Origins and the Revival of Trade*. Princeton, NJ: Princeton University Press.

de Planhol, Xavier (1968) *Les Fondements géographiques de l'histoire de l'Islam*. Paris: Nouvelle Bibliothèque Scientifique.

de Planhol, Xavier and Claval, Paul (1994) *An Historical Geography of France*. Cambridge: Cambridge University Press.

Pleticha, Heinrich and Schönberger, Otto (eds) (1977) *Die Römer. Ein enzyklopädisches Sachbuch zur frühen Geschichte Europas*. Gütersloh.

Pollack, Mark A. (1997) 'Delegation, Agency, and Agenda Setting in the European Community', *International Organization*, 51 (1): 99–134.

Pollack, Mark A. (1998) 'The Engines of Integration? Supranational Autonomy and Influence in the European Union', in Wayne Sandholtz and Alec Stone Sweet (eds), *European Integration and Supranational Governance*. Oxford: Oxford University Press.

Porter, Michael (1990) *The Competitive Advantage of Nations*. London: Macmillan.

Postan, Michel (ed.) (1966) *The Agrarian Life of the Middle Ages: Cambridge Economic History of Europe 1*. Cambridge: Cambridge University Press.

Pounds, N.G.J. (1994) *An Economic History of Medieval Europe*. London: Longman.

Putnam, Robert D. (1993) *Making Democracy Work. Civic Traditions in Modern Italy*. Princeton, NJ: Princeton University Press.

Raiffa, Howard (1982) *The Art and Science of Negotiation*. Cambridge, MA: Harvard University Press.

Randers-Pehrson, Justine D. (1983) *Barbarians and Romans*. Oklahoma: University of Oklahoma Press.

Reich, Robert B. (1991) *The Work of Nations. Preparing Ourselves for 21st-century Capitalism*. New York: Alfred A. Knopf.

Reilly, Bernhard F. (1993) *The Medieval Spains*. Cambridge: Cambridge University Press.

Renfrew, Colin (1987) *Archaeology and Language: The Puzzle of Indo-European Origins*. New York: Cambridge University Press.

Renna, Thomas (1986) 'Theories of Kingship', *Dictionary of the Middle Ages*, vol. 7 (Joseph R. Strayer editor-in-chief). New York: Charles Scribner's Sons. pp. 259–71.

Richards, Erle H. (1912) *Sovereignty over the Air*. Oxford: Clarendon Press.

Richardson, Jeremy (1996) 'Policy-Making in the EU: Interests, Ideas and Garbage Cans of Primeval Soup', in Jeremy Richardson (ed.), *European Union: Power and Policy-Making*. London/New York: Routledge.

Ritschl, Dietrich (1981) 'Historical Development and Implications of the Filioque Controversy', in Lukas Vischer (ed.), *Spirit of God, Spirit of Christ*. Geneva: WCC.

Rivano-Fischer, Marcelo (1987) 'Human Territoriality', *Psychological Research Bulletin*, 1987: 6.

Rörig, Fritz (1975) *The Medieval Town*. Berkeley, CA: University of California Press.

Rosecrance, Richard (1986) *The Rise of the Trading State*. New York: Basic Books.

Rosecrance, Richard (1996) 'The Rise of the Virtual State', *Foreign Affairs*, 75 (4): 45–61.

Rosenau, James N. (1990) *Turbulence in World Politics*. London: Harvester Wheatsheaf.

Rosenau, James N. (1995) 'Governance in the Twenty-first Century', *Global Governance*, 1 (1): 13–43.

Rosenau, James N. (1997) *Along the Domestic–Foreign Frontier: Exploring Governance in a Turbulent World*. Cambridge: Cambridge University Press.

Rosenau, James N. and Czempiel, Ernst-Otto (eds) (1992) *Governance Without Government: Order and Change in Word Politics*. Cambridge: Cambridge University Press.

Rouche, Michel (1979) *L'Aquitaine des Wisigoths aux Arabes: Naissance d'un région*. Paris: Touzot.

de Rougemont, Denis (1961) *Vingt-huit siècles d'Europe: la conscience européenne à travers les textes*. Paris: Gallimard.

de Rougemont, Denis (1966) *The Idea of Europe*. New York: Collier–Macmillan.

Ruggie, John G. (1993) 'Territoriality and Beyond: Problematizing Modernity in International Relations', *International Organization*, 47 (1): 139–74.

Ruggie, John G. (1998) *Constructing the World Polity: Essays on International Institutionalization*. London/New York: Routledge.

Russett, Bruce (1993) *Grasping the Democratic Peace: Principles for a Post-Cold War World*. Princeton, NJ: Princeton University Press.

Sack, Robert D. (1986) *Human Territoriality: Its Theory and History*. Cambridge: Cambridge University Press.

Sassen, Saskia (1991) *The Global City: New York, London, Tokyo*. Princeton, NJ: Princeton University Press.

Sawyer, Birgit and Sawyer, Peter (1993) *Medieval Scandinavia*. Minneapolis: University of Minnesota Press.

Saxenian, Annelie (1994) *Regional Advantage: Culture and Competition in Silicon Valley and Route 128*. Cambridge, MA: Harvard University Press.

Scharpf, Fritz W. (1988) 'The Joint-Decision Trap: Lessons from German Federalism and European Integration', *Public Administration*, 66 (3): 239–78.

Schivelbusch W. (1977) *Geschichte der Eisenbahnreise. Industrialisierung von Raum und Zeit im 19. Jahrhundert*. Munich/Vienna: Carl Hanser Verlag.

Schmitter, Philippe C. (1996) 'Examining the Present Euro-Polity with the Help of Past Theories', in Gary Marks, Fritz W. Scharpf, Philippe C. Schmitter and Wolfgang Streeck, *Governance in the European Union*. London: Sage.

Schmitter, Philippe C. (1996) 'Imagining the Future of the Euro-Polity with the Help of New Concepts', in Gary Marks, Fritz W. Scharpf, Philippe C. Schmitter and Wolfgang Streeck, *Governance in the European Union*. London: Sage.

Schneider, Volker (1992) 'The Structure of Policy Networks: A Comparison of the "Chemicals Control" and "Telecommunications" Policy Domains in Germany', *European Journal of Political Research*, 21 (1): 109–29.

Schneider, Volker, Dang-Nguyen, Godefroy and Werle, Raymund (1994) 'Corporate Actor Networks in European Policy-Making: Harmonizing Telecommunications Policy', *Journal of Common Market Studies*, 32 (4): 473–98.

Schön, Donald A. (1979) 'Generative Metaphor: A Perspective on Problem-Solving in Social Policy', in Andrew Ortony (ed.), *Metaphor and Thought*. Cambridge: Cambridge University Press.

Seibt, Ferdinand (1978) *Karl IV: Ein Kaiser in Europa 1346–1378*. Munich: Süddeutscher Verlag.

Seth, Sanjay (1995) 'Nationalism in/and Modernity', in Joseph A. Camilleri, Anthony P. Jarvis and Albert J. Paolini (eds), *The State in Transition: Reimagining Political Space*. Boulder, CO: Lynne Rienner.

Sinor, Denis (1990) 'The Hun Period', in Denis Sinor, (ed.), *Cambridge History of Early Inner Asia*. Cambridge: Cambridge University Press.

Smith, Adam (1776) *An Inquiry into the Nature and Causes of the Wealth of Nations*. London: W. Strahan and T. Cadell.

Smith, Anthony D. (1986) *The Ethnic Origins of Nations*. Oxford: Blackwell.

Smith, Anthony D. (1995) *Nations and Nationalism in a Global Era*. Oxford: Basil Blackwell.

Smith, Michael (1996) 'The European Union and Concepts of Negotiated Order in Europe'. Paper presented at the annual conference of the British International Studies Association, Durham, December 1996.

Sölvell, Örjan, Zander, Ivor and Porter, Michael (1991) *Advantage Sweden*. Stockholm: Norstedts.

Sörlin, Sverker (1994) *De lärdas republik: Om vetenskapens internationella tendenser*. Malmoe: Liber-Hermods.

Spruyt, Hendrik (1994) *The Sovereign State and Its Competitors*. Princeton, NJ: Princeton University Press.

Stengers, Jean (1959) 'La formation de la frontière linguistique en Belgique', *Collection Latomus*, XLI. Brussels: Latomus.

Stone Sweet, Alec and Sandholtz, Wayne (1998) 'Integration, Supranational Governance, and the Institutionalization of the European Polity', in Wayne Sandholtz and

Alec Stone Sweet (eds), *European Integration and Supranational Governance*. Oxford: Oxford University Press.

Stopford, John and Strange, Susan (1991) *Rival States, Rival Firms: Competition for World Market Shares*. Cambridge: Cambridge University Press.

Strange, Susan (1994) 'Rethinking Structural Change in the International Political Economy: States, Firms, and Diplomacy', in Richard Stubbs and Geoffrey R.D. Underhill (eds), *Political Economy and the Changing Global Order*. London: Macmillan.

Strange, Susan (1996) *The Retreat of the State: The Diffusion of Power in the World Economy*. Cambridge: Cambridge University Press.

Sugar, Peter F., Hanák Péter and Frank, Tibor (eds) (1990) *A History of Hungary*. London: Tauris.

Sweden in the World: National Atlas of Sweden (1993) Stockholm: Almqvist & Wiksell.

Tabacco, Giovanni (1989) *The Struggle for Power in Medieval Italy: Structures of Political Rule*. Cambridge: Cambridge University Press.

Tägil, Sven (1983) 'The Question of Border Regions in Western Europe: An Historical Background', in Malcolm Anderson (ed.), *Frontier Regions in Western Europe*. London: Frank Cass.

Tägil, Sven (ed.) (1998) *Europa – Historiens återkomst*, 3rd edn. Hedemora: Gidlunds.

Tägil, Sven (1999) 'The German Stem Duchies', in Sven Tägil, (ed.), *Regions in Central Europe. The Legacy of History*. London: Hurst & Co.

Tägil, Sven (ed.) (1999) *Regions in Central Europe. The Legacy of History*. London: Hurst & Co.

Tägil, Sven, Gerner, Kristian, Henriksson, Göran, Johansson, Rune, Oldberg, Ingmar and Salomon, Kim (1977) *Studying Boundary Conflicts: A Theoretical Framework*. Stockholm: Esselte.

Taylor, Paul (1990) 'Consociationalism and Federalism as Approaches to International Integration', in A.J.R. Groom and Paul Taylor (eds), *Frameworks for International Co-operation*. London: Pinter.

Tellenbach, Gerd (1993) *The Church in Western Europe from the Tenth to the Early Twelfth Century*. Cambridge: Cambridge University Press.

Thomson, Edvard A. (1996) *The Huns*. Oxford: Blackwell.

Thomson, Janice E. (1994) *Mercenaries, Pirates and Sovereigns: State-Building and Extraterritorial Violence in Early Modern Europe*. Princeton, NJ: Princeton University Press.

Thomson, Janice E. (1995) 'State Sovereignty in International Relations: Bridging the Gap Between Theory and Empirical Research', *International Studies Quarterly*, 39 (2): 213–33.

Tilly, Charles (1975) *The Formation of National States in Western Europe*. Princeton, NJ: Princeton University Press.

Tilly, Charles (1985) 'War Making and State Making as Organized Crime', in Peter B. Evans, Dietrich Rueschmeyer and Theda Skocpol (eds), *Bringing the State Back In*. Cambridge: Cambridge University Press.

Tilly, Charles (1992) *Coercion, Capital, and European States, AD 990–1992*, rev. edn. Oxford: Blackwell.

Tilly, Charles and Blockmans, Wim P. (eds) (1994) *Cities and the Rise of States in Europe AD 1000 to 1800*. Boulder, CO: Westview Press.

Törnqvist, Gunnar (1963) 'Studier: industrilokalisering', *Meddinlandern från Geografiska institutionen vid Stockholms Universitet no. 153*. Stockholm: Department of Geography, Stockholm University.

Törnqvist, Gunnar (1970) *Contact Systems and Regional Development*. Lund: C.W.K. Gleerup.

Törnqvist, Gunnar (1996) *Sverige i nätverkens Europa: Gränsöverskridandets former och villkor*. Malmoe: Liber-Hermods.

Törnqvist, Gunnar (1998) *Renässans för regioner: Om tekniken och den sociala kommunikationens villkor*. Stockholm: SNS Förlag.

Veggeland, Noralv (1994) *Regionbygging over grenser i det nye Europa – aktører, arenaer og regimer*. NordREFO 1994: 96. Copenhagen/Stockholm: Nordiska institutet för regionalpolitisk forskning.

Veit-Brause, Irmline (1995) 'Rethinking the State of the Nation', in Joseph A. Camilleri, Anthony P. Jarvis and Albert J. Paolini (eds), *The State in Transition: Reimagining Political Space*. Boulder, CO: Lynne Rienner.

de Vet, Jan (1993) 'Globalisation and Local and Regional Competitiveness', *STI Review*, 13, 89–121.

Vidal de la Blache, Paul (1911) *Tableau de la géographie de la France*. Paris: Armand Colin.

Vidal de la Blache, Paul (1917) *La France de l'Est*. Paris: Armand Colin.

Virilio, Paul (1977) *Vitesse et politique*. Paris: Hachette/Reclus.

Virilio, Paul (1984) *L'espace critique*. Paris: Hachette/Reclus.

Waarden, Frans van (1992) 'Dimensions and Types of Policy Networks', *European Journal of Political Research*, 21 (1): 29–52.

Waever, Ole (1995) 'Identity, Integration and Security: Solving the Sovereignty Puzzle in E.U. Studies', *Journal of International Affairs*, 48 (2): 389–431.

Wahle, Ernst (1970) 'Ur- und Frühgeschichte im Mitteleuropäischen Raum', in Herbert Grundmann (ed.), *Gebhardt: Handbuch der Deutschen Geschichte 1*, 9th edn. Stuttgart: Klett.

Waley, Daniel (1988) *The Italian City-Republics*. London: Longman.

Walker, R.B.J. (1993) *Inside/Outside: International Relations as Political Theory*. Cambridge: Cambridge University Press.

Walker, R.B.J. (1995) 'From International Relations to World Politics', in Joseph A. Camilleri, Anthony P. Jarvis and Albert J. Paolini (eds), *The State in Transition: Reimagining Political Space*. Boulder, CO: Lynne Rienner.

Wallace, Helen (1996) 'Politics and Policy in the EU: The Challenge of Governance', in Helen Wallace and William Wallace (eds), *Policy-Making in the European Union*. Oxford: Oxford University Press.

Wallace, William (1996) 'Government without Statehood: The Unstable Equilibrium', in Helen Wallace and William Wallace (eds), *Policy-Making in the European Union*. Oxford: Oxford University Press.

Wallerström, Thomas (1997) 'On Ethnicity as a Methodological Problem in Historical Archaeology', in Hans Andersson, Peter Carelli and Lars Ersgård (eds), *Visions of the Past. Trends and Traditions in Swedish Medieval Archaeology*. Stockholm: Central Board of National Antiquities.

Wandruszka, Adam (1978) *Das Haus Habsburg: Die Geschichte einer europäischen Dynastie*. Vienna: Herder.

Weber, Cynthia and Bierstecker, Thomas J. (1996) 'Reconstructing the Analysis of Sovereignty: Concluding Reflections and Directions for Future Research', in Thomas J. Bierstecker and Cynthia Weber (eds), *State Sovereignty as Social Construct*. Cambridge: Cambridge University Press.

Webster, Graham (1969) *The Roman Imperial Army*. London: Adam & Charles.

Weiss, Linda (1998) *The Myth of the Powerless State*. Ithaca, NY: Cornell University Press.

Whittaker, C. R. (1994) *Roman Empire: A Social and Economic Study*. Baltimore, MD/London: Johns Hopkins University Press.

Williams, Derek (1996) *The Reach of Rome: A History of the Roman Imperial Frontier 1st–5th Centuries AD*. London: Constable.

Wolfers, Arnold (1962) *Discord and Collaboration: Essays in International Politics*. Reprinted 1988. Baltimore, MD: Johns Hopkins University Press.

Wolfram, Herwig (1988) *History of the Goths*. Berkeley/Los Angeles, CA: University of California Press.

Wolfram, Herwig (1997) *The Roman Empire and its Germanic Peoples*. Berkeley, CA: University of California Press.

World Investment Report (1993) Geneva: UNCTAD.

von Wright, Georg Henrik (1993) *Myten om framsteget*. Stockholm: Bonniers.

Young, Oran R. (1989) *International Cooperation: Building Regimes for Natural Resources and the Environment*. Ithaca, NY: Cornell University Press.

Zartman, I. William (1994) 'Two's Company and More's a Crowd: The Complexities of Multilateral Negotiation', in I. William Zartman (ed.), *International Multilateral Negotiation*. San Francisco: Jossey–Bass.

Index